STONE COTTAGE

STONE COTTAGE

Pound, Yeats, and Modernism

❧

James Longenbach

New York   Oxford
OXFORD UNIVERSITY PRESS
1988

Oxford University Press

Oxford   New York   Toronto
Delhi   Bombay   Calcutta   Madras   Karachi
Petaling Jaya   Singapore   Hong Kong   Tokyo
Nairobi   Dar es Salaam   Cape Town
Melbourne   Auckland

and associated companies in
Beirut   Berlin   Ibadan   Nicosia

Published by Oxford University Press, Inc.,
200 Madison Avenue, New York, New York 10016

Oxford is a registered trademark of Oxford University Press

Library of Congress Cataloging-in-Publication Data
Longenbach, James.
Stone Cottage.
Bibliography p.
Includes index.
1. Pound, Ezra, 1885–1972.   2. Yeats, W. B. (William Butler),
1865–1939—Influence—Pound.   3. Modernism (Literature)
4. Poets, American—20th century—Biography.
5. Authors, Irish—20th century—Biography.
6. Sussex—Intellectual life.   I. Title.
PS3531.082Z386   1988   821'.912'09   87–18545
ISBN 0-19-504954-3

2 4 6 8 9 7 5 3 1
Printed in the United States of America
on acid-free paper

Acknowledgment is made to the following:

New Directions Publishing Corp. and Faber and Faber Ltd. for permission to reprint lines from Cantos 3, 5, 7, 8, 13, 14, 16, 74, 76, 77, 80–83, 95, and 113, *The Cantos of Ezra Pound*, copyright © 1934, 1948, 1962 by Ezra Pound; "La Fraisne," "In Durance," "In Exitum Cuiusdam," "Und Drang," "The Fault of It," "Homage to Wilfrid Scawen Blunt," "Poem: Abbreviated from the Conversation of Mr. T. E. H.," from *The Collected Early Poems*, copyright © 1976 by Ezra Pound; "The Return," "Dance Figure," "The Temperaments," "The Coming of War: Actaeon," "Liu Ch'e," "In a Station of the Metro," "Heather," "The Lake Isle," "Provincia Deserta," "Exile's Letter," "Salutation the Third," "Post Mortem Conspectu," "Near Perigord," "Villanelle: The Psychological Hour," "Hugh Selwyn Mauberley," "Abu Salammamm—A Song of Empire," "Fratres Minores," from *Personae*, copyright 1926 by Ezra Pound; previously unpublished or uncollected material by Ezra Pound, copyright © 1988 by the Trustees of the Ezra Pound Literary Property Trust.

A. P. Watt Ltd. on behalf of Michael B. Yeats and Macmillan London Ltd., and Macmillan Publishing Co. for permission to reprint from *The Variorum Edition of the Poems of W. B. Yeats*, copyright 1916, 1918, 1919, 1924, 1928 by Macmillan Publishing Co., renewed 1944, 1946, 1947, 1952, 1956 by Bertha Georgie Yeats; copyright 1940 by Georgie Yeats, renewed 1968 by Bertha Georgie Yeats, Michael Butler Yeats and Anne Yeats; copyright 1957 by Macmillan Publishing Co.

Oxford University Press for excerpts from previously unpublished letters by W. B. Yeats, copyright © 1988 by Michael Yeats and Anne Yeats.

Harcourt Brace Jovanovich and Faber and Faber Ltd. for permission to reprint from "Sweeney Among the Nightingales" in *Collected Poems 1909–1962* by T. S. Eliot, copyright 1936 by Harcourt Brace Jovanovich, Inc.; copyright © 1963, 1964 by T. S. Eliot; and "Little Gidding" in *Four Quartets* by T. S. Eliot, copyright 1943 by T. S. Eliot; renewed 1971 by Esme Valerie Eliot.

Parts of Chapter 3 appeared in *Yeats Annual No. 4* (London: Macmillan, 1986).

TO JOANNA

Preface

Reminiscing about his fellow poets in the Rhymers' Club, Yeats pauses in his autobiography to consider that "the dream of my early manhood, that a modern nation can return to Unity of Culture, is false; though it may be we can achieve it for some small circle of men and women, and there leave it till the moon bring round its century." When Yeats first published these words in 1922, the small circle of the Rhymers had been gone for over a generation. Yeats mourned their loss, recognized their limitations, but remembered the ideal of an artistic community—a secret society—which the tragic generation embodied.

A generation later, Ezra Pound, incarcerated at Pisa at the end of the Second World War, looked back to the small circle of men and women he knew in his youth. "God knows what else is left of our London / my London, your London," he wrote in the *Pisan Cantos*. All Pound had were memories, and, like Yeats, he invoked the companions of an earlier age one by one.

> Lordly men are to earth o'ergiven
> these the companions:
> Fordie that wrote of giants
> and William who dreamed of nobility
> and Jim the comedian singing:

"Blarrney castle me darlin'
you're nothing now but a StOWne"
and Plarr talking of mathematics
or Jepson lover of jade
Maurie who wrote historical novels
and Newbolt who looked twice bathed
are to earth o'ergiven.

Henry Newbolt, Maurice Hewlett, Edgar Jepson, Victor Plarr, James Joyce, Ford Madox Ford, and most of all Yeats himself, the poet who had passed on the noble dream of an artistic community to Pound: these were some of the members of Pound's small circle, and when he wrote the *Pisan Cantos* they were every one of them dead. Pound had his tragic generation too, but he lived long enough to discover that his own fate was the most tragic of all.

Pound belonged to an even smaller artistic circle during three of his London years, a community that included just Yeats and himself, sequestered in a six-room cottage at the edge of Ashdown Forest in Sussex. The situation is unique: two of the great poets of the twentieth century—and two poets so different in temperament—living in desolate close quarters for months at a time. Yet we are used to thinking of artistic communities when we think of the rise of modern art: Bloomsbury, Paris in the twenties, even the group of writers that gathered around Conrad and James in Rye. If two is not a large enough number to constitute a community, then the communal spirit in which Pound and Yeats secluded themselves in Ashdown Forest should be enough to make us add their collaboration to this list. More than the story of a literary friendship, the chronicle of their three winters together reveals that their interactions were a crucial part of the rise of Anglo-American literary modernism. In retrospect, Stone Cottage may be seen as a workshop or (to borrow a phrase that Pound employed with increasing frequency during those years) a "secret society" of modernism. Together Pound and Yeats canonized many of the practices and (even more important) the aristocratic tone that would characterize modernist literature for many years to come.

Pound's relationship with Yeats passed through several stages. In his student years, long before he met Yeats in 1909, Pound absorbed the aesthetic of *Ideas of Good and Evil* and imitated the rhythms of

The Wind Among the Reeds. When Pound met the man he considered the greatest living poet, he and Yeats began several years of close association, which culminated in the three winters at Stone Cottage (1913–1916). And when Pound left London after the conclusion of the First World War, the two poets were sustained by their affection, but no longer united by the feeling that their work was part of the same movement.

During the Stone Cottage years Pound and Yeats often felt that their work was closely linked, and it is the story of that collaboration which this book chronicles. In the autumn of 1913 the two poets went to Stone Cottage with the idea that Pound would serve as Yeats's secretary. Pound, who had just received the Fenollosa papers, began translating Noh plays. Yeats read the translations and was inspired to make a new start with his own drama. These episodes in the story of Stone Cottage are well known. But the story as it is known is incomplete: the premiere of Yeats's *At the Hawk's Well*, just after their final winter together, was originally scheduled as a double bill; one of Pound's own plays (probably *The Consolations of Matrimony*, itself a marriage of Syngean folk-drama and Japanese farce) was to precede the first of Yeats's plays for dancers.

The two poets did far more than write and translate plays. Pound became interested in Yeats's occult studies and began to read widely in esoteric literature, finding confirmation for his own esoteric theories of Imagism and Vorticism. Yeats looked back to his days in the Rhymers' Club, and began to write his autobiographies with Pound's admiring assistance. Pound read Browning's *Sordello* aloud to Yeats and began working steadily on *The Cantos*; his early drafts reveal the influence of the occult doctrines Yeats was preparing to explain in *Per Amica Silentia Lunae*. At the same time, the poets tracked the progress of the Great War from the safety of Stone Cottage and wrote war poems that express a sensibility close to that of the poets who suffered in the trenches. Yeats introduced Pound to Joyce, and Pound presented Eliot to Yeats: the builders of literary modernism came to know one another during the Stone Cottage winters. Most important of all, Pound began to think of Yeats and himself as an artistic and social elite—a secret society—that excluded even some of their closest friends. Stone Cottage was a seedbed for *The Cantos* and for Yeats's later esoterica, but it was also a breeding ground for some of the unfortunate excesses of *Jefferson and/or Mussolini* and *On the*

Boiler. As it grew, the secret society of modernism was marked by a tension between the noble dream of an artistic enclave and the less admirable realization of that dream in the open spaces of politics.

The conception of Anglo-American literary modernism which this book investigates is a familiar one: Pound, Yeats, Eliot, and Joyce play large parts in the story, while Stevens, Moore, Hardy, and Woolf have minor roles. But part of my intention is to show how the modernists gained their hegemony and became a society which excluded many writers whom we today recognize as their equals. That process of exclusion began when Pound left his younger friends in London to sequester himself in the country with the greatest living poet.

Yeats's and Pound's relationship has always been an integral part of the mythology of modernism's break with nineteenth-century poetics, especially the largely apochryphal story of how Pound transformed Yeats from the whispering poet of *The Wind Among the Reeds* to the stark modern poet of *Responsibilities.* More recently, Yeats's readers have seen that he began the transformation long before he met Pound, and attention has turned to the far more profound influence of the early Yeats on Pound's work—just as modernism has more often been revealed as an extension of nineteenth-century poetics. This is a more fruitful avenue of exploration, but limiting a discussion of Yeats's effect on Pound to the relationship of Symbolism and Imagism obscures the depth of their collaborative effort and the importance of that effort for modernism as a whole. Not just literary, but social and political attitudes were forged at Stone Cottage. In examining the poetry written by Pound and Yeats, it is important to remember that the two poets knew each other intimately. They lived in the same small rooms. They went for walks in the woods, drove motorcars, and watched soldiers hold maneuvers on the heath. Their poems do not exist only in a rarified world of textuality; the turns of influence and counter-influence occurred in concrete and identifiable ways. Consequently, my study of Pound and Yeats proceeds from my belief that it is impossible to separate their lives and work from the intellectual and cultural matrix in which they existed. Both the walls of Stone Cottage and the battles of the Great War play a part in the story of their friendship—just as current debates about the nature of literary criticism and the national debt have shaped the way I tell the story.

As I have structured it, the story is told more from Pound's point of view than Yeats's; in 1913 Pound was the more pliable poet (being twenty years Yeats's junior), and the mark of the three winters is stamped more strongly on his work. I should also caution that the story is not strictly chronological. The prologue follows Pound and Yeats from the time they met in 1909 to the time they left for Stone Cottage in November 1913. The three major divisions of the chapters correspond roughly to the three winters, but each winter is subdivided thematically to address the topics that preoccupied the poets, and each chapter dips into the years before and after the Stone Cottage winters to elucidate the full significance of the poets' collaboration. The final chapter, "Ghosts Patched with Histories," sets Pound's *Three Cantos* and Yeats's *Per Amica Silentia Lunae* (both of which were completed in 1917) side by side to show that these apparently vastly different works each form a diary of three years of collaborative research. The epilogue places Pound, Yeats, and the ideals they shared in the context of the secret society of modernism—the most enduring product of their friendship.

⤙⤚

In writing the story of a collaboration, I have had many collaborators. Beginning with pioneering work by Richard Ellmann and Thomas Parkinson, the Pound-Yeats relationship has accumulated a critical history that is interesting in its own right, and I am grateful to those scholars who made my work possible. I am also indebted to the staffs of the Princeton University Library, the University of Chicago Library, the Beinecke Rare Book and Manuscript Library at Yale University, the Harry Ransom Humanities Research Center at the University of Texas at Austin, and both the Berg Collection and the Manuscripts Division of the New York Public Library. I would also like to thank the University of Rochester for the research grants that facilitated my research in England, and the National Endowment for the Humanities for the fellowship that enabled me to complete the book.

Other debts are more personal. First, by the example of his own work and later by his interest in mine, Hugh Kenner has been an unflagging source of inspiration. John Kelly graciously allowed me to read his transcriptions of Yeats's unpublished correspondence. Rosemary Hammond made my search into the history of the terrible pair more profitable than I could possibly have imagined. Ronald Bush, Frederick Crews, Warwick Gould, and Thomas Reed each read part or all of the manuscript and offered essential advice.

For information on particular matters I am indebted to Mary Fitzgerald, Donald Gallup, George Mills Harper, Samuel Hynes, Stephen Myers, Omar Pound, Ann Saddlemyer, Ronald Schuchard, Donald Stanford, Emily Wallace, Roy and Barbara Welfare, and Barbara Willard. Kenneth Gross, Bette London, and Russ McDonald, my colleagues at the University of Rochester, offered me both intellectual challenge and friendly support. At Oxford University Press, William Sisler and Susan Meigs attended to the manuscript with admirable efficiency and sensitivity.

Finally, there remain two people without whom this book would not have been written. A. Walton Litz first encouraged me to undertake the project, and his continuing enthusiasm and advice made its completion possible. Along the way, my prime collaborator has been Joanna Scott, who read and reread every page, reminding me of both the difficulty and the joy of telling stories.

Rochester, NY   J.L.
September 1987

Contents

Illustrations

STONE COTTAGE

The Order of
the Brothers Minor

In the eighth century the Venerable Bede described the region including Ashdown Forest as "thick and inaccessible; a place of retreat for large herds of deer and swine." The ninth-century Anglo-Saxon Chronicle records that the forest extended 120 miles from east to west and 30 miles from north to south. After the year 1066, William the Conqueror granted the region including Ashdown Forest to his half brother Robert, Earl of Moretain. A survey conducted in 1273, five years after the district once again came under the direct control of the king, records that 208 commoners lived at the forest's edge; they were permitted the right to collect any wood blown from the trees in the forest—unless the tree were torn up by the roots, in which case it belonged to the king. In 1372 Edward III granted the "Forest of Ashdon" to his son John of Gaunt, Duke of Lancaster, and it remained part of the Duchy of Lancaster for over three centuries. In 1822 William Cobbett described the land as "a heath, with here and there a few birch scrubs upon it, verily the most villainously ugly spot I ever saw in England." The poet Thomas Pentecost, writing later in the nineteenth century, called the forest "A healthy waste of huts and dens, / Where human nature seldom mends." In the *Pisan Cantos* Pound remembered the landscape as a "waste moor."

Perhaps Stone Cottage portions out the landscape in the same way that Wallace Stevens's jar took dominion in the hills of Tennessee, for despite this history of abuse, the land surrounding Stone Cottage remains lovely and unspoiled even today. Yeats described the vista in a letter to the dying Mabel Beardsley:

> I am on the border of a great heath and there are woods on the other side and the only village near is scattered about a crossroads with a little old country inn. My walk which is always after dark to save time is to the post office or to the inn to order cyder, and then out on to the heath and at night when the clouds are not too dark and heavy a great heath is beautiful with a beauty that is not distracting. One comes in full of thoughts. When I am in the country like this I find that life grows more and more exciting till at the last one is wretched when one goes back to London.

The village at the crossroads is named Coleman's Hatch; the inn where Pound and Yeats drank their cider is still called the Hatch. In 1913 their walk would have looked much the same as it did when Stone Cottage was built a century before; the Hatch has been serving cider for several hundred years. Walking south from the crossroads, the poets would have turned onto an unpaved lane. They would have passed a small chapel built in 1867 so that the residents of Ashdown Forest did not need to ride to the church in Hartfield during winter. Just at the time Pound and Yeats installed themselves in the cottage in 1913, the Parish of Coleman's Hatch was carved from the Hartfield parish, and a larger church was erected at the crossroads opposite the Hatch. In January 1915 the local vicar paid Pound and Yeats a visit, which Pound told his companion they had brought on themselves by reading too much Wordsworth. The poets considered themselves members of a more enduring priesthood.

After the chapel (now converted into a cottage named Spinningdale), the poets passed a cottage named White Plat and then came to Stone Cottage, just where the lane bends sharply to the left. In the front, a waist-high wall of gray stone divides the cottage garden from the lane; across the lane lies a heath of birch and bracken. To the rear, the cottage is surrounded by hedgerows, and the lane dips down the hill to reach five more cottages, the last named The Prelude when Yeats stayed there in 1913. Now called End House, The Prelude sits at the very edge of Ashdown Forest and opens onto a more spectacular view than its neighbors. Standing in their secluded garden behind Stone Cottage, Pound and Yeats would have seen just the edge of the Five Hundred Acre Wood rising on the hill on the oppo-

Stone Cottage as it appeared in 1913, with the heath before it and the Five Hundred Acre Wood in the distance.

site side of the valley. The trees are familiar from Ernest Shepard's illustrations for A. A. Milne's Pooh books: tall pines stripped for most of their height and topped with a crest of boughs. The trees fascinated Dorothy Shakespear and Georgie Hyde-Lees (cousins, best friends, and the women Pound and Yeats would marry) when they were staying at The Prelude. "Georgie had an amusing dream about you two nights ago," Dorothy Shakespear wrote to Pound in October 1913. "You were hanging to the top of a very straight pine tree—all-stem-&-a-burst-of-branches-at-the-top-kind, and you had not climbed it—but got there 'by translation' as she says." Dorothy Shakespear also warned Pound that "You and W.B.Y. will certainly get lost in the woods here." If the poets walked through the woods northeast of the cottage they would have crossed the bridge, immortalized by Ernest Shepard on the frontispiece to *The House at Pooh Corner*, where Christopher Robin and his friends played Poohsticks. Once they were staying at Stone Cottage, Pound reported that he had "not yet got lost in the wild, tho' the eagle [Yeats] tried to go the wrong way once, with amazing persistence." For the moment, the poets' powers of translation remained purely linguistic.

During the winters when Pound and Yeats made Ashdown Forest their home, their cottage had only six rooms, stacked in an "L" shape two stories high. The empty corner has since been filled in to make

The Prelude (now called Endhouse) today.

the cottage rectangular, but the double-gabled roof and the subtle gradations in the stone betray the history of additions. When William Welfare bought Stone Cottage in 1858, in time for his marriage to Eliza Staplehurst, the cottage had only four rooms built of gray stone with a rust-colored grain. Welfare, who was a stonemason by trade, soon added two more rooms in stone of a deeper gray, giving the cottage the shape it had when Pound and Yeats came to stay. Welfare's son, William Jr., remembered Stone Cottage as the place of his birth:

> When my father bought Stone Cottage, Coleman's Hatch, it had four rooms only. He enlarged it and the sitting room with bedroom over was done in time for my birth. That event brought joy to his parents, he being the first boy.
>
> My father had borrowed money to buy and build, and he and my mother lived a life of self denial in order to repay the money. He used to walk miles to his work leaving the small farm to my mother until he returned at the end of the week. It was a hard life for them both. He hoped by his industry to save enough for old age. He died in July 1876, aged 54 of consumption. . . . When he knew his end was near he said [my mother] must sell the place

and live on the money, but she determined not to do so if she
could manage and she succeeded.

Many people at the time I was a child could not read or write
[but] both my parents could. I remember my father reading aloud.
He was a very quiet man, strictly honorable.

The younger William Welfare had two sisters, Ellen and Alice,
who lived at Stone Cottage during the time Pound and Yeats rented
rooms. Alice Welfare looked after the poets. Many years later she recalled the day Yeats came to inquire: "I can see Mr Yeats standing
there at the door the day he called with Mrs Shakespear; they were
staying with friends who rented The Prelude, up the road you know.
He'd been to see another place but no, he wanted to be on the forest.
It was the year the church was consecrated I remember."

A letter Dorothy Shakespear wrote to Pound from The Prelude
suggests the reasons for Yeats's desire to live at the forest's edge. "It
is a pretty place—common, heather, & woods—Georgie [Hyde-Lees]
says the latter are haunted. . . . Your cottage is next door nearly to
us. Its plain grey stone & right on the moor. There is a queer lake in
the forest—with wonderful-coloured trees reflecting in it—It is a weird

A late nineteenth-century photograph of Stone Cottage showing William
Welfare's addition.

place—and possibly faerie." Not only did Pound and Yeats move to an enchanted forest, but (more important) they lived down the lane from a cottage where eligible young women sometimes stayed. Both Lady Gregory and Olivia Shakespear were encouraging Yeats to marry at this time, and in the introductory rhymes of *Responsibilities,* written during Yeats's first winter at Stone Cottage, he complained that he had no child, "nothing but a book" to offer his ancestors. In his reminiscences of Stone Cottage in the *Pisan Cantos* Pound recalled

> the advice to the young man to
> breed and get married (or not)
> as you choose to regard it.

Once Pound and Yeats were settled in the cottage, Alice Welfare prepared their meals and did their housekeeping. She remembered the day the poets arrived to stay at Stone Cottage in November 1913: "After dinner the first evening, Mr Pound said to me, 'I haven't had a meal like that for a long time,' and he told me how his things were put out on the pavement. 'Why' I asked, 'Oh because I couldn't pay the rent.'" Pound's economic situation was one reason for living by the waste moor; another reason, as Alice Welfare remembered, was the solitude: "When breakfast was over they would get to work as if life depended on it. 'Don't disturb him' Mr Pound used to say, if I wanted to dust, and Mr Yeats would be humming over his poetry to himself in the little room."

In 1914 and 1915 the poets did not arrive at Stone Cottage until after Christmas, but during their first winter they spent the holiday season in Sussex. Yeats was particularly deeply involved in his humming on Christmas 1913. "Very dreamy he was," recalled Alice Welfare. "One morning, when Mr Pound was away visiting friends I think, he came back from the post office and said, 'Why, there's nothing doing; all shut up.' 'But Mr Yeats,' I said, 'Didn't you know, it's Christmas Day!'" Such was the extent to which Pound and Yeats left the everyday world behind when they came to Ashdown Forest. Their cottage was literally an enclave, in walking distance of the post office, but otherwise completely secluded. Yeats returned to the real world of London only for his Monday Evenings and his weekly sessions with his medium.

It is easy to overlook the peculiarity of what happened at Stone Cottage, if only because the protagonists' idiosyncrasies are so fa-

Alice Welfare.

miliar to us. W. B. Yeats, an Irish poet who had already achieved international fame, had chosen to spend his winters in desolate isolation with an American poet twenty years his junior who had published little more than what we read today as his juvenilia. There was not much that the young Pound could teach the author of *The Wind Among the Reeds* about poetry, especially since Pound had learned to write his own poems by reading the early Yeats. And one must wonder why Pound (who as an undergraduate at Hamilton College in 1905 had written that there "don't seem much sense in scrawling trifles with history making itself on the other side of the world") would come to feel that a six-room cottage in the middle of the waste moor was the center of his vortex.

Pound knew what he was doing. "The problem for the modern poet," wrote W. H. Auden, "as for every one else to-day, is how to find or form a genuine community." The young Pound would have agreed. Just before he left for Europe in 1907, he took a job teaching Romance languages at Wabash College in Indiana. There he wrote these lines of the poem "In Durance."

> I am homesick after mine own kind
> And ordinary people touch me not.
>   Yea, I am homesick
> After mine own kind that know, and feel
> And have some breath for beauty and the arts.

Pound sailed to Europe in search of "kindred e'en as I am, / Flesh-shrouded bearing the secret." A community was what he sought, a society of poets who would share the secrets of their craft with only one another—something like the Rhymers' Club he read about. Even more, Pound wanted to know the man whom he considered "the greatest living poet."

First Pound settled in Venice, and although the city satisfied his Byronic yearnings for the exotic, he could not remain there. He wrote his mother that he wanted "to have a month up the Thames somewhere and meet Bill Yeats." Pound had idolized Yeats and his fellow Rhymers for years. In *Profile* (1932), an annotated anthology of modern poetry, he recalled that from "1902 to 1908 'we' read Symons, Dowson, and Yeats." A *Lume Spento* (1908), the volume of poetry Pound published privately in Venice, is filled with echoes of the poet he longed to meet. In the "Note Precedent" to "La Fraisne," he explained that he had found himself in the "mood" of "Mr. Yeats in his 'Celtic Twilight,' " and the Yeatsian cadences of the poem reveal the depth of his admiration for the older poet: "Naught but the wind that flutters in the leaves."

When Pound arrived in London at the end of August 1908 with copies of *A Lume Spento* under his arm, he would not meet Yeats for several months. But the young poet was as canny as he was star struck, and he quickly became involved in several of the "gangs" (as he called them) that made up London's literary society. In February 1909 Pound wrote his father that he had shared lunch with Elkin Mathews, the publisher of Yeats, Wilde, and several of the Rhymers: "he is introducing me at the Poets' Club dinner on the 23rd. Sturge Moore and Hilaire Belloc are the other attractions." At the Poets' Club, a new society of the arts, Pound met T. E. Hulme and Florence Farr, Yeats's good friend and collaborator. Soon Hulme split from the Poets' Club, forming a secession group. There and at the meetings of the Irish Literary Society, Pound met F. S. Flint, Padraic Colum, and two former members of the Rhymers' Club itself, Ernest Radford and Ernest Rhys. Rhys began to have small groups of poets to his house for supper, as he recalled in his autobiography, "resuming the nights at the old Cheshire Cheese of the Rhymers' Club."

Pound now had more community than he had time for. Yet he was in his glory. He met Selwyn Image, another former Rhymer, "who does stained glass and has writ a short book of poems and was one of the gang with Dowson, Johnson, Symons, Yeats, etc. Talks of 'when old Verlaine' came over, etc." All of these acquaintances helped "to make the milieu 'London' a mecca" for Pound, but he had still to meet the greatest living poet—despite the fact that he lunched with that poet's publishers and dined with the friends of his youth.

During the winter of 1908–1909 Yeats was actually in Ireland, attending to the Abbey Theatre, so Pound had no chance to meet him. His invitation to do so eventually came from Olivia Shakespear, Yeats's former lover, Pound's future mother-in-law, and the focal point of yet another literary circle that included Frederic Manning and Arthur Galton. At the end of January 1909 Pound had tea with her and reported that she was undoubtedly "the most charming woman in London." In February he read from his manuscript collection of poems called *The Dawn* at the Shakespear home; he bragged to his friend Mary Moore of Trenton that he had been "sitting on the same hearth rug" in the Shakespear home where Yeats had sat.

Dorothy Shakespear described a more casual visit to the Shakespear
home that took place two days before the reading:

> At first he was shy—he spoke quickly, (with a strong, odd, ac-
> cent, half American, half Irish) he sat back in his chair; but after-
> wards, he suddenly dropped down, cross-legged, with his back to
> the fire: then he began to talk—He talked of Yeats, as one of the
> Twenty of the world who have added to the World's poetical mat-
> ter—He read a short piece of Yeats, in a voice dropping with emo-
> tion, in a voice like Yeats's own—He spoke of his interest in all the
> Arts, in that he might find things of use in them for his own—
> which is the Highest of them all.
> "Have you ever seen things in a crystal?" I asked—And he looked
> at me, smiling, & answered "I see things without a crystal."

Considering that Pound had already been able to mimic Yeats's
style so successfully in poems such as "La Fraisne," it is not surprising that he already spoke with the older poet's voice. Pound may
have heard that voice when Yeats lectured at the University of Pennsylvania in 1903, but he did not actually meet his mentor until May
1909 when Olivia Shakespear brought him to Yeats's rooms at 18
Woburn Buildings. Yeats then invited Pound to attend his Monday
Evenings—London's most exclusive society of poets. Seven months
after arriving in London Pound had penetrated the inner sanctum,
and now he worked even harder to show his peers that this young
American poet was the only colleague Yeats required. Douglas Gold-
ring remembered how Pound presided over one of Yeats's Monday
Evenings later in 1909: "I shall never forget my surprise . . . at the
way in which he dominated the room, distributed Yeat's [sic] ciga-
rettes and Chianti, and laid down the law about poetry. Poor golden-
bearded Sturge Moore, who sat in a corner with a large musical
instrument by his side (on which he was never given a chance of per-
forming) endeavoured to join in the discussion on prosody, a subject
on which he believed himself not entirely ignorant, but Ezra promptly
reduced him to a glum silence." To be part of Yeats's inner circle
was not enough. Pound set out—and he would succeed—to establish
just Yeats and himself as London's most exclusive, most mysterious
society of all. At the same time he kept up his other memberships.
"No special furor during the last week," he wrote his father. "I find
one Victor Plarr of the old Rhymers' Club most congenial. He is in

on Sunday supper-and-evenings, Yeats Monday evenings; a set from
the Irish Lit. Soc. eats together on Wednesdays and a sort of new
Rhymers gang on Thursdays." Still Yeats remained "the only living
man whose work has more than a most temporary interest."

Even in 1909 Yeats remained more important for Pound as a former member of the legendary Rhymers' Club, a poet of the eighteen-
nineties rather than a poet of the new century. Pound wrote to his
father that the "things of Yeats that you want to read" are *The
Wind Among the Reeds* and "Red Hanrahan's Song About Ireland."
This poem, published in *The Secret Rose* (1897), remains a quintes-
sential example of Yeats's early manner, even in the substantially
revised version of *In the Seven Woods* (1903), which Pound knew
and quoted in *The Spirit of Romance* (1910):

> The old brown thorn-trees break in two high over Cummen Strand,
> Under a bitter black wind that blows from the left hand;
> Our courage breaks like an old tree in a black wind and dies,
> But we have hidden in our hearts the flame out of the eyes
> Of Cathleen, the daughter of Houlihan.

In *The Spirit of Romance* Pound went so far as to compare Yeats's
use of epithets in this poem to Dante's in the *Inferno:* "There are
also epithets of 'emotional apparition,' transensuous, suggestive as in
Yeats' line, 'Under a bitter *black* wind that blows from the left
hand.' Dante's coloring and qualities of the infernal air, although
they are definitely symbolical and not indefinitely suggestive, fore-
shadow this sort of epithet."

But "Red Hanrahan's Song About Ireland" sat side by side in *In
the Seven Woods* with poems such as "Adam's Curse," which sig-
naled the development of a new and starker style in Yeats's verse.
Whether Pound read his favorite of Yeats's poems in *In the Seven
Woods* or the 1908 *Collected Works,* he would have seen it printed
beside one of the first glimpses of the "new" Yeats. Given Pound's
growing desire to forge a modern idiom for poetry, it is surprising
that he singled out "Red Hanrahan's Song About Ireland" rather than
"Adam's Curse" or the title poem from *In the Seven Woods* for his
highest praise. "In the Seven Woods" was Yeats's first poem to
leave the world of shades and shadows and refer openly to contemporary events (the coronation of Edward VII: "new common-

ness / Upon the throne")—something Pound would not do until he began to write the epigrammatic poems collected in *Lustra* (1916). Unable to perceive how this newer style would crystallize in the poems of *Responsibilities* (1914), *In the Seven Woods* seemed to Pound less a transitional volume than a volume that fell away from the standard of "pure" poetry established by *The Wind Among the Reeds*. "Red Hanrahan's Song About Ireland" stood out to Pound because it is the poem that most recalls the voice of Yeats's poetry of the Nineties—the voice that Pound was trying to make his own. Even after *Responsibilities* was published and the Imagist manifestos had come and gone, this poem remained one of Pound's favorites; in 1915 he wrote that "Mr. Yeats has perfect mastery in *Red Hanrahan's Song About Ireland*, and in the verse of *The Wind Among the Reeds*."

Pound came to London to meet the author of *The Wind Among the Reeds*, but by 1909 Yeats was a different man. One of the friends of his youth, Arthur Symons, had recently lost his sanity; Yeats visited him in January and reported to John Quinn that Symons was writing continually but in handwriting that nobody could read. At around the same time Yeats discovered that John Synge was ill: "if he dies," Yeats wrote in his journal, "it will set me wondering whether he could have lived if he had not had his long, bitter misunderstanding with the wreckage of Young Irelandism." Yeats wondered if the same involvement with Irish theatre and politics might not have destroyed his own career. He had published his *Collected Works* in 1908 and was struggling to silence the voices who claimed his career was finished. The loudest voice came from within Yeats himself, a poet watching his close companions die young or go mad. Between 1902 and 1908 Yeats had written almost no lyric poetry, and his journal records his despair:

> I often wonder if my talent will ever recover from the heterogeneous labour of these last few years. The younger Hallam says that vice does not destroy genius but that the heterogeneous does. I cry out vainly for liberty and have ever less and less inner life. Evil comes to us men of imagination wearing as its mask all the virtues. I have known, certainly, more men destroyed by the desire to have wife and child and to keep them in comfort than I have seen destroyed by harlots and drink. . . . I thought myself free, loving neither vice nor virtue; but virtue has come upon me and given me a nation instead of a home. Has it left me any lyric faculty?

Ironically, Yeats's one victory as a lyric poet in the early months of 1909 came by default. In April he heard that Symons now believed himself to be in heaven: "All the great poets were there, of other times. He was helping to prepare the reception of Swinburne. The angels were to stand in groups of three." Swinburne died on April 10th. Yeats, when he met his sister on the street the following day, proclaimed that he was now "King of the Cats."

Swinburne's death was deeply overshadowed by the death of Synge, which occurred on March 24th. Now Symons, the poet who helped him create the city of the imagination, was mad; Synge, the man who urged him to "renounce the deliberate creation of a kind of Holy City in the imagination, and express the individual," was dead. Yeats had little time for mourning; the month of April was spent selecting a new manager for the Abbey Theatre, wrangling with Synge's brother-in-law over the manuscript of *Deirdre of the Sorrows*, and negotiating with the Municipal Gallery over a proposed bust of Synge. Yeats left Dublin with relief. When he arrived in London in May, he was ready to begin again.

To remake himself as a lyric poet, Yeats first needed to push the successes of the eighteen-nineties securely behind him. In order to show his public that he was more than one of the members of the Rhymers' Club who happened to live into the twentieth century, he began to lecture about his dead companions, fixing them at a point in history that only he himself had transcended. These public reminiscences (eventually given their final form in the "Tragic Generation" chapters of his autobiographies) pleased Pound enormously, for they provided him with yet another conduit to the poets he had admired since childhood. On March 9, 1910 Yeats delivered a talk on "Friends of my Youth," the second of three lectures given in London to raise money for the Abbey Theatre. Yeats described the talk in his journal: "I shall read from the books of the Rhymers' Club—Plarr, Johnson, Dowson—and then from Sturge Moore and explain how, coming after the abundance of the Swinburne-Rossetti-Morris movement, we sought not abundance or energy, but preciseness of form. . . . We sought for new subject matter, and many of us were men of passionate living, expressing our lives. Our forerunners [had] been more contemplative, more calm." In the lectures, Yeats offered the first expression of his sense of the tragedy of the rhymers, later canonized in "The Grey Rock" and *The Trembling of the Veil*, as their heroic expression of personal ecstasy in an increasingly impersonal and mechanical world: "In the generation that came after us," Yeats wrote in his lecture, "and somewhere at the end of the nineties, the tide changed and our brief movement was over. The young poets, or at any rate the poets younger than myself and my friends, are impersonal, and if their lives are active, or dissipated or vehement they do not sing them."

As Pound looked forward to attending Yeats's lecture on "Friends of my Youth," he wrote his mother that it "is rumored that Yeats intends to say something decent about me in one of his lectures next week." Pound had previously heard that Yeats had said in private that he considered Pound "a solitary volcano" among the younger generation of poets: "If he writes rhyme like an amateur he writes rhythm like a master." Pound brought his old friend William Carlos Williams to the lecture, but Yeats failed to repeat this praise in public. Williams recalled the event in his autobiography:

> I sat alone, Ezra and his crowd being at some other section of the hall. I was fascinated by the proceedings, listening closely to what was being said. The hour was drawing to a close when Yeats began to speak of those young men, Lionel Johnson among them, who had been consistently denied an audience in England though in his opinion they well merited it and more.
>
> What was there left for them to do, then, but to live the decadent lives they did? What else, neglected as they found themselves to be, but drunkenness, lechery or immorality of whatever other sort?

Williams's recollections of the lecture are partly conditioned by the accounts of the Rhymers Yeats would publish in *The Trembling of the Veil*; in the lecture itself he said almost nothing about how the Rhymers died. Of Johnson he merely remarked that gradually "the darkness gathered about him. I think I need not speak to you of the infirmity that in the end brought him to his death."

Through the first year of his friendship with Yeats, Pound was more interested in anecdotes about the past than in the poetry Yeats was writing in the present. Not until Yeats wrote "Reconciliation" and "No Second Troy," as A. Walton Litz has pointed out, did Pound become more interested in the Yeats of the new century than the Yeats of the eighteen-nineties. In "No Second Troy" Yeats pictured Maud Gonne with "beauty like a tightened bow" and "nobleness made simple as a fire," and these were just the qualities Pound saw in the poem itself. The unrelenting tautness of these lines convinced him that Yeats was establishing a new manner in his poetry and not merely falling away from the perfected style of *The Wind Among the Reeds*. On November 27, 1910, Pound quoted "No Second Troy" in a letter to a friend in Paris, adding that "That is the spirit of the new things as I saw them in London. The note of personal defeat which one finds in [Yeats's] earlier work has gone out of it." No longer simply a living relic from the past, Yeats had now become a great contemporary in Pound's eyes:

> Yeats has been doing some new lyrics—he has come out of the shadows & has declared for life—of course there is in that a tremendous uplift for me—for he and I are now as it were in one movement with *aims* very nearly identical. That is to say the movement of the "90"ies (nineties) for drugs & the shadows has worn itself out. There has been no "influence"—Yeats has found within himself spirit of the new air which I by accident had touched before him.
>
> He is in transit I think from the *"dolce stile"* to the *"stile grande"*—and he looks to his new work & *l'avenir* rather than playing cenotaph to [the] memory of the dead "rhymers" and their period.

Considering how interested Pound had been in Yeats's recollections of the Rhymers, this judgment is more indicative of Pound's perception of Yeats than Yeats's own poetic development. The older poet had been trying to unburden himself of the Nineties for some time (in 1903 he stated explicitly in the notes to *In the Seven Woods* that he was trying to "bring a less dream-burdened will" into his verse); but not until Pound found his own poetry of shadows and dreams old-fashioned was he able to perceive the value of Yeats's newer style. A few years later T. S. Eliot was similarly persuaded that Yeats was not merely a faded Rhymer but a powerful contemporary when he attended the first performance of *At the Hawk's Well*: "Yeats did not appear, until after 1917, to be anything but a minor survivor of the '90's."

Pound's sense that he and Yeats were now "in one movement" led him to write "The Fault of It," a poem that begins with a tag from the opening line of Yeats's "Reconciliation" and elaborates that poem's promise to abandon songs "about but kings, / Helmets, and swords, and half-forgotten things":

"Some may have blamed you—"

Some may have blamed us that we cease to speak
Of things we spoke of in our verses early,
Saying: a lovely voice is such and such;
Saying: that lady's eyes were sad last week,
Wherein the world's whole joy is born and dies;
Saying: she hath this way or that, this much
Of grace, this little misericorde;
Ask us no further word;
If we were proud, then proud to be so wise
Ask us no more of all the things ye heard;
We may not speak of them, they touch us nearly.

This poem, published in the July 1911 issue of the *Forum*, was Pound's public declaration that he and Yeats were "in one movement with *aims* very nearly identical": although the poets wrote in different idioms, their common aim was to rejuvenate the lyric tradition by finding a new language for the poetry of modern love. In "Au Jardin" (the final poem in *Canzoni*, also published in July 1911), Pound offered a similar response to Yeats's "The Cap and Bells" from *The Wind Among the Reeds*. In "The Cap and Bells" Yeats had sung of a jester who dies of unrequited love, leaving his lady his cap and bells. In "Au Jardin" Pound is unwilling to adopt the language of the courtly lover: "there's no use your loving me / That way, Lady; / For I've nothing but songs to give you." Yet "Au Jardin" is not a condemnation of Yeats's love poetry; rather it is a repetition of Yeats's own rejection of his early style and sensibility. In repudiating the courtly lover of "The Cap and Bells," Pound's "Au Jardin" borrows the language of Yeats's "Adam's Curse":

I had a thought for no one's but your ears:
That you were beautiful, and that I strove
To love you in the old high way of love;
That it had all seemed happy, and yet we'd grown
As weary-hearted as that hollow moon.

Just a year before Pound wrote "Au Jardin" he passed by "Adam's Curse" for the more seductive sonorities of "Red Hanrahan's Song About Ireland." Now, like the Yeats of the new century, he realizes that to keep the lyric tradition alive he must create a fresh style for his poetry. Both poets had forsaken "the old high way of love."

Although Pound is often thought of as the poet who dragged the reluctant Yeats into the twentieth century, the actual turns of influence reveal Yeats as the dominant force. Pound himself felt that Yeats's transformation was due to Synge's influence more than his own:

> There is little use discussing the early Yeats, everyone has heard all that can be said on the subject. The new Yeats is still under discussion. Adorers of the Celtic Twilight are disturbed by his gain of hardness. Some of the later work is not so good as the Wind Among the Reeds, some of it better, or at least possessed of new qualities. Synge had appeared. There is a new strength in the later Yeats on which he & Synge may have agreed between them. Poems like "The Magi" & "The Scholars," and "No Second Troy" have in them a variety that the earlier work had not.

Pound wrote these sentences in 1915 for an aborted book called *This Generation*; had he published them, our sense of his role in Yeats's artistic development might have been quite different. Over the last fifty years, Pound's supposed influence on the Yeats of *Responsibilities* has become part of the mythology of literary modernism, primarily because of the well-known story of Pound's minor revisions of poems Yeats offered to *Poetry* magazine late in 1912. While the young Pound may have been proud of his brazened "corrections" of the older poet, Yeats thought of the corrections as nothing more than that—"misprints" he called them in a letter to Lady Gregory, "Ezra's fault." A transformation of style is not founded on misprints. Yet Yeats did come to accept Pound's suggestions, and at the same time he wrote to Lady Gregory praising his young critic: "He is full of the middle ages and helps me to get back to the definite and the concrete away from modern abstractions. To talk over a poem with him is like getting you to put a sentence into dialect. All becomes clear and natural." In a speech Yeats gave at a *Poetry* magazine banquet the following year he repeated this praise, claiming that he "had a young man go over all my work with me to eliminate the abstract." If Yeats thought Pound had taught him this lesson, Pound himself felt he had first learned about the clarity of poetic diction from Yeats; he wrote in *This Generation* that some of the poems in *The*

Wind Among the Reeds "run with the simplicity of a good prose sentence, and that, I think, shows a very fine art."

Yeats did not need Pound's criticism to transform his style, yet one senses that his praise of Pound's critical eye is not disingenuous. The extravagance of his statements to Lady Gregory and at the *Poetry* magazine banquet grew from his desire to reciprocate the praise Pound had been heaping on him for several years. The words William Horton wrote to Yeats in 1916 are probably true: "What is astonishing is that you do not see what Ezra is to you." To Yeats, Pound was most valuable as a great admirer during a time when Yeats himself was enormously insecure about the quality of his work. Pound helped to fill the gap left by Synge, the man who first taught Yeats to "express the individual." It is not difficult to see why Yeats would have found the opening sentences of Pound's "Status Rerum" (January 1913) flattering: "I find Mr. Yeats the only poet worthy of serious study. Mr. Yeats' work is already a recognized classic and is part of the required reading in the Sorbonne. There is no need of proclaiming him to the American public." Pound's typescript for this essay reveals that this lavish praise for Yeats was originally far more personal. When he sent the essay to Harriet Monroe for publication in *Poetry*, the first sentence read, "I find Mr. Yeats the only poet worthy of *my* serious study."

Pound sometimes did make pejorative comments about Yeats during the early years of their friendship, but it is important to see that these statements were conditioned by the audience for which they were intended. In the spring of 1912 Pound wrote "The Return" and Yeats pronounced it "distinguished." Yeats was now interested enough in the younger poet's career to cast his horoscope; when Pound received Yeats's request for his birth date from Dorothy Shakespear, his response was predictable:

> The Eagle [Yeats] is welcome to my dashed horoscope tho' I think Horace was on the better track when he wrote
>
> "Tu ne quaesaris, scire nefas, quem
>   mihi quem tibi
>   Finem dii dederunt" [sic]
>
> [Ask not—we cannot know—what end the gods have set for me, for thee]

Despite this skepticism, Pound did provide Yeats with the necessary information. He had actually written to his mother two years earlier, requesting the exact hour of his birth, and had at the same time defended his own interest in astrology, including himself among the "half a million people, some of them intelligent, who still believe in the possibility of planetary influences. . . . When astrology is taken hold of systematically by modern science there will be some sort of discoveries. In the meantime there is no reason why one should not indulge in private experiment and investigation."

These two responses to Yeats's stargazing, so different in tone, epitomize a duality that runs through all Pound's work. To impress his fiancée, the brash young poet rejects the authority of both metaphysical speculation and the elder Yeats; writing to his parents, the anxious disciple emerges, eager to emulate his mentor. When Pound writes to Harriet Monroe in August 1913 that "Yeats is already a sort of great dim figure with its associations set in the past," one must remember that Pound was trying to assert his own superiority to a sometimes resistant editor. In the same month Pound praised Willard Huntington Wright, the editor of the *Smart Set*, for having "the good sense to divide all of the poets here [in London] into two classes: Yeats and I in one class, and everybody else in the other." And in a letter printed in the *New Age* in September 1913, Pound asked, "is not the greatest 'English poet' of to-day an Irishman?" These statements, written just before his first winter at Stone Cottage, should be weighed against Pound's more famous remark in a letter to his mother that his "stay in Stone Cottage will not be in the least profitable." Although he sometimes quarreled with Yeats, Pound continued to think of himself and Yeats as members of an artistic class that excluded all his other friends. Pound mocked Yeats's aristocratic pretensions by calling him the "Eagle"—but not until he had been accepted into that noble company.

Whatever Pound's statements about his relationship with Yeats, from 1911 to 1913 the two poets shared their poems and opinions, often working together closely to promote the arts in London. When Yone Noguchi sent Pound a copy of his new book of poems, *The Pilgrimage*, Pound wrote back suggesting that "we who are artists should discuss the matters of technique & motive between ourselves. Also if you should write about these matters I would discuss your letters with Mr. Yeats & likewise my answers." During one of these private discussions at 18 Woburn Buildings, Pound met G.R.S. Mead, formerly secretary to Madame Blavatsky and now the founder of the Quest Society, whose aims were to "promote investigation and

comparative study of religion, philosophy, and science, on the basis
of experience" and to "encourage the expression of the ideal in beautiful forms." Mead was also the editor of *The Quest*, and he persuaded both Pound and Yeats to contribute to this theosophical
quarterly. The April 1913 issue included Yeats's "The Mountain
Tomb," a poem Pound had already published in *Poetry* magazine:

> In vain, in vain; the cataract still cries;
> The everlasting taper lights the gloom;
> All wisdom shut into his onyx eyes,
> Our Father Rosicross sleeps in his tomb.

If Yeats thought that an age of imagination and faith had been
eclipsed, Pound reassured him that Father Rosicross was alive and
well. He had written in the *New Age* that "to say we are faithless
in an age without faith is an absurdity." And a few months before
Yeats's "The Mountain Tomb" appeared in *The Quest*, Pound
lectured to the Quest Society on "Psychology and Troubadours."
(The lecture was then published in the October 1912 issue of *The
Quest* and after 1932 reprinted in *The Spirit of Romance*.) While
Pound was drafting the talk, Dorothy Shakespear suggested that he
claim to be "a re-incarnation [of a troubadour] so you *know*," but
instead Pound employed what he called the method of "visionary
interpretation" to translate himself back into the age of Arnaut
Daniel. In the lecture, he explained his theory of the "phantastikon":
"the consciousness of some seems to rest, or to have its center more
properly, in what the Greek psychologists called the *phantastikon*.
Their minds are, that is, circumvolved about them like soap-bubbles
reflecting sundry patches of the macrocosmos." In a letter to Harriet
Monroe, Pound explained the word in a slightly less esoteric manner: "It is what Imagination really meant before the term was debased presumably by the Miltonists, tho' probably before them. It
has to do with the seeing of visions." In "Psychology and Troubadours" Pound emphasized that these visions, especially as primitive
man experienced them, were more "real" than everyday reality itself.
"I know, I mean, one man who understands Persephone and Deme-
ter, and one who understands the Laurel, and another who has, I
should say, met Artemis. These things are for them *real*."
Although Pound borrowed the term "phantastikon" from the

Greeks, he found the inspiration for his theory of visionary experience in the early Yeats. When he wrote to his father in 1909 suggesting that he read *The Wind Among the Reeds* and "Red Hanrahan's Song About Ireland," he also said that Robert Hugh Benson's *The Light Invisible* "compares interestingly with Yeats' mystical studies." *The Light Invisible* is a collection of tales, each of which culminates in a visionary experience that reveals "how the world of spirits was the real world, and the world of sense comparatively unreal." In "such moments," remarks the protagonist of one tale, "although I generally know the difference between the spiritual and the natural, yet they appear to me simultaneously, as if on the same plane." This sense of the concrete reality of visionary experience was attractive to Pound, and he found the same idea in Yeats's essay on "Magic" in *Ideas of Good and Evil*. Yeats wrote in this early manifesto that there is evidence "that the memories of primitive man and his thoughts of distant places must have had the intensity of hallucination." Many "imaginative writers to-day," he continued, seek to reclaim this visionary power by "imagining themselves to be stocks and stones and beasts of the wood, till the images were so vivid that the passers-by became but a part of the imagination of the dreamer." For Yeats as for Pound, a visionary experience is the one unquestionable reality for the person who undergoes it. The older poet would have had no trouble entering into Pound's own "phantastikon" during his Quest Society lecture.

A few months after Pound gave his lecture, the Bengali poet Rabindranath Tagore arrived in London. Given the widespread interest in mystical and theosophical studies at the time, Tagore's ethereal poetry attracted an enormous readership. His two most devoted readers were Yeats and Pound, and they put together what Pound would later call "the cleverest boom of our day" in order to promote his work. Between June 1912, when Yeats first met Tagore at the home of William Rothenstein, and August 1913, when Tagore sailed home to India, Pound and Yeats fell over one another to see who could lavish more ostentatious praise on the Bengali poet. When Yeats first told Pound about Tagore he said that he was "someone greater than any of us—I read these things and wonder why one should go on trying to write." Early in July 1912, when Yeats was the host of a dinner for Tagore sponsored by *The Nation*, he introduced the poet, proclaiming that "To take part in honoring Mr. Rabindra Nath

Tagore is one of the great events in my artist life. I know of no man in my time who has done anything in the English language to equal these lyrics."

While Yeats was busy making a selection of Tagore's poems to be published by the India Society, Pound wrote to Harriet Monroe that he would "try to get some of the poems of the very great Bengali poet, Rabindranath Tagore. They are going to be *the* sensation of the winter. . . . W.B.Y. is doing the introduction to them." When six poems by Tagore appeared in the December 1912 issue of *Poetry*, Pound wrote an introduction in which he said that the appearance of Tagore's poems on the London literary scene was comparable to the rediscovery of Greek literature in the Renaissance: "And we feel here in London, I think, much as the people of Petrarch's time must have felt about the mysterious lost language, the Greek that was just being restored to Europe after centuries of deprivation. That Greek was the lamp of our renaissance and its perfections have been the goal of our endeavor ever since." In another essay on Tagore, in the March 1913 number of the *Fortnightly Review*, Pound repeated this praise, stating that readers of the Bengali poet felt as "Boccaccio must have felt" when he first heard "the curious music of Theocritus" and adding that the only "fitting comparison" for Tagore's poetry was "the *Paradiso* of Dante."

In the meantime, Yeats had completed his introduction to Tagore's *Gitanjali*, published by the India Society in November 1912, and there he confided that "I have carried the manuscript of these translations about with me for days, reading it in railway trains, or on top of omnibuses and in restaurants, and I have often had to close it lest some stranger would see how much it moved me." Yeats's praise for Tagore had its own peculiar beauty, as Marianne Moore recognized in "To William Butler Yeats on Tagore," published in the special Imagist number of the *Egoist* (1 May 1915).

> It is made clear by the phrase,
> Even the mood—by virtue of which he says
>
> The thing he thinks—that it pays,
> To cut gems even in these conscience-less days;
>
> But the jewel that always
> Outshines ordinary jewels, is your praise.

Moore realized that Yeats's introduction to *Gitanjali* outshone the ordinary beauty of Tagore's poetry, and her words addressed to Yeats are instructive: the outlandish praise which Pound and Yeats heaped on Tagore would be odd enough in itself, but what makes it even more curious is that both poets considered Tagore's verse to be uneven. After *Gitanjali* was published, Yeats wrote Edmund Gosse to suggest that Tagore be made an honorary member of the Academic Committee of the Royal Society of Literature. He admitted that Tagore's work "is unequal and there are dull pages" but urged that his election to the committee would be "a piece of wise imperialism": "I believe that if we pay him honour, it will be understood that we honour India also for he is its most famous man to-day." Pound overpraised Tagore for the same reason. In his note in *Poetry* magazine he wrote that "world-fellowship is nearer for the visit of Rabindranath Tagore to London." But Pound also had more self-serving reasons for joining Yeats to "boom" Tagore so strenuously: by doing so, he emphasized his position as the single poet of the younger generation with whom Yeats would associate. Before *Gitanjali* was reprinted by Macmillan in March 1913 (and then reprinted twenty times over the following two years), the book was available only in the limited edition published by the India Society. Pound relished this opportunity to include himself among the "few," as he wrote in the *Fortnightly Review*, "who have been privileged to receive the work of Mr. Tagore before the public had heard it." He told Harriet Monroe that the appearance of Tagore produced "the only real fever of excitement among the *inner circle* of literature that I've ever seen here."

Pound worked to keep that inner circle limited to Yeats, himself, and a handful of novitiates. When he organized a piano recital by Walter Rummel in honor of Tagore during the summer of 1913, he tried to restrict the guest list to four people—excluding even the wife of the pianist. This stunt caused Dorothy Shakespear (in whose drawing room the recital would take place) to retort that on "this occasion W[alter Rummel] & Tagore would be the important people—not yourself." Richard Aldington recalled in his autobiography that he "wasn't allowed to see Tagore, as being too profane; but I could always tell when Ezra had been seeing him, because he was so infernally smug. The snob appeal was worked with consummate skill, and the first edition of Tagore's book was limited to five hundred

expensive copies." Pound's extravagant praise of Tagore was designed
to emphasize his own position as one of the "inner circle" to a public
who could not even obtain a copy of the poems.

By the time Rummel's honorary recital took place, Pound no
longer kept up the pretense of admiring Tagore's work. In May 1912,
while vacationing in Italy, he wrote Dorothy Shakespear that Yeats's
" 'Grey Rock' is very fine—but his syntax is getting obscurer than
Browning's. I'm fed up with Tagore. I wish he'd get thru' lecturing
before I get back. I don't want to be any more evangelized than I
am already—which is too dam' much. And I much prefer the eagle's
gods to any oriental beetle with 46 arms." Yeats was the man Pound
was after, not Tagore, and his need for Yeats's support and approval
only grew stronger as they approached their first winter together at
Stone Cottage.

By sequestering himself in the country with Yeats, Pound was
finally able to recreate the aspect of the Rhymers' Club that he admired most: the sense of a poetic aristocracy, meeting in private,
ignoring the demands of a vastly inferior public. In the months just
before his first pilgrimage to the cottage, Pound was feeling the pressure of that public rather strongly. He needed a respite from what
he would call in a letter to James Joyce "the whirl of a metropolis
with the attrition of endless small amusements and endless calls on
one's time, and endless trivialities of enjoyment (or the reverse)."
Just a month before he left for Sussex he read an article in the
October 13, 1913 issue of the *New Freewoman* which advertised the
formation of a new religious order called the "Angel Club." Pound
wrote a letter in response, asking the "Chancellor" of the club to
consider the request of what Pound called the "unfounded order"
of the "Brothers Minor": "I have longed for some order more hu-
mane than the Benedictines who should preserve even the vestiges
of our present light against that single force whereof the 'ha'penny'
press and the present university and educational systems are but the
symptoms of surface. . . . I want an order to foster the arts as the
church orders fostered painting." Pound was only half joking. His
"unfounded order" of the "Brothers Minor" was comprised of two
members, Yeats and himself, and he wanted to forge a social system
that would not demean the "order" by forcing them to worry about
the roof over their heads and the source of their next meal.

For the moment, the Order of the Brothers Minor was self-
sustaining and did not require the assistance of the "Angel Club" or

Pound photographed by Alvin Langdon Coburn in 1913.

any other higher order. Pound and Yeats were watching out for each other. Beginning in the summer of 1913, Pound had begun badgering Harriet Monroe into awarding *Poetry* magazine's first annual Guarantor's Prize to Yeats. "About the $250 prize," he wrote to Harriet Monroe,

> It must be offered to Yeats. If he is so dam'd opulent as not to need it, he will probably return it. As for it's not being adventurous to offer it to him, I don't see that it is our job to be adventurous in this case but to be just. He has fought a long fight and had damn little reward (in the way of cash and comfort). . . .

If you give it to Yeats, you FIRST, make the giving of this particular prize serious, you establish a good tradition. The person
who receives it after Yeats is considerably more honoured than if
he receives it after Lindsay, or after any other man who can not
yet be taken quite seriously as an author.

Yeats was Pound's all-purpose answer to the problem of prestige.
When Pound first became the foreign editor of *Poetry* in 1912 he
insisted that they print Yeats's work immediately, telling Harriet
Monroe that Yeats's presence in the magazine "ought to be enough
to establish the fact . . . that we are a serious international publication, to be 'taken seriously' by all the elect." In campaigning for
Yeats to receive the Guarantor's Prize, then, Pound was looking out
not only for Yeats's welfare but for the continued prestige of *Poetry*
magazine.

Yeats did turn down the prize, but not because of opulence. He
explained his consternation and embarrassment to Lady Gregory:
"My first thought was to send it all back but that looked like pride,
so much as to say I am too important to take a prize." Yeats's solution was to keep £10 to spend on a bookplate and to return the remaining £40 to Harriet Monroe, suggesting that it be given to "some
unknown needy young man in a garret." Pound suggested that the
money be divided between Richard Aldington and Vachel Lindsay,
but Yeats wrote another letter to Harriet Monroe explaining that
the needy young man he had in mind was Pound: "I suggest him
to you because, although I do not really like with my whole soul the
metrical experiments he has made for you, I think those experiments
show a vigorous creative mind. He is certainly a creative personality
of some sort, though it is too soon yet to say of what sort."

If Yeats's praise of Pound in this letter is somewhat qualified,
Pound's praise of Yeats in a letter he wrote to accept the prize was
as lavish as usual: "I am very glad to receive *Poetry*'s annual award
at Mr. Yeats' suggestion as he is about the only poet now writing
in English for whom I have any appreciable respect, or I might say
more exactly for whom I have any feeling of deference." This sentence, intended for publication, was modified by Harriet Monroe
(before she decided not to publish it at all) to make it clear that
Pound was receiving only the money—not the award. While Yeats
was looking after Pound's finances, Pound was both preserving Yeats's
reputation and, by association, enhancing his own.

The two poets continued this system of mutual support by arranging to spend the winter of 1913–14 together at Stone Cottage. Yeats first explained his plan to Lady Gregory in July: "I want to arrange for Ezra Pound to act as my secretary this winter. I propose that he take rooms for himself & me an hour out of London & I go straight there after Coole. I shall then do my best not to go anywhere except to London for my Mondays until I start for America. . . . Ezra is to do my correspondence & read to me after dark." As a result of a civil list pension, Yeats was able to employ Pound as his part-time secretary. Pound increased his own prestige by associating with Yeats and saved himself the necessity of indulging in hack journalism to support himself; Yeats had the pleasure of having his greatest admirer close at hand and saved his eyesight by having the admirer read to him. Both poets had the time to pursue their research and write their poems without interruption.

At first Yeats thought that he and Pound would stay at Daisy Meadow, a cottage in Kent owned by Eva Fowler, one of Yeats's collaborators in psychic experiments. "Mrs Fowler has lent me this cottage for the winter," he wrote Lady Gregory, "so my experiment with Ezra will not be too expensive. It will be a great thing to get nearly five months—September to end of January—unbroken routine. Ezra will have the cottage ready for me when I leave Coole." By August 1913 the plans had been changed. While Yeats was visiting the Tucker family (Olivia Shakespear's brother Henry Tucker, his wife, Edith Ellen Tucker, and her daughter by a previous marriage, Georgie Hyde-Lees), he discovered that the Welfare's cottage, near The Prelude, was available for the winter. Stone Cottage lay "on the edge of Ashdown Forest," Yeats told Lady Gregory, and "on the other side of the House [is] a great Heath. It is a most perfect and most lonely place and only an hour and a half from London." At the same time Pound reported gleefully to Dorothy Shakespear that Yeats had sent him "a signed photograph of the winter quarters" at Stone Cottage. His dream of the Brothers Minor was about to come true.

Yet that dream was more complicated than Pound would have had some of his contemporaries believe. Despite the fact that Pound reiterated his feelings of unity with Yeats several times between 1911 and 1913, both poets were still involved in many other activities during that time. The ambitious and energetic Pound had more to benefit from this sense of unity and probably felt it rather more strongly than Yeats. Without Pound, the older poet was spending a good amount of time and energy running the Abbey Theatre and fighting

The postcard of Stone Cottage Yeats sent to Pound in November 1913.

to keep Hugh Lane's collection of Impressionist paintings in Dublin. He pursued his experiments in psychic research with a new intensity. In the spring of 1912 he met Elizabeth Radcliffe, a medium whom he would consult intermittently throughout 1912 and intensively between May and August 1913. Early in 1913, when Pound visited Eva Fowler at Daisy Meadow along with Yeats and Olivia Shakespear, he reported that Yeats "insisted on talking ghosts." Yeats continued talking: later that year he completed an account of Elizabeth Radcliffe's automatic writing ("Preliminary Examination of the Script of E.R."), and on All Hallows' Eve he gave a lecture in Dublin titled "Ghosts and Dreams," in which he described his research and concluded that the "great controversy was closed": for Yeats there was no longer any question that the soul survived the body and that supernatural phenomena could be explained by the theories of spiritualism. His account of those theories in "Preliminary Examination" would be extended in "Swedenborg, Mediums, and the Desolate Places" (1914), *Per Amica Silentia Lunae* (1918), and finally in "The Gates of Pluto," the last chapter of the 1925 version of *A Vision.*

While Yeats was holding court for ghosts at Daisy Meadow, Pound was instructing younger poets to "go in fear of abstractions." Despite his use of the Tagore "boom" to emphasize his exclusive relationship with Yeats, Pound was involved with a circle of younger artists (Aldington, H. D., Gaudier-Brzeska, Epstein, Lewis) who had little interest in anyone of Yeats's generation. Pound felt the tensions of this double life. The Imagist manifestos seem designed to counteract the dreamy symbolism of both Yeats's and (more to the point) Pound's early verse. But in writing the manifestos, Pound was formulating a literary movement for "les jeunes." Even though Yeats had come to the same conclusions about poetic diction a decade earlier, he could have no part in the movement.

From the start, though, Pound maintained a private conception of Imagism, distinct from the publicized goals of "A Few Don'ts by an Imagiste"; and for his own purposes, Pound considered Yeats a seminal part of the movement. In "Imagisme," first drafted by Pound and then rewritten by F. S. Flint, Flint reported that "they" (meaning Pound) "held also a certain 'Doctrine of the Image,' which they had not committed to writing; they said that it did not concern the public, and would provoke useless discussion." Twenty-five years later Flint would remark that "we had a doctrine of the image, which none of us knew anything about." Only a very select few knew the secret. Pound did commit the doctrine to writing and then unveiled it in "Ikon," a prose poem published in the December 1913 issue of the *Cerebralist*. "Ikon" is preceded in the *Cerebralist* by a long article that was probably written by Richard Aldington. Many of Pound's readers have suspected that some kind of visionary impulse lurks behind the clipped precision of Imagist poetics, and while Aldington's essay rehearses the litany of Imagist "Don'ts," "Ikon" makes the visionary impulse of Pound's own work clear:

> It is in art the highest business to create the beautiful image; to create order and profusion of images that we may furnish the life of our minds with a noble surrounding.
> And if—as some say, the soul survives the body; if our consciousness is not an intermittent melody of strings that relapse between whiles into silence, then more than ever should we put forth the images of beauty, that going out into tenantless spaces we have with us all that is needful—an abundance of sounds and patterns to entertain us in that long dreaming; to strew our path to Valhalla; to give rich gifts by the way.

This prose-poem is Pound's most revealing statement about the nature of Imagist poetics. And the Yeatsian quality of both the language and the sentiment of "Ikon" is striking. In his notes to *The Wind Among the Reeds* Yeats had written that "The image—a cross, a man preaching in the wilderness, a dancing Salome, a lily in a girl's hand, a flame leaping, a globe with wings, a pale sunset over still waters—is an eternal act; but our understandings are temporal and understand but a little at a time." "Ikon," which describes how the Image is a necessary accompaniment to life after death, almost seems to be a response to Yeats's excursions into the spirit world with Elizabeth Radcliffe: while Yeats decided that the "great controversy was closed"—that the soul does indeed survive the body— Pound described how art can "entertain us in that long dreaming" and "strew our path to Valhalla" with the eternal Image.

The first winter at Stone Cottage strengthened Pound's belief that Yeats held a seminal position in his secret "Doctrine of the Image." When he reviewed Yeats's *Responsibilities* in May 1914, he asked, "Is Mr. Yeats an Imagiste?" and answered "No, Mr. Yeats is a symbolist, but he has written *des Images* as have many good poets before him." While Yeats (like Pound himself) did not always conform to the Imagist "Don'ts" that Aldington belabored in the *Cerebralist*, he did subscribe to the secret "Doctrine of the Image." It is not coincidental that the lines from Yeats's "The Magi" which Pound quotes as "a passage of *imagisme*" present a visionary experience:

> Now as at all times I can see in the mind's eye,
> In their stiff, painted clothes, the pale unsatisfied ones
> Appear and disappear in the blue depth of the sky
> With all their ancient faces like rain-beaten stones,
> And all their helms of silver hovering side by side.

Pound goes on in his review of *Responsibilities* to hint that the poet who best achieved the visionary goals of Imagism described in "Ikon" was Yeats himself. First Pound repeats the opening phrases of "Ikon": "It is perhaps the highest function of art that it should fill the mind with a noble profusion of sounds and images, that it should furnish the life of the mind with such accompaniment and surrounding." Then he adds, in homage to the man whom he still considered "the best poet in England," that "Mr. Yeats' work has done this in the past and still continues to do so."

Only the initiated members of the Brothers Minor would understand that Pound was presenting Yeats as the ultimate poet of the secret "Doctrine of the Image." By the time "Ikon" appeared in the *Cerebralist*, Pound and Yeats were hiding by the waste moor in Sussex, writing letters and poems, reading Swedenborg and Noh plays. The Yeatsian cadences of Pound's "Ikon" lead us to the door of Stone Cottage. A few days after they settled in, Pound wrote to William Carlos Williams that he was "getting our little gang after five years of waiting." Pound was referring to "les jeunes," but the irony of the letter is that Pound wrote it while alone with the older master, having left his contemporaries behind. The first meeting of the Brothers Minor, a club even more exclusive than the Rhymers', had convened.

I

1

Initiation

Yeats thought of it as an "experiment." In a moment of uncertainty Pound admitted that he feared his stay at Stone Cottage would "not be in the least profitable." Neither poet knew exactly what to expect when he arrived in Sussex in the second week of November 1913. Having boasted to family and friends of his privileged position in Yeats's coterie, Pound needed to express his doubts about the experiment in case his mentor decided it had failed. But the worries were unnecessary. Yeats told Lady Gregory that his new plan of life was a great success: "Ezra is a pleasant companion & a learned one. He never shrinks from work." At the same time Pound told William Carlos Williams that "Yeats is much finer *intime* than seen spasmodically in the midst of the whirl. We are both, I think, very contented in Sussex." A few months before, Pound had boasted to his parents that he had spent an evening alone with Yeats. Now they were full-time companions. And in his most candid moments, Pound could not disguise his pride at being Yeats's chosen protégé. His sense of the exclusiveness of their Stone Cottage retreat was enhanced, as he told Dorothy Shakespear, by the presence of an unidentified "elderish female" who "gazed from the road into our study at about 2.45 this P.M. with undisguised awe & curiosity." Perhaps this woman had never heard of W. B. Yeats—much less Ezra Pound—but to Pound she represented the entire world. Although the

manor house of Earl de la Warr was within walking distance,
Pound was coming to see that the "aristocracy of entail and of title
has decayed" and that "the aristocracy of the arts is ready again for
its service." He would remember that "at Stone Cottage in Sussex
by the waste moor" Yeats

> would not eat ham for dinner
> because peasants eat ham for dinner
> despite the excellent quality
> and the pleasure of having it hot.

Pound sometimes mocked Yeats's aristocratic pretensions, but it
was Pound who entertained fantasies of an aristocracy of the arts
while living in the middle of the waste moor. He indulged himself
in what Yeats wistfully considered "the prerogative of youth"—making
enemies. "A few weeks ago he took a great distaste to another poet's
work [Lascelles Abercrombie] and sent him a challenge to meet him

Stone Cottage today.

in France and fight a duel on the ground that such poetry was an
affront to the reader. The other poet, poor man, was deeply depressed
for many days at the thought of being so disliked. I feel I have a
very vigorous sec[retary]. I am careful however to dictate my letters."
The impulse that made Pound challenge a fellow poet to a duel
(even in jest), like his glimpse of "undisguised awe" in the face of
a woman who looked in the cottage window, came from the same
self-consciousness as a member of a select few. The awe was Pound's;
the woman was merely curious. In the event that his lusty challenges
were taken seriously, Pound spent the winter practicing his fencing.
In the evenings he and Yeats would venture out into the garden,
foils in hand, to play at the prerogative of youth.

Some of the more mundane obligations of the literary life were
fulfilled. While reading Confucius and the *Mahābhārata*, Pound
wrote reviews of William Carlos Williams's *The Tempers*, Paul
Castiaux's "*Lumières du monde*" *poèmes*, and the *Collected Poems*
of Ford Madox Hueffer [Ford]. "Because of his long prose training,"
wrote Pound, "Mr. Hueffer has brought into English verse certain
qualities which younger writers would do well to consider." He added
that "one need not carp at his occasional lapses," but no doubt remembered that he had done just that in his Imagist manifestos. Hueffer's *Collected Poems* included "On a Marsh Road," which ended
with these lines:

> Past all the windings of these grey, forgotten valleys,
> To west, past clouds that close on one dim rift—
> The golden plains; the infinite, glimpsing distances,
> The eternal silences; dim lands of peace.

In "A Few Dont's by an Imagiste" Pound singled out this poem
without naming its title or author, advising younger writers to avoid
"such an expression as 'dim lands *of peace.*' It dulls the image. It
mixes an abstraction with the concrete." Although Pound would
write in a subsequent review of Hueffer's poems that he considered
"On Heaven" to be "the best poem yet written in the 'twentieth-
century fashion,'" he would also say (once again skirting the opportunity to carp at Ford's inadequacies as a verse writer) that "it is absolutely the devil to try to quote snippets from a man whose poems
are gracious impressions, leisurely, low-toned." This kind of verse had
none of the intensity Pound sought in poetry, no beauty like a tight-

ened bow. Ford was a critic and prose writer of the highest rank
in Pound's mind, but when it came to verse, Yeats remained the
authority. Many years later Pound would set Hueffer beside Yeats
in the *Pisan Cantos* to show that "old Ford's conversation was better" than Yeats's, "consisting in *res* non *verba.*" But in "On Criticism in General" (1923), written closer to the time when he knew
his mentors best, Pound pointed out that Ford "goes wrong because
he bases his criticism on the eye, and almost solely on the eye."
Ford's impressionistic method could not reach "the quality that
Yeats calls 'intensity.'" Even more important for Pound, Ford's
aesthetic "let in 'too many people'"; Yeats's method was a mystery
Pound did not want to share.

   Pound practiced the rites of that mystery at Stone Cottage while
putting the finishing touches on the Chinese-style poems he would
publish in *Des Imagistes* (March 1914): "After Ch'u Yuan," "Liu
Ch'e," "Fan-Piece, for her Imperial Lord," and "Ts'ai Chi'h." Pound
worried over his own choice of the *mot juste* because Richard Aldington accused him of using "the word delicate 947 times in 'Lustra.'" Aldington would soon make his point even more strongly in
a parody of Pound's verse published in the January 15, 1914 issue
of the *Egoist*:

> She stands by the rail of the Old Bailey dock,
> Her intoxication is exquisite and excessive,
> and delicate her delicate sterility.
> Her delicacy is so delicate that she would feel affronted
> If I remarked nonchalantly, "Saay, stranger, ain't you dandy."

Aldington also took a jab at Pound's delicate admiration for Tagore:

> Come, my songs, let us go to America.
> Let us move the thumbs on our left hands
> And the middle fingers on our right hands
> With the delicate impressive gestures
> Of Rabindranath Tagore. (Salaam, o water-cress of the desert.)

And at Pound's smugness:

> Come my songs,
> Let us praise ourselves;

I doubt if the smug will do it for us,
The smug who possess all the rest of the universe.

Aldington's criticism left its mark on Pound even before the parodies were published. For help with his uninspired vocabulary, Pound
turned not to Ford but to Yeats: on January 6th he told Dorothy
Shakespear that he had "much improved one passage by changing
['delicate'] to 'sensuous.' The other places are more difficult. . . . I
have just thought of the eagle's *own* word 'elaborate.' " Yeats had
used the word only once in all his poetry, but since it was in "The
Two Kings," a poem Pound had helped to make "a new thing" before he published it in *Poetry* magazine, he remembered the lines
well: Yeats described a battle raging on amid "the elaborate wilderness of the air." This line appealed to Pound because it accomplished
what Pound often attempted in his Imagist poems: it presents an
ethereal reality in sensuous terms. But Dorothy Shakespear finally
supplied the crucial word for Pound's "Liu Ch'e": "I shouldn't think
you could change 'delicate' to 'elaborate'? The latter is rococco &
heavy surely? Might do—can't tell minus context. What about 'discontinued'!!!" With that suggestion, "Liu Ch'e" was finished.

> The rustling of the silk is discontinued,
> Dust drifts over the court-yard,
> There is no sound of foot-fall, and the leaves
> Scurry into heaps and lie still,
> And she the rejoicer of the heart is beneath them:
>
> A wet leaf that clings to the threshold.

Although Pound received Ernest Fenollosa's papers just before
coming to Stone Cottage in 1913, "Liu Ch'e" was not derived from
the sinologist's transliterations; Pound would soon begin work on
the Noh plays, but he did not break into Fenollosa's notes on Chinese poetry until the autumn of 1914. Along with "Fan-Piece, for her
Imperial Lord," "Liu Ch'e" was reworked from English versions of
the poems in H. A. Giles's *History of Chinese Literature*. While
Pound alternately thought of "the rustling of the silk" as "delicate,"
"sensuous," "elaborate," and "discontinued," Giles wrote that it was
"stilled"—which he then rhymed with "filled": "The sound of rustling silk is stilled, / With dust the marble courtyard filled." Pound's
search for the *mot juste* was exacerbated by Aldington's criticism,

but it was initially fueled by his struggle to free "Liu Ch'e" from Giles's couplets; Dorothy Shakespear's "discontinued" struck a note quite foreign to the easy music of Giles's rhymes. And while Giles ended "Liu Ch'e" by explaining that "she, my pride, my lovely one, is lost / And I am left, in hopeless anguish tossed," Pound distilled the emotion into its Imagist residue: "A wet leaf that clings to the threshold."

Besides fussing with his own verse, Pound fulfilled his duty as Yeats's secretary. The older poet's eyesight became "practically useless after artificial light begins" so Pound read aloud in the evenings and took dictation in the afternoons. Yeats was a busy man: on January 11th he dictated twenty-one letters. Two of his most impassioned missives were written soon after he arrived at Stone Cottage in early November. In the last week of November, the Abbey players' production of Synge's *The Playboy of the Western World* at the Liverpool Repertory Theatre provoked such a disturbance that the authorities persuaded the theatre to cancel the play after two performances. Yeats responded from the seclusion of Stone Cottage in a letter that appeared in the December 4th issue of the London *Times*:

> The Irish Players have been giving a number of plays during the last week at the Repertory Theatre, Liverpool. The *Playboy* was performed on Monday and on Thursday evenings. The audience, on the whole, were exceedingly enthusiastic, but from time to time fervoured Irish patriots, who are a little old-fashioned in their opinions, interrupted and were thrown out. Yesterday our manager received a message from the police asking that the play should not be produced at the Saturday *matinée*. If the police are to be allowed to suppress plays at their will, a very serious issue has been raised affecting the reputations and financial interests of managers and dramatic authors. That for the first time a performance of the *Playboy* should have been prevented by the mob, reinforced by the police, matters little to the Irish players. . . . [But it] cannot be in the interest of the public or the police that the police should be left under the temptation to suppress the victim to avoid the trouble of suppressing the more formidable malefactor. They might as well forbid a man whose watch had been stolen to leave his house because of the indignation his complaint had caused among the thieves, as forbid without process of law or public inquiry the production of a famous play which lies under no charge of immorality

and is held by most educated Irishmen to be the master-work of the dramatic literature of Ireland.

The thought of the police supporting the whims of the ignorant "mob" was anathema to Yeats. In "To a Wealthy Man," published in *Poems Written in Discouragement* (October 1913), he had just remonstrated against Lord Ardilaun for making his gift to the city of Dublin contingent upon the approval of the people. When Godfrey Edwards, the manager of the Liverpool Repertory Theatre, responded to Yeats's letter, protesting that the police had "simply suggested" that they cancel Synge's play and that the theatre had accepted the suggestion "entirely upon their own responsibility," Yeats responded even more strongly: "*The Playboy* has been played in many towns in America, in England, and in Ireland, and besides those, always increasing in number, who consider the play a classic, others resenting the sarcastic genius of its creator have organized demonstrations. But nowhere outside Liverpool have the police made 'suggestions' which are a precedent for mob law and a menace to all playwrights who would serve their art and not their purse and have enough imagination and power to be loved and hated." These letters are official pronouncements from the Brothers Minor: the poets were enraged by a social system which forced artists to bend their gifts to economic concerns.

Pound was also raging at the ignorance of his public, but like Yeats he did so from a comfortable distance. The week after Yeats dictated his letters to the *Times*, he told Pound about an unknown artist named James Joyce who had done fine work but could not find a publisher. Pound wrote to Joyce from Stone Cottage to offer assistance: "Mr Yeats has been speaking to me of your writing. I am informally connected with a couple of new and impecunious papers . . . about the only organs in England that stand and stand for free speech and want (I don't say get) literature." Pound also asked for permission to print Joyce's "I Hear an Army" in *Des Imagistes*, and Joyce wrote back granting permission and enclosing a copy of a letter he had circulated in Irish newspapers in 1911. Pound published it as "A Curious History" in the January 15, 1914 issue of the *Egoist* (a few pages away from Richard Aldington's parodies). Joyce updated the letter to reveal his continuing struggle over the publication of *Dubliners*:

I wrote this book seven years ago and hold two contracts for its publication. I am not even allowed to explain my case in a prefatory note: wherefore, as I cannot see in any quarter a chance that my rights will be protected, I hereby give Messrs. Maunsel publicly permission to publish this story with what changes or deletions they may please to make, and shall hope that what they may publish may resemble that to the writing of which I gave thought and time. Their attitude as an Irish publishing firm may be judged by Irish public opinion. I, as a writer, protest against the systems (legal, social, and ceremonious) which have brought me to this pass.

Pound and Yeats found an ally in Joyce. Like Yeats, he protested against the authorities that controlled the avenues of public taste; like Pound, he objected to the present social and economic systems which forced the artist into exile or silence. Pound wrote to Joyce that "W.B.Y. says . . . we have a hate or two in common." A new candidate for the Brothers Minor had been found.

By writing letters about the Abbey Theatre or Joyce's publishing history, however, Pound and Yeats were indulging in just the kind of activity they had come to Stone Cottage to escape. Pound "found some consolation" by digging deeper into Oriental esoterica, reading about the practice of "listening to incense" in the chapters on "Refinements and Pastimes of the Military Epoch" in Brinkley's *Japan and China: Their History, Arts, and Literature*. Although the phrase "listening to incense" was a misreading of the ideogram for "smelling," both Pound and Yeats were taken with the acute sensitivity which the phrase implied. In his introduction to *Certain Noble Plays of Japan* (1916) Yeats wrote: "when I remember that curious game which the Japanese called, with a confusion of the senses that had seemed typical of our own age, 'listening to incense,' I know that some among them would have understood the prose of Walter Pater, the paintings of Puvis de Chavannes, the poetry of Mallarmé and Verlaine." Listening to incense had nothing to do with the mob who rejected *The Playboy* or *Dubliners*, and for Pound, the practice remained a touchstone for his sense of a cultural elite. In his *Guide to Kulchur* (1938) he wrote that to define civilization, "we may start with the 'Listening to Incense.' This displays a high state of civilization. In the Imperial Court of Nippon the companions burnt incense, they burnt now one perfume, and now another, or a mixture of perfumes, and the accomplishment was both to recognize what had gone materially into the perfume and to cite apposite poems. . . . It is a pastime neither for clods nor for illiterates." Nor for a public who ignored Joyce and Synge. In "Refinements and Pastimes of the Military Epoch" Brinkley explained that this practice "was not merely a question of smelling incense: it was a literary pursuit, designed in great part for testing the players' knowledge of classical poetry and their ability to apply the knowledge." A name derived from classical literature had to be assigned to each aroma, and Brinkley pointed out that a phrase taken from these verses—

> When autumn's wind breathes
> Chill and lone my chamber through,
> And night grows aged,
> Dark shadows of the moonlight,
> Cast athwart my couch,
> Sink deep into my being

—was superior to one derived from the "freight of perfumed dewdrops / Sipped from sweet chrysanthemum" because the scent of flowers is "an every-day simile in praising incense; whereas the first, while its derivation had no material allusion to anything suggestive of incense-burning, conveyed a rarely forcible idea of the profoundly penetrating influence of a fine aroma." Pound took this advice seriously, for he was writing poems such as "Liu Ch'e" in which a departing woman is equated with the materially unrelated image of "A wet leaf that clings to the threshold."

Pound read about other pastimes of the Japanese nobles—gardening, flower arranging, and the tea ceremony—but Brinkley's account of the Noh drama naturally interested him most of all. When he arrived at Stone Cottage, Pound had just received "all old Fenollosa's treasures in mss" and by December 16th he had finished adapting *Kinuta* from Fenollosa's notes. Yeats found the play "charming" (the same word he used to describe Pound's *A Lume Spento*) and must have soon realized that the Noh could provide the solution to the kind of problems he was having with the Abbey Theatre in Liverpool. It was Brinkley who offered the word "accomplishment" as the translation for the word "Noh," and Yeats pointed out that this "accomplishment" in theatre was limited to the aristocracy: "a few cultivated people who understand the literary and mythological allusions and the ancient lyrics quoted in speech or chorus, their discipline, a part of their breeding." Brinkley explained that the Noh drama was designed for "princes, nobles, and high officials" who "did not cease to study it assiduously, and were prepared at any moment to organise performances or to take part in them. . . . Common folks in the Military epoch had no opportunity of witnessing a histrionic performance unless a drama of the Nô type was put upon one of the religious stages for purposes of charity, and even then a certain measure of selection was applied to the audience." The Noh theatre required neither an ignorant "mob" to watch it nor a public theatre to support it. Yeats would write in "Certain Noble Plays of Japan" that "with the help of Japanese plays 'translated by Ernest Fenollosa and finished by Ezra Pound,' I have invented a form of drama, distinguished, indirect, and symbolic, and having no need of mob or Press to pay its way—an aristocratic form."

Brinkley's account of the Noh helped to shape Pound's translations. While some Noh plays "have been skilfully translated into English of purity and grace," Brinkley remarked, "the learned sinologues, . . . by substituting the smoothly moving, majestic Iambic metre for the short, crisp pulsations of the Japanese line, and by obeying exigencies of rhyme whereas the original demands rhythm only, have obtained elegance at the partial expense of fidelity." Pound followed Brinkley's advice in *Kinuta*, *Hagoromo*, and *Nishikigi*, the three plays he finished during the first winter, and when he sent the manuscript of *Nishikigi* to Harriet Monroe he explained that the "earlier attempts to do Japanese in English are dull and ludicrous. That you needn't mention . . . [when *Nishikigi* appears in *Poetry*] as the poor scholars have done their bungling best. One can not commend the results. The best plan is to say nothing about it. This present stuff ranks as re-creation."

Brinkley offered a sample translation of one Noh play, *The Ataka No*, which Pound followed in *Nishikigi*, employing alternating passages of prose and free verse to render the Japanese into English. Yet a more distinctive voice crept into Pound's "re-creation" of the Noh. Fenollosa translated a longer speech in the beginning of *Nishikigi* into prose: "It is this very colored-branch, (set up) time after time, as if it were brocade woven into the narrow fabric of Kefu, which shall set up the rumor (of love) . . . (just as) the grass-patterns of Shinobu cloth in Land's End." Pound's version of the passage reveals the influence of Yeats chanting his poetry in the next room: "Times out of mind am I here setting up this bright branch, this silky wood

with the charms painted in it as fine as the web you'd get in the grass-
cloth of Shinobu, that they'd be still selling you in this mountain."
The Irish lilt of the prose in Pound's translations, which has often
been noticed, is not merely the casual result of his proximity to
Yeats: the effect is calculated to express the similarity that both
poets sensed between Noh drama, Irish folklore, and the literature of
the occult. "These plays are full of ghosts," Pound wrote in 'Noh' or
Accomplishment (1916), "and the ghost psychology is amazing. The
parallels with Western spiritist doctrines are very curious." In the
Noh drama, "The suspense is the suspense of waiting for a supernatural manifestation—which comes. Some will be annoyed at a form of
psychology which is, in the West, relegated to spiritistic séances.
There is, however, no doubt that such psychology exists. All through
the winter of 1914–15 I watched Mr. Yeats correlating folk-lore
(which Lady Gregory had collected in Irish cottages) and data of
the occult writers, with the habits of charlatans of Bond Street."
While Pound was busy translating Noh plays, Yeats had "his nose
kept down to his demon's" and was busy correlating Lady Gregory's
collection of Irish folklore with other tales and myths from occult
and esoteric literature. His work resulted in thirty pages of explanatory notes for Lady Gregory's Visions and Beliefs in the West of Ireland as well as two essays, "Witches and Wizards and Irish Folklore"
and "Swedenborg, Mediums, and the Desolate Places." The two poets immediately realized that their studies were linked: correspon-
dences between folk legends could be found not simply within the
western tradition but with the traditions of the east as well.

   In a footnote in 'Noh' or Accomplishment Pound specified the connection between Japanese and Irish traditions that the language of
his translations implied: "In Nishikigi, the ghosts of the two lovers
are kept apart because the woman had steadily refused the hero's offering of charm sticks. The two ghosts are brought together by the
piety of a wandering priest. Mr. Yeats tells me that he has found a
similar legend in Arran, where the ghosts come to a priest to be married." Yeats had indeed found such a legend. In Visions and Beliefs
in the West of Ireland Lady Gregory relates the story of a priest who
is visited by the ghost of his recently deceased servant girl: "And she
said, 'I have a comrade now, and I came for you to marry us as you
gave your word.' And he said, 'I'll hold to my word since I gave it,'
and he married them then and there, and they went away again." In
his notes to this tale, Yeats added that the "same story as that [oc-

curs] in one of the most beautiful of the 'Noh' plays of Japan. I tell
the Japanese story in my long terminal essay." In this essay on "Swedenborg, Mediums, and the Desolate Places," Yeats does tell the
story of *Nishikigi*, prefacing it by saying that "Last winter Mr. Ezra
Pound was editing the late Professor Fenollosa's translations of the
Noh Drama of Japan, and read me a great deal of what he was doing."

This connection that both Yeats and Pound sensed between Irish
folklore, the Noh, and the occult was a turning point in both their
careers; *Four Plays for Dancers, Per Amica Silentia Lunae*, and the
early *Cantos* each in its own way grew from their collaborative research at Stone Cottage. And while the influence of Pound's studies
in the Noh on Yeats's plays has long been evident, the influence of
Yeats's occult interests on Pound has been obscured—partly by Pound
himself, writing to his mother in 1913 that Yeats would "bore [him]
to death with psychical research" at Stone Cottage. Pound was far
from bored. When Yeats dictated a letter to W. T. Horton on November 23, 1913, he asked Horton to "repeat . . . the prophecy you
made about Ezra Pound." Horton, who participated in many of
Yeats's occult experiments, had mailed Yeats a sequence of prophecies a few months before Yeats and Pound came to Sussex, including
this one "to Ezra Pound": "You'll do, only climb higher, ever higher
& thus forget *the* burden." While taking dictation from Yeats, Pound
must have requested that the prophecy be repeated for his own benefit.

The systematic investigation of occult literature which Yeats undertook at Stone Cottage did not initiate but rekindled Pound's own
interest. In 1909 Pound had noted the similarity of Yeats's mystical
studies and Father Benson's *The Light Invisible*; in "La Fraisne,"
written before Pound met Yeats in 1909, he linked the tales of spirits
and fairies in Yeats's *The Celtic Twilight* with *De Daemonialitate, et
Incubis et Succubis*, a nineteenth-century occult tract which was presented as the work of a seventeenth-century Franciscan theologian
named Lodovico Maria Sinistrari. In his note to "La Fraisne" in *A
Lume Spento* Pound wrote that he found himself in the "mood" of
"Mr. Yeats in his 'Celtic Twilight.' " The footnote to this "Note
Precedent" links Pound's Yeatsian "mood" with *De Daemonialitate*:
"Referendum for contrast. 'Daemonalitas' of the Rev. Father Sinistrari of Ameno (1600 circ). 'A treatise wherein is shown that there
are in existence on earth rational creatures besides men, endowed like
him with a body and soul, that are born and die like him, redeemed

by our Lord Jesus-Christ, and capable of receiving salvation or dam-
nation.' " The Latin manuscript of *De Daemonialitate* was first "discovered" in 1872 and published with a French translation in 1875.
Pound owned the 1879 edition, which contained an English translation, and in his note to "La Fraisne" he quotes from the summary of
the book printed on the title page of this edition.

During the first winter at Stone Cottage Pound must have remembered the connection he had made between Yeats's fairies and Sinistrari's demons because he wrote to his father, "Yeats is doing various
books. He wants my *Daemonalitas*. Will you try to find it along with
the other thing I asked for." When the book arrived, Yeats made use
of it in his notes on "the faery people" in *Visions and Beliefs:* "Were
these beings but the shades of men? Were they a separate race? Were
they spirits of evil? Above all, perhaps, were they capable of salvation?
Father Sinistrari in *De Daemonialitate et Incubis, et Succubis*, reprinted in Paris with an English translation in 1879, tells a story
which must have been familiar through the Irish Middle Ages, and
the seed of many discussions." Yeats goes on to paraphrase a tale that
Sinistrari tells about a spirit who asks St. Anthony if his soul can be
saved. He then remarks, "I heard or read that tale [in a different ver-
sion] somewhere before I was twenty, for it is the subject of one of
my first poems." Yeats does not name the poem, but it is clear from
his description of the tale that he remembers "The Priest and the
Fairy," originally published in *The Wanderings of Oisin and Other
Poems* (1889) and never reprinted in Yeats's lifetime. The poem
itself is a piece of juvenilia, but what is interesting is that Yeats
made the same connection between *De Daemonialitate* and his early
"Celtic" work that Pound had made in his note to "La Fraisne"—and
he probably did so at Pound's urging.

Pound also urged Dorothy Shakespear to read *De Daemonialitate*,
and like Yeats she delighted in its tales of spooks and spirits. When
Pound first wrote to her that he was "reading ghosts" to Yeats at
Stone Cottage, she wrote back asking him to "glean anything you can
for the suppression of ghosts, or else of the fear of them." Pound's
response is characteristically jocular, but it also highlights an important aspect of his work: " 'Intellectual vision' is, acc. Wm. Blake & others, the surest cure for ghosts. You'd better begin by seeing fire, or
else by doing that visualization of points that I recommended. Fix a
point, colour it, or light it as you like, start it moving, multiply it, etc.

Make patterns, colours, pictures, whatever you like. You will end as a great magician & prize exorcist."

Pound probably first learned about Blake's "intellectual vision" from Yeats's essays on Blake in *Ideas of Good and Evil*. After he met Yeats his interest in "intellectual vision" was no doubt strengthened by the older poet's descriptions of the method of symbolic vision he had practiced in the Order of the Golden Dawn. In the first draft of his autobiography Yeats described how the cabalist Mac-Gregor Mathers instructed Florence Farr to "fix her attention on a certain symbol, and by a process she could not describe a seashore and a flight of seagulls had risen before her. Then my turn came for a visit, and I was made to look at a coloured geometric form and then, closing my eyes, see it again in the mind's eye. I was then shown how to allow my reveries to drift, following the suggestion of the symbol. I saw a desert, and a gigantic Negro raising up his head and shoulders among great stones." Yeats added that he "allowed [his] mind to drift from image to image, and these images began to affect [his] writing, making it more sensuous and more vivid." In the final version of his autobiography, Yeats revised this account of his vision to describe "a desert and black Titan raising himself up by his two hands from the middle of a heap of ancient ruins," making it clear (as Richard Ellmann first noticed) that the poem it had enriched was "The Second Coming."

Yeats also used this method of "intellectual vision" at Stone Cottage. In the *Pisan Cantos* Pound drifted back to his first winter with Yeats and recalled the older poet's incantation of "The Peacock," a poem Pound would publish in the May 1914 issue of *Poetry*.

> The Kakemono grows in a flat land out of mist
> 　　sun rises lop-sided over the mountain
> 　　　　so that I recalled the noise in the chimney
> as it were the wind in the chimney
> 　　　　but was in reality Uncle William
> downstairs composing
> that had made a great Peeeeacock
> 　　in the proide ov his oiye
> 　　　　had made a great Peeeeeeecock in the . . .
> made a great peacock
> 　　in the proide of his oyyee

proide ov his oy-ee
as indeed he had, and perdurable

a great peacock aere perennius.

"The Peacock" is itself a justification of poetry made from the intellectual vision of the poet rather than the public world around him.
Like Blake, whom Yeats described in his early essay on the illustrations of the *Divine Comedy* as an artist who becomes "drunk with
intellectual vision," Yeats had indeed made his peacock in the pride
of his eye.

> What's riches to him
> That has made a great peacock
> With the pride of his eye?
> The wind-beaten, stone-grey,
> And desolate Three Rock
> Would nourish his whim.
> Live he or die
> Amid wet rocks and heather,
> His ghost will be gay
> Adding feather to feather
> For the pride of his eye.

"The Peacock," written on November 23rd, was a justification for a
kind of poetry that excluded the "mob," who were interested in accumulating different sorts of riches. The quotidian inspiration for
the poem was not the peacock dinner that Blunt served Pound and
Yeats almost two months later on January 18th. Yeats's peacock was
purely imagined but the "wet rocks and heather" were not; Dorothy
Shakespear described the heath before Stone Cottage as covered with
heather and "a drippy kind of place." A more likely inspiration for
the peacock, as Hugh Kenner has pointed out, was Pennell's *Life of
Whistler*. There Yeats would have learned about Whistler's proposal
for "a great peacock ten feet high" at the same time that he read the
painter's own condemnation of material riches: "it is better to live on
bread and cheese and paint beautiful things than to live like Dives
and paint pot-boilers." Whistler's peacock existed nowhere except in
the pride of his eye; he conceived the design for a panel at the head
of the stairs in the Boston Library, but it was never executed.

The fireplace in Stone Cottage.

Pound also used intellectual vision to make poems for his mind's eye at Stone Cottage. In "The Wisdom of Poetry" (1912), he wrote—sounding much like Yeats—that "perception by symbolic vision is swifter and more complex than that by ratiocination." And in the same letter in which he described the method of "intellectual vision" to Dorothy Shakespear, he also wrote that he had "found a black panther." He was referring to "Heather," a dream-vision poem he wrote at Stone Cottage.

> The black panther treads at my side,
> And above my fingers
> There float the petal-like flames.

> The milk-white girls
> Unbend from the holly-trees,
> And their snow-white leopard
> Watches to follow our trace.

"Heather" is a good example of the kind of Imagist poem Pound de-scribes in "Ikon." Like Dante, Pound shows us that the Image he de-scribes is the product of a vision by including white leopards and flames that float calmly without singeing a sleeve. He explained the visionary mechanism of the poem in a letter to his father: "The title is put on it to show that the poem is a simple statement of facts oc-curing to the speaker, but that these facts do not occur in the same plane with his feet, which are solidly planted in a climate producing Heather and not leopards etc." Like Yeats's "The Peacock," Pound's poem begins in the heather-covered heath before Stone Cottage but at the same time transcends the world of perishable riches.

Another of Pound's Imagist poems, "His Vision of a Certain Lady Post Mortem" (published in the 1914 issue of *Blast*), presents a vi-sion of his dead friend Margaret Cravens.

> A brown, fat babe sitting in the lotus,
> And you were glad and laughing
> > With a laughter not of this world.
> It is good to splash in the water
> And laughter is the end of all things.

Two years before this poem was published and shortly after her sui-cide, Pound wrote that he imagined Margaret Cravens as "a small, fat, brown god sitting in a huge water-lily, splashing over the edge. . . . Said image may sound ridiculous, but it is a great comfort to one, and is so unanswerably true that I don't dare mention it to anyone else." Pound took these visions seriously, and the Imagist poems he crafted from them, as he wrote in "Ikon," are designed to prepare us for "that long dreaming" of the afterlife by offering a preliminary glimpse of the world beyond the senses. In an unpublished version of "His Vi-sion of a Certain Lady Post Mortem," Pound made his vision of Mar-garet Cravens clearer with an opening line that he eventually cut from the poem: "They call you dead, but I saw you."

Given Pound's interest in the poetry of vision, it is easy to see why

he was eager to include Joyce's "I Hear an Army" in *Des Imagistes*.
Not only was the poem, as Yeats remarked, "a technical and emotional masterpiece," but like Yeats's "The Magi" (which Pound singled out in his review of *Responsibilities* as an Imagist poem), "I
Hear an Army" presents a visionary experience. The opening stanzas
of Joyce's poem even recall the apocalyptic vision of Yeats's "The
Valley of the Black Pig" (from *The Wind Among the Reeds*), in
which "the clash of fallen horsemen and the cries / Of unknown per-
ishing armies beat about my ears."

> I hear an army charging upon the land,
>> And the thunder of horses plunging, foam about their knees:
> Arrogant, in black armour, behind them stand,
>> Disdaining the reins, with fluttering whips, the charioteers.

> They cry unto the night their battle-name:
>> I moan in sleep when I hear afar their whirling laughter.
> They cleave the gloom of dreams, a blinding flame,
>> Clanging, clanging upon the heart as upon an anvil.

In a 1918 review of Joyce's work, Pound praised the poem for the intensity of its "phantom vision." For most of the contributors to Pound's
anthology, Imagism was (in the words of John Gould Fletcher, who
like Flint was never permitted entry to the inner sanctum) "an attitude towards technique, pure and simple." But while Pound was com-
piling *Des Imagistes* at Stone Cottage, the visionary "Doctrine of the
Image" was as important as the "Don'ts."

Pound's esoteric theories of the Image would not be so interesting
(as he himself wrote of the occult aspect of the Noh) if they "were
not bound up with a dramatic and poetic interest of the very highest
order." And it seems likely that part of Pound's attraction to the
occult, and his desire to maintain an esoteric doctrine of the Image distinct from the exoteric trinity of "Don'ts," came from the same impulse that led him to boom Tagore: it was another way to set himself apart from the mob, to differentiate himself from artists such as
Aldington or Fletcher whom he otherwise included in his circle. Everything Pound and Yeats studied at Stone Cottage was chosen for
its esoteric value: Noh drama, Chinese poetry, western demonology,
even Lady Gregory's folklore—these were not subjects that preoccupied the "elderish female" who peered into the windows of Stone
Cottage with what Pound took to be curiosity and awe. In their ef-

forts to separate themselves from what they perceived as an ignorant public who rebelled at Synge and ignored Joyce, Pound and Yeats delved deeper and deeper into the esoterica from which their later works would grow. But Pound and Yeats could not remain inside this hermetic world for long, and when the January 1914 issue of the *English Review* containing George Moore's attack on "Yeats, Lady Gregory, and Synge" arrived at their door, they returned from the rarefied air of Stone Cottage to the concerns of public life. And they emerged with a vengeance that fueled their attacks on the public as never before.

2

The Bourgeois State of Mind

When Pound recreated Yeats's incantation of "The Peacock" in the *Pisan Cantos* he also remembered Yeats

> hearing nearly all Wordsworth
> for the sake of his conscience but
> preferring Ennemoser on Witches.

These lines not only allude to Joseph Ennemoser's *The History of Magic*, which the two poets read during their first winter in Sussex, but also recall "The Witch," a poem Yeats published as a companion to "The Peacock."

> Toil and grow rich,
> What's that but to lie
> With a foul witch
> And after, drained dry,
> To be brought
> To the chamber where
> Lies one long sought
> With despair?

Pound had particular reason to remember these verses, because in his own copy of *Responsibilities* he had made a note which reveals that

56

Yeats originally wrote a much grittier poem: Pound crossed out the words "a foul witch" from the third line and wrote in the margin, "emended by W.B.Y. to 'some stale bitch' & then castrated by the greasy Macmillan. E.P. 1917."

The word "greasy" had special significance for Pound. Yeats used it memorably in "September, 1913" to castigate the Irish middle classes who (in Yeats's eyes) had no interest in the kinds of riches he accumulated in "The Peacock":

> What need you, being come to sense,
> But fumble in a greasy till
> And add the halfpence to the pence
> And prayer to shivering prayer, until
> You have dried the marrow from the bone?

Pound borrowed the word again in "The Lake Isle" (a riposte to Yeats's "The Lake Isle of Innisfree") in which he beseeched the gods for "a little tobacco-shop" with

> the little bright boxes
>   piled up neatly upon the shelves
> And the loose fragrant cavendish
>   and the shag,
> And the bright Virginia
>   loose under the bright glass cases,
> And a pair of scales not too greasy.

Pound's use of the word "greasy" is emblematic of the influence Yeats had on his social attitudes during the Stone Cottage years. From Yeats, Pound learned an entire vocabulary. In "On Criticism in General" (1923), the "De Vulgari Eloquentia" he wrote to accompany the early *Cantos*, Pound described this "honorable debt": "To W. B. Yeats (with whom one disagrees on nearly all possible points, save in the belief that a poem should attain some degree of intensity): that he backs one in the belief that one should make NO compromise with the public." By 1923 Pound's and Yeats's poetic practices had diverged dramatically, but they still shared a belief in the privilege of an artistic elite. A decade earlier, during their first winter at Stone Cottage, Yeats first impressed Pound with his ability to "make NO compromise with the public" and provided him with a

model for the hostile attitude he would project in his Vorticist manifestos and for many years to come.

Yeats's impact on Pound can best be measured by comparing the
two poets' attitudes toward their audience just before their first winter together. In October 1913 Yeats published his *Poems Written in
Discouragement*, five poems provoked by the Hugh Lane controversy:
"To a Wealthy Man, who promised a second subscription if it were
proved the people wanted pictures," "September, 1913," "To a Friend
whose Work has Come to Nothing," "Paudeen," and "To a Shade."
Hugh Lane, Lady Gregory's nephew, had offered his collection of
French impressionist paintings to Dublin if the city would agree to
house them properly. A proposal for a bridge-gallery that would span
the Liffey was rejected by the Dublin corporation. Yeats explained
the controversy in a note he added to *Poems Written in Discouragement* when he republished them as part of *Responsibilities*: "One
could respect the argument that Dublin, with much poverty and
many slums, could not afford the £22,000 the building was to cost the
city, but not the minds that used it. One frenzied man compared the
pictures to Troy horse which 'destroyed a city,' and innumerable cor-
respondents described Sir Hugh Lane and those who had subscribed
many thousands to give Dublin paintings by Corot, Manet, Monet,
Degas, and Renoir, as 'self-seekers,' 'self-advertisers,' 'picture-dealers,'
'log-rolling cranks and faddists.' "

One of these subscribers, Lord Ardilaun, made his support of the
gallery contingent upon the public's acceptance of the project and
provoked some of Yeats's finest invective in "To a Wealthy Man":

> You gave, but will not give again
> Until enough of Paudeen's pence
> By Biddy's halfpennies have lain
> To be 'some sort of evidence,'
> Before you'll put your guineas down,
> That things it were a pride to give
> Are what the blind and ignorant town
> Imagines best to make it thrive.
> What cared Duke Ercole, that bid
> His mummers to the market-place,
> What th'onion sellers thought or did
> So that his Plautus set the pace
> For the Italian comedies?

> And Guidobaldo, when he made
> That grammar school of courtesies
> Where wit and beauty learned their trade
> Upon Urbino's windy hill,
> Had sent no runners to and fro
> That he might learn the shepherds' will.

In contrast to the wealthy man, who consulted the "blind and ignorant" public, Yeats offers the examples of Ercole d'Este and Guidobaldo di Montefeltro, the fifteenth-century dukes of Ferrara and Urbino. These rulers, immortalized in Castiglione's *The Book of the Courtier*, did not depend upon their public's approval for their support of the arts. Yeats felt that if the city of Dublin were to become the cultural center it deserved to be, the Corporation should do the same: no compromise should be sought with the ignorant middle classes. Yeats made this sentiment explicit in his note for *Responsibilities*: "Against all this we have but a few educated men and the remnants of an old traditional culture among the poor. Both were stronger forty years ago, before the rise of our new middle class which made its first public display during the nine years of the Parnellite split, showing how base at moments of excitement are minds without culture."

In the same month that Yeats published *Poems Written in Discouragement*, Pound published "The Serious Artist," and his attitude toward the public projected in this essay could not be more different from Yeats's. While Yeats demanded that both the artist and his patron ignore public taste, Pound offered a justification of art which stressed its social obligation. Situating his essay in what he thought of as the "humanist" tradition of Sidney's *Defense of Poesy*, he asserted that "the good of the greatest number [of people] cannot be attained until we know in some sort of what that good must consist" and that it is the artist's job to isolate this "lasting and unassailable data regarding the nature of man." Should the artist lie, "his offence is of the same nature as the physician's and according to his position and the nature of his lie he is responsible for future oppressions and for future misconceptions." Pound would never give up this belief that the health of a culture depends upon the health of its arts, but at Stone Cottage his respect for his audience dwindled rapidly as he witnessed Yeats's response to George Moore's attack on the aristocracy of the arts.

The attack appeared in "Yeats, Lady Gregory, and Synge," a chapter from the third volume of Moore's trilogy of memoirs (*Hail and Farewell*), which arrived at Stone Cottage in the January 1914 issue of the *English Review*. In the second volume of the trilogy, Moore had poked fun at Yeats's occult studies, and at the time of its publication (1912) Pound had reported Yeats's reaction in a letter to his parents: "As W.B.Y. says of Moore's book, 'it's a very amusing book, only it ought not to have been written.' I haven't bothered to read it. Have seen Moore once or twice at teas or dinners. He is regarded mostly as a joke or a 'stupid old man' or what you like."

In the new chapter of his memoirs in the *English Review*, Moore's attack on Yeats's pretensions to an aristocratic ancestry came too close to the bone for Yeats to be amused. Moore recalled a lecture he delivered on the French Impressionists to publicize a temporary exhibition of paintings that Hugh Lane organized for the city of Dublin in 1904. "As soon as the applause died away," according to Moore, Yeats stood up and

> began to thunder like Ben Tillett himself against the middle classes, stamping his feet, working himself into a great passion, and all because the middle classes did not dip their hands into their pockets and give Lane the money he wanted for his exhibition. It is impossible to imagine the hatred which came into his voice when he spoke the words "the middle classes"; one would have thought that he was speaking against a personal foe; but there are millions in the middle classes! And we looked round asking each other with our eyes where on earth our Willie Yeats had picked up such extraordinary ideas. He could hardly have gathered in the United States so ridiculous an idea that none but titled and carriage-folk can appreciate pictures. And we asked ourselves why Willie Yeats should feel himself called upon to denounce the class to which he himself belonged essentially: on one side excellent mercantile millers and ship-owners, and on the other a portrait painter of rare talent.

Moore was recalling an expression of the same ire that fueled Yeats's attack on the middle classes in *Poems Written in Discouragement*, but Yeats felt that Moore had badly misrepresented his sentiments. In his diary entry for January 1914, Yeats recorded his first response to Moore's attack:

> George Moore in an outrageous article in *English Review* attacks Lady Gregory and myself. Lady Gregory has threatened a libel ac-

tion and Moore has apologized and withdrawn a statement about her proselytizing in early life. The statements about me are too indefinite for any action, though equally untrue. Some years ago I made a speech at a lecture of Moore's for which Lane thanked me at the time, saying it was the one speech that might have some good effect. It was an appeal to the Irish aristocracy to support Lane's gallery, and I heard afterwards that it offended Lady Ardilaun. Moore has turned this into an attack on the middle classes.

Yeats went on to turn Moore's insinuations about his ancestry back on Moore himself, attributing his "crudity" to his family, "half-peasants in education and occupation." In the privacy of his journal, Yeats addressed Moore in his own terms; his public response required a more disinterested stance. When Dorothy Shakespear asked Pound how Yeats felt about the attack, Pound replied from Stone Cottage that Yeats "does nowt but write lofty poems to his ancestors, thinking that the haughtiest reply." Pound was referring to the two poems that frame *Responsibilities*, "Pardon, old fathers" and "While I, from that reed-throated whisperer." The second poem, titled "Notoriety (*suggested by a recent magazine article*)" when it first appeared in the *New Statesman* in this slightly different form, offered a rather indelicate image of Moore's crudity: at Stone Cottage, sequestered with one young companion, Yeats wrote that so long as he could

> surmise companions
> Beyond the fling of the dull ass's hoof—
> Ben Jonson's phrase—and still may turn my feet
> To Kyle-na-Ino and to that ancient roof
> By the woods edge where only equals meet,
> I can forgive even that wrong of wrongs,
> Those undreamt accidents that have made me—
> Seeing that Fame has perished this long while,
> Being but a part of ancient ceremony—
> Notorious, till all my priceless things
> Are but a post the passing dogs defile.

The "ancient roof / By the woods edge where only equals meet" near "Kyle-na-Ino" is meant to be Coole Park, Yeats's summer retreat, but the phrase applies equally as well to Stone Cottage, the retreat at the edge of Ashdown Forest in which Yeats wrote the poem. When

Yeats reprinted it in *Responsibilities* he amended these lines to "that ancient roof / A sterner conscience and a friendlier home," but the poem remains the lofty pronouncement of a tiny aristocracy of the arts, meeting in Sussex by the waste moor.

These poems were all Yeats had to say to Moore until he published his own recollections of the Irish dramatic movement in *Dramatis Personae* (1935), but Pound soon offered an even stronger reply. The suppression of the Abbey players in Liverpool probably angered Pound as much as it did Yeats, but it did not move him to make a public response. Yet an attack on his Stone Cottage companion could not go unanswered. First Pound advised Lady Gregory on the best way to approach William Heinemann, Moore's publisher, in order to have the libelous sentences deleted. On January 4th Yeats explained an alternate plan to Lady Gregory.

> In the inconceivable case of Heinemann refusing you, you should not shrink from law. It is a good general rule to avoid law, but there are exceptions. In this case the matter is entirely clear, Moore would be told by his counsel that an attempt to defend the case would increase the damages. Your simple statement would be all the court would ask. I say this not because I think there will be any necessity for law but because readiness for it will strengthen your hand, though Ezra says your decided manner will scare Heinemann into docility.

On the same day that he conveyed this advice to Lady Gregory, Yeats also wrote to Mabel Beardsley about Moore's remarks and commented that Pound wanted to attack Moore in print. Yeats dissuaded him from doing so since he felt that Pound had begun to write fine verse; an attack on Moore would be a waste of his energy. The poetry of aristocratic disdain—not what Yeats had previously called Pound's prerogative of youth, "making enemies"—was most important to the elder poet. Yet Pound could not keep silent. As a postscript to "A Curious History" (the survey of Joyce's troubles over the publication of *Dubliners* that appeared in the January 15th issue of the *Egoist*), Pound added these sentences: " 'The English Review' for the month contains the outpourings of Messrs. Crowley, Edmund Gosse, and George Moore. Mr. Moore has succeeded in falling below even his usual level of mendacious pusillanimity."

This brief comment did not exhaust Pound's anger. The next number of the *Egoist* (February 2nd) contained an essay called

"The Bourgeois" by a certain Bastien von Helmholtz. Written pseudonymously by Pound, it repeats almost everything Yeats wrote about Moore in his journal but was unwilling to say in public. Without naming Moore, Pound wrote that "One of the boudoir school of journalists . . . has attacked Mr. Yeats because Mr. Yeats has, according to him, attacked the bourgeoisie." Like Yeats in his journal, Pound then pointed out that "Mr. Yeats was, in the particular speech refered to, attacking the aristocracy, which needs it, but no matter." In reply to Moore's allegation that "Mr. Yeats talks as if he wasn't born of the bourgeoisie," Pound explained:

> The word "bourgeois" is not applied to the middle classes to distinguish them from the aristocracy. It might be but that is scarcely its historical usage. The bourgeoisie is a state of mind. It is as a term of opprobrium, used by the bohemian, or the artist in contempt of the citizen. The bourgeoisie is digestive. The bourgeois is the lineal descendant of the "honest citizen" of the Elizabethan. The "honest citizen" was the person who was so overjoyed when he found out that Ben Jonson had made him a cuckold. He gained in distinction not because Ben Jonson was a great author, but because Ben Jonson sometimes appeared at court. The bourgeois is, roughly, a person who is concerned solely with his own comfort or advancement. He is, in brief, digestive. He is the stomach and gross intestines of the body politic and social, as distinct from the artist, who is the nostrils and the invisible antennae.

Here too Pound was acting as Yeats's public (and probably unauthorized) mouthpiece: as early as 1900 Yeats had written that he used the words "middle class" to "describe an attitude of mind more than an accident of birth." And in his response to George Moore in his journal Yeats wrote that "The word 'bourgeois' which I had used is not an aristocratic term of reproach, but, like the old 'cit' which one finds in Ben Jonson, a word of artistic usage." Pound and Yeats must have been reading Jonson at Stone Cottage, for Yeats refers to lines from *The Poetaster* in "Notoriety," describing himself as "Beyond the flint of the dull asse's hoof— / Ben Jonson's phrase." For both Pound and Yeats, their time at Stone Cottage was an escape from the pressures of what Pound called the bourgeois "state of mind." Perhaps the poets read Ben Jonson because Stone Cottage is just seven miles from Penshurst, the ancient home of the Sidney family, which Jonson idealized as the aristocratic ideal—a place where "all the muses met."

When their own private meeting of the muses at Stone Cottage was interrupted by Moore's outburst of "middle class" values, Pound responded at the end of his article—as Yeats had at the end of his journal entry—by attributing Moore's crudity to his inferior breeding: "He has mistaken a term which is the censure of a whole code of morals and of ethics for a term of social snobbery, which is perhaps natural, as he himself would fall under either censure." This conception of social class as a "state of mind" rather than an economic condition, which Pound articulated with the help of Yeats and Jonson, would become a cornerstone of his social criticism over the next few years.

Except for *Patria Mia* (1913), Pound's account of his Jamesian return to America in 1910, "The Bourgeois" is his first piece of explicitly social criticism and his first piece of writing to exhibit the exaggerated arrogance which would cloud Pound's work for the next three decades; it is also a virtual paraphrase of Yeats's private thoughts. Once "The Bourgeois" was published, Pound did not let his aggressive persona "Bastien von Helmholtz" rest quietly. Sometimes replacing him with his brother, "Baptiste von Helmholtz," Pound went on to address a wide range of topics. In "John Synge and the Habits of Criticism" Helmholtz attacked the "democracy of commentators who believe not only that every man is created free and equal with a divine right to become an insignificant part of a social system but that all books are created equal and that all minds are created equal and that any distinct and distinguishing faculty should be curtailed and restricted." Pound was attacking the (for his purposes) appropriately named Maurice Bourgeois, whose biography of Synge Yeats found equally offensive. In "On the Imbecility of the Rich," Pound wrote, like the Yeats of *Ideas of Good and Evil*, that "the only true religion is the revelation made in the arts," offering a vision of a social system much like Yeats's ideal feudal society: "One can only hope for some protection of the arts like the churchly protection of knowledge of the middle ages. This 'truce of the arts' will come; this security of artistic creation. But the foundation will not be from the rich. It will not be a 'rich young man of Assisi' who shall found it; it will be a guild of the intelligent poor and near-poor. It will be as fanatical almost as the mediaeval religious. It will hate and condemn the world. It will be a damnable nuisance." When "Helmholtz" turned his caustic eye to the "Suffragettes" he reiterated the principle which supports all this criticism: "The duty of literate men and of all women is to keep alight some spark of civilisation at the summit of things. . . . It is not our duty to fuss about Sunday closing or minimum wage or any other attempt to make hell less hell-like for the lower classes." Throughout these articles Pound continued to deny the importance of real social and economic conditions, urging instead the consolations of an en- lightened spiritual condition attainable only by and through the artist.

Pound's stance toward the public also became more and more aggressive throughout the "Helmholtz" essays; the response to George Moore seemed justified in some ways, but Pound's ideal of an artistic community became progressively more unpalatable. During the first winter in Sussex, Yeats participated in two ceremonies honoring two different poets; the contrast between them points out the potential nobility of Pound's dream of an aristocracy of the arts. On November 28th Yeats returned to London for a meeting of the Academic Com- mittee of the Royal Society of Literature (of which he had been a founding member in 1910) to award the Edmond de Polignac Prize (£100) to James Stephens. Pound did not attend the ceremony, but he was able to read this account of Yeats's speech in the December 15th issue of the *New Freewoman*:

> Mr. Yeats? Ah, Mr. Yeats. Mr. Yeats explained with Dublin Theatre gestures and parsonic elocution that he had no manuscript to read from. He had given his to the press. He smiled benignly, and recited his memorised speech perfectly. He spoke in his beau- tiful voice; he expressed Celtic lore with his more beautiful face; he elevated and waved his yet more beautiful hands. He blessed us with his presence. He spoke of spirits and phantasmagoria. He spoke of finding two boots in the middle of a field and the owner of the boots listening for the earth-spirits under a bush. He said that in Ireland the hedge-rows were rushing upon the towns. He praised Mr. Stevens' Crock of Gold. He read one of Mr. Stevens' poems, which was admirable as he read it.
>
> Mr. Yeats concluded the performance by giving Mr. Stevens a hundred pounds. We could not hear Mr. Stevens promising to be a good boy and not spend it all in toffee and fairy-books.

The Academic Committee's published record of Yeats's remarks reveals that he did speak of "spirits and phantasmagoria" but not of boots in a field. Yeats also hinted at his lack of real interest in

Stephens's verse ("when I first met with his name I was not interested") and went on to discuss the young Irish poet's career in terms
more relevant to his own dilemma: Stephens's work offered "proof
that my native city has begun to live with a deeper life. . . . No
matter how much we seem to create ourselves in solitude, wren or
eagle, we proclaim the twigs we have sprung from. I think that if
[Stephens] had grown up in Dublin any time before these last twenty
years he would have found it hard to escape from rhetoric and insincerity. I hope he will not be offended if I say that even his rich soul
might not have saved him from being, like some writer of Young
Ireland, but a gallant journalist." As these sentences echo his own
"Upon a House Shaken by the Land Agitation," they also describe
the work Yeats himself had set out to accomplish in the solitude of
Stone Cottage; having been born more than twenty years before
(and having wondered if Synge's death was caused by his "misunderstanding with the wreckage of Young Irelandism"), Yeats was working hard to escape rhetoric and insincerity. "During these last years,"
he continued in his speech, "the Dublin that reads and talks has
begun to interest itself in the ancient legends and in the living
legends of Connaught and Munster, and here in this book it discovers them weighty with new morals, lofty and airy with philosophy.
The town has begun to make, it seems also, in Mr. Stephens' mouth
new legends, new beliefs, new folk-lore, and instead of rhetoric, the
hard-driven logic—natural wherever the interest was political—there
is a beautiful, wise, wayward phantasy."

That is precisely the transformation Yeats was enacting in his own
work as he left his *Poems Written in Discouragement* behind and
buried himself in his commentary on Lady Gregory's collection of
folklore. George Moore had forced him back to the world of politics,
and even the excursion to London to offer this praise for James
Stephens was a distraction. Dorothy Shakespear attended the ceremony, and suggested that, for Yeats, the Academic Committee
"must be a terrible & solid phalanx of A. C. Bensonism to battle
against." Pound agreed that the award to Stephens was neither
adventurous nor warranted, responding from Stone Cottage that
Yeats "talks of the academic committee's 'passion for the absolutely
harmless.'" In his speech, Yeats even offered a playful acknowledgment of the committee's stodginess: "We of the Academic Committee are much wiser than we seem. You will listen to us for an hour,
and you will be surprised at how little we shall have said, and even

if you do not admire our books very much, you will go away wondering that we could have written them."

As if to counter the Academic Committee's public award ceremony to an undeserving poet, Pound began to organize a private award ceremony for a poet he had once called "the grandest of old men, the last of the great Victorians": Wilfrid Scawen Blunt (1840–1922). In 1911 Yeats had made an unsuccessful attempt to have Blunt elected to the Academic Committee. Part of the problem was that Blunt was better-known for his outspoken anti-imperialism and for breeding Arabian horses than for his poetry. Yeats had known him both as a political activist and as a playwright: Blunt had joined in the Irish revolt against absentee-landlordism, and his *Fand of the Fair Cheek* had been produced by the Abbey Theatre. Lady Gregory, who called Blunt "the first Englishman put in prison for Ireland's sake," knew Blunt better than Yeats did. In November 1913 Yeats wrote to her explaining Pound's idea for an honorary dinner in London, asking "if you think Blunt would come and if he would care about it." With Lady Gregory's approval, the dinner was proposed to Blunt, who then invited the poets to Newbuildings Place, his Sussex estate, instead. Yeats hired a motorcar to drive them from Stone Cottage; looking forward to the journey Pound mused that "if it is as dammmmM cold sunday next as it is now we'll arrive like a box of marrons glacés."

So that the honor would be meaningful, Pound invited only poets he respected: besides Yeats, Sturge Moore, Victor Plarr, Richard Aldington, and F. S. Flint attended the dinner for Blunt; Hilaire Belloc arrived after the meal, and John Masefield declined the invitation but sent a poem. Blunt served the poets a roast peacock, carried to the table in full plumage. Yeats told Lady Gregory that it tasted like turkey but noted that Pound thought it was "a more divine turkey." For Pound, who was not accustomed to such things, the entire experience was profoundly aristocratic—the antithesis of the bourgeois Academic Committee; he told his mother that the peacock "went very well with the iron-studded barricades on the stairway and other mediaeval relics and Burne-jones tapestry." Newbuildings Place was Blunt's Penshurst, a home where poets could truly dwell.

After the feast, the company of poets presented Blunt with a reliquary carved by Gaudier-Brzeska, which contained copies of verses they read in tribute. Yeats offered "When Helen Lived," a poem he had not yet published.

> We have cried in our despair
> That men desert,
> For some trivial affair
> Or noisy, insolent sport,
> Beauty that we have won
> From bitterest hours;
> Yet we, had we walked within
> Those topless towers
> Where Helen walked with her boy,
> Had given but as the rest
> Of the men and women of Troy
> A word and a jest.

The trouble with *The Playboy* lingered in Yeats's mind as he wrote this poem: in "The Death of Synge" he recorded that on July 8, 1909 he had "dreamed this thought two nights ago: 'Why should we complain if men ill-treat our Muses, when all that they gave to Helen while she still lived was a song and a jest?'" "When Helen Lived" was a sobering reflection on the despair-ridden cries that both Yeats and Pound had released at a public who failed to recognize the hard-won beauties of Joyce and Synge; Yeats confessed that even he might not have been so perceptive in more noble times. In *Responsibilities* Yeats emphasized this aspect of the poem by placing it immediately after his "Poems Written in Discouragement," allowing it to temper his haughty condemnations of middle-class values with a touch of self-consciousness.

The verses Pound composed for the dinner expressed his more radical sense of the poet's aristocratic "state of mind."

> Because you have gone your individual gait,
> Written fine verses, made mock of the world,
> Swung the grand style, not made a trade of art,
> Upheld Mazzini and detested institutions;
>
> We, who are little given to respect,
> Respect you, and having no better way to show it,
> Bring you this stone to be some record of it.

The "stone" refers to Gaudier-Brzeska's reliquary, carved with the motto "Homage to W. S. BLVNT" on one side and a reclining female nude on the other. Guiseppe Mazzini, the Italian revolutionary who was Swinburne's hero, is cited in error; Blunt had been associated with the Egyptian rebel Ahmed Arabi. But these details were not so important as the tone of the poem. When Pound was composing these verses at Stone Cottage, Yeats told Lady Gregory that Pound had spent the morning trying to revive his knowledge of Elizabethan English but was having trouble since he considered poems of salutation to be obsolete. Pound recognized the inadequacy of his poem when he later wrote that Blunt himself was "the last man who has been able to use the old-fashioned Elizabethan 'grand style' effectively." When Pound's salutation was completed, Yeats sent it to Lady Gregory, lamenting its lack of rhyme but noting that if one read it as "an attitude of mind" one approved of it. That attitude of mind was deeply arrogant, the proclamation of a secret society of the arts meeting in medieval splendor—not the Academic Committee of the Royal Society of Literature, holding open court in Caxton Hall. Pound later wrote, rather disingenuously, that the dinner for Blunt was "a fairly complete sort of tribute, representing no one clique or style," but when at Lady Gregory's request Yeats wrote an account of the affair for the *Times*, Pound said, "Tell Lady Gregory we hate the newspapers as Blunt hates the British Empire." He was delighted after the Great War began when he learned that Blunt had hung a sign on his front door: "BELLIGERENTS WILL PLEASE GO ROUND TO THE KITCHEN." Blunt lived like the Medici prince of Yeats's "To a Wealthy Man," idealized for devoting himself to the arts, "indifferent how the rancour ran."

For Pound, it was not so much Blunt's poetry as his aristocratic life and thought which were worthy of emulation. Yeats approved of Pound's "attitude of mind," but sometimes the vehemence of his companion's attacks on the "middle-classes" worried him; Pound's poetry was slipping into the public rhetoric of politics that Yeats had rejected in his speech for the Academic Committee. At the dinner for Blunt, Yeats gave another short speech in which he catalogued the movements in verse which had come and gone in Blunt's lifetime. After discussing the Victorian "abstract" poet, Blunt's poetry of "actual life," and his own conversion to a poetry "of a man who is simply giving the thoughts which he had in some definite situation in life," Yeats ended by remarking that "Ezra Pound has a desire personally to insult the world."

Yeats was thinking of poems such as Pound's "Salutation the

Third," verses which show just what Pound meant when he told
Yeats that poems of salutation were obsolete. When he sent this
poem to Harriet Monroe, Pound mentioned that Yeats "trembles for
my 'unrestrained language' " and added that he would "change 'pot-
bellied' and write 'obese.' " But when the poem appeared in *Blast*
Pound ignored Yeats's advice and wrote "slut-bellied":

> Let us deride the smugnesss of "The Times": GUFFAW!
>   So much for the gagged reviewers,
> It will pay them when the worms are wriggling in their vitals;
> These are they who objected to newness,
> Here are their tomb-stones.
>   They supported the gag and the ring:
> A little BLACK BOX contains them.
>   So shall you be also,
> You slut-bellied obstructionist,
> You sworn foe to free speech and good letters,
> You fungus, you continuous gangrene.

Yeats's early diagnosis of Pound's "desire to personally insult the
world" would eventually lead him to place the younger poet in phase
12 of *A Vision*, where one is driven "into all sorts of temporary
ambitions" which one "defends by some kind of superficial intellectual action, the pamphlet, the violent speech, the sword of the
swashbuckler." The older poet would rather have seen Pound write
lofty poems such as "Pardon, old fathers" instead of "Salutation the
Third" or the aggressive Bastien von Helmholtz essays. While Yeats
entertained all the same thoughts about George Moore in his diary,
he would not air them in public.

Pound was perceptive when he told Harriet Monroe that Yeats
trembled at his "unrestrained language"; it was not Pound's attitude
so much as his mode of expressing it that bothered the older poet.
The image of George Moore as a urinating dog in "Notoriety" is at
least as ribald as anything in Pound's "Salutation the Third," but
the coarseness of the image is contained by Yeats's finely honed
pentameters—what Pound called his "Elizifbeefan" style. Similarly,
Yeats made a condemnation of middle-class economic striving as in-
sulting as any of Pound's in "Beggar to Beggar Cried," but unlike
Pound he tempered the coarseness in traditionally sanctioned verse
forms:

'Time to put off the world and go somewhere
And find my health again in the sea air,'
Beggar to beggar cried, being frenzy-struck,
'And make my soul before my pate is bare.'

'And get a comfortable wife and house
To rid me of the devil in my shoes,'
Beggar to beggar cried, being frenzy-struck,
'And the worse devil that is between my thighs.'

Yeats's impulse to insult the world was always more dignified than Pound's, a difference in mode that, despite the two poets' common arrogance, created a tension in their relationship. This tension was exacerbated by a feature of their relationship suggested by a photograph taken of the poets who came to honor Blunt: standing to Blunt's right is the older generation (Victor Plarr, Sturge Moore, and Yeats) while on the left are Pound, Richard Aldington, and

The poets at Blunt's peacock dinner *(from left to right)*: Victor Plarr, Sturge Moore, Yeats, Blunt, Pound, Richard Aldington, and F. S. Flint.

F. S. Flint. What joined these two generations was their admiration
for Blunt, but Pound, having close friends in both camps, felt the
generation gap more severely. In the *Pisan Cantos* Pound would
remember that old Colonel Jackson "said to Yeats at a vorticist
picture show: / 'You also of the brotherhood?' " The confusions here
are manifold. Yeats was not a Vorticist, and the Vorticists were not
the Pre-Raphaelite Brotherhood, a secret society which, as Pound
mentions in the *Guide to Kulchur*, Colonel Jackson was "old
enough" to remember. As *Hugh Selwyn Mauberley* (Pound's history
of the British avant-garde from the P.R.B. through the Nineties to
his own war-torn "gang") reveals, Pound did sense a real connection
between these "brotherhoods," but it was not a comparison his
younger friends welcomed. Pound addressed this tension between
the different generations of moderns in "Ferrex on Petulance" and
"Porrex on Ferrex," two articles written during the first Stone Cottage winter. The esssays appeared side by side in the *Egoist*, signed
by "Ferrex" and "Porrex," names Pound took from Thomas Sack-
ville and Thomas Norton's *Gorboduc or Ferrex and Porrex* (1561–
62), the first English Renaissance play written in blank verse.

Both essays are concerned with Pound's relationship with Yeats,
and more specifically with the two poets' different ways of responding
to George Moore. In "Ferrex on Petulance" Pound refers to Yeats
only as his "elder friend":

> My gracious, superior and I need scarcely say elder friend con-
> stantly remonstrates with me for the petulance of me and my gen-
> eration. He says I cannot get Lord Howard de Walden to buy
> "The Times" and suppress it, or Lord Alfred Douglas to assassi-
> nate the most odious editor of a very odious monthly, or, in short,
> have any effect on superior circles unless I lay aside all petulance,
> and persuade my generation to do so.
> "In short [says my elder friend], the younger generation is ill-fed,
> and its petulance betrays its ill-feeding, and therefore no superior
> person will believe in the loftiness and unbiasedness of its ill-fed
> opinion."

Pound says that his "elder friend" suggests that "we should preserve a lofty indifference" (as Yeats himself had done in response to
George Moore) and Pound now agrees that the "young writer" must
"seek out henceforth a not too honied suavity in dealing with 'current questions,' for by this means alone shall he gain empery over

the moderate minds of his elders." In making this statement, Pound had taken to heart Yeats's critique of his more violent work, but he nevertheless remained of two minds on the issue; in the second essay, "Porrex on Ferrex," he adopted the more aggressive stance of Wyndham Lewis or Gaudier-Brzeska to criticize this Yeatsian indifference: "It may be that we as the youngest generation are truly well opinioned of our parts, that we write with truculence rather than with that air of triumph which designates and distinguishes those authors who are getting well on toward forty. . . . As for influencing the suet-like minds of our prosperous forerunners—why should we bother? These men will probably die in due season and we shall be left to insult above their tribe with a placid insouciance." In his contributions to the Vorticist movement, launched after he returned from Stone Cottage in 1914, Pound followed the advice of the aggressive "Porrex" rather than the deferential "Ferrex." Throughout all his Vorticist manifestoes and reviews, Pound never mentions Yeats, and he exhibits what Yeats had called his "desire personally to insult the world."

Despite the aggressiveness of Pound's prose, however, the lessons he learned from Yeats at Stone Cottage stand behind his Vorticist pronouncements. As many observers at the time noticed, that aggressive persona was not natural for Pound. When Aldington reviewed the 1914 issue of *Blast* he remarked that "Mr. Pound is one of the gentlest, most modest, bashful, kind creatures who ever walked the earth; so I cannot help thinking that all this enormous arrogance and petulance and fierceness are a pose." At heart, Pound's feelings were closer to Ferrex's respect for Yeats's reticence than to Porrex's emulation of Lewis's aggressive rhetoric.

Yeats's influence was naturally not the only source of Pound's growing arrogance, but it is important to see that subtle gradations of tone are present in the younger poet's blasts against the middle-classes. Just after Pound returned from Stone Cottage at the end of January, just before Yeats boarded the Lusitania, bound for his American lecture tour, Pound spoke at the Quest Society with Lewis and Hulme. Hulme delivered his lecture on "Modern Art and its Philosophy," declaring the "break up of the Renaissance humanistic" ideal of man's natural place in the world and the artist's obligation to represent and nurture that relationship. Having just witnessed Yeats's aristocratic denials of his public, Pound found Hulme's statements attractive. In an account of the Quest Society lectures published in the *Egoist,* Pound rejected the humanist values he had projected in "The Serious Artist" just a few months before: "The artist has been for so long a humanist! He has been a humanist out of reaction. He has had sense enough to know that humanity was unbearably stupid and that he must try to disagree with it. But he has also tried to lead and persuade it; to save it from itself." Pound will have no more of the symbiotic relationship of the artist and society and instead proclaims that "the war between [the artist] and the world is a war without truce." "The aristocracy of entail and of title has decayed, the aristocracy of commerce is decaying, the aristocracy of the arts is ready again for its service. . . . We artists who have been so long the despised are about to take over control."

While the occasion for these remarks was the lectures by Lewis and Hulme, Pound had already honed the sentiments in the privacy of Stone Cottage, watching Yeats preserve "the aristocracy of the arts." The phrase itself has the Yeatsian tone; Vorticists did not commonly speak of aristocracies without irony. For the three months prior to the Quest Society lectures, Pound had been spending every day not with his Vorticist friends but with Yeats. And his rejection of the humanist values he himself had recently espoused in "The Serious Artist" was nurtured by the "elder poet" before "les jeunes" gave him the opportunity to express it in their aggressive style. The example of *Poems Written in Discouragement* and "Notoriety" was just as important to the Ferrex side of Pound as Hulme and Lewis were to Porrex. In his 1915 essay on Vorticism, Pound did not invoke Lewis when he wanted to explain the public's antipathy to modern painting; instead, he summarized Yeats's struggle with the Dublin Corporation: "Sir Hugh Lane tried to give Dublin a collection of pictures, Degas, Corot and Manet, and they called him a charlatan and cried out for real pictures 'like the lovely paintings which we see reproduced in our city art shops.'" Pound does not mention Yeats directly in this essay; the "elder poet" could have no open role in forging an avant-garde movement. But in a review of *Responsibilities* Pound published while *Blast* was going to press, he wrote that "to date no one has shown any disposition to supersede [Yeats] as the best poet in England." The true aristocracy of the arts remained quite select.

Pound depended upon the vocabulary of Yeats's vision of society not only in his critical prose but in his poetry. Unlike Hulme, Pound did not forsake his Paterian idealization of the Renaissance along

with his humanist vision of the artist's obligation to the "mob."
Like Yeats, he saw a return to certain aspects of the quattrocento as
a cure for modern culture's inadequacies. When Yeats completed a
draft of "To a Wealthy Man" in the last week of December 1912,
he told Lady Gregory that before he published it he planned to
show it to Masefield and Pound (whom he considered the sterner
critic). Pound approved, and the poem appeared in the January 11th
issue of the *Irish Times* as "The Gift." Pound admired the poem
so much that he quickly sent a copy to Harriet Monroe, saying that
Poetry could "print this as soon as possible" because the *Irish Times*
did not own the copyright; although Yeats dismissed "To a Wealthy
Man" as "a bit of propaganda," Pound thought the poem "better
than anything" in the previous batch of Yeats's poems they had published.

Poetry did not publish "To a Wealthy Man," but the poem remained a kind of touchstone for Pound's sense of the Renaissance
ideal of an aristocracy of the arts. In "To a Wealthy Man" Yeats
excuses the despotism of Cosimo de' Medici because of his patronage of the arts:

> And when they drove out Cosimo,
> Indifferent how the rancour ran,
> He gave the hours they had set free
> To Michelozzo's latest plan
> For the San Marco Library,
> Whence turbulent Italy should draw
> Delight in Art whose end is peace,
> In logic and in natural law
> By sucking at the dugs of Greece.

At Stone Cottage Pound quickly made this ideal his own, writing to
that poet most unlike Yeats, William Carlos Williams, that his "La
Flor" was "gracious" and "dignified": "It has the air of Urbino." A
few months later, in his essay "The Renaissance," Pound wrote that
the "scholars of the quattrocento . . . did not give the crowd what
it wanted." Pound's ideal of the Renaissance artist was first nurtured by Pater and then reinforced by the living example of Yeats;
in his notes to "Redondillas" (one of the poems cut from *Canzoni*
in 1911) Pound had named Yeats a "specialist in renaissances." The
point of Pound's *Patria Mia* was that America was the only place

where a second Renaissance could take place: "we will rebuild
Venice on the Jersey mud flats." So even as Pound praised Williams,
New Jersey's laureate, for resurrecting the spirit of Urbino, he looked
to Yeats as the model leader of a cultural renaissance. In his efforts
to make Dublin a cultural center, Yeats had shown Pound that a
renaissance must be "a thing made by conscious propaganda." No
direct link exists between Yeats's "To a Wealthy Man" and Pound's
Malatesta Cantos, but it is not coincidental that Pound lionizes
Sigismundo Malatesta, the Venetian despot who engaged the greatest artists of the Renaissance to build his *tempio*, in the same terms
Yeats uses to praise Cosimo de' Medici: the artistic foresight of
each man is presented as a justification of political atrocity. In
Canto 8 Pound portrays the ideal relationship between an artist and
his patron; Malatesta instructs his chancellor to tell his painter
(probably either Filippo Lippi or Gentile da Fabriano),

> That there can be no question of
> His painting the walls for the moment,
> As the mortar is not yet dry
> And it wd. be merely work chucked away
>   (*buttato via*)
> But I want it to be quite clear, that until the chapels are ready
> I will arrange for him to paint something else
> So that both he and I shall
> Get as much enjoyment as possible from it,
> And in order that he may enter my service
> And also because you write me that he needs cash,
> I want to arrange with him to give him so much per year
> And to assure him that he will get the sum agreed on.
> You may say that I will deposit security
> For him wherever he likes.
> And let me have a clear answer,
> For I mean to give him good treatment
> So that he may come to live the rest
> Of his life in my lands—
> Unless you put him off it—
> And for this I mean to make due provision,
> So that he can work as he likes,
> Or waste his time as he likes.

As Canto 8 progresses, Pound makes it clear that Malatesta wrote this letter while he was leading the Venetian army against Francesco Sforza, later the duke of Milan, at the city of Cremona. Like Yeats, Pound believed that civilization was saved not so much by political action as by artists who gave us the peace of antiquity by "sucking at the dugs of Greece." If a political leader such as Yeats's Cosimo or Pound's Malatesta provides properly for his artists, all manner of political atrocity might be excused. For Pound it was the "state of mind" that mattered.

It is a short step from Pound's veneration of Malatesta to his support of Mussolini. But during the first winter at Stone Cottage, Pound remained torn between political engagement and indifferent retreat. George Moore's attack on Yeats provoked Pound to return to the very world he had come to Sussex to escape. Yet even as he and Yeats remained in the seclusion of Ashdown Forest, studying Japanese plays and Irish folklore, their work remained political; they could not escape engagement with the outside world. The occult studies Yeats shared with Pound provided the younger poet with confirmation of his own esoteric doctrine of the Image—what he would call " 'symbolism' in its profounder sense" in his essay on Vorticism. But it also gave him a vocabulary for describing the initiated few, whether artistic or social: the doctrine of the Image was reserved for the priesthood of the arts, not the uninitiated mob. Or as Pound would write in his *Guide to Kulchur*, borrowing the metaphors of the occult, poetry expresses "the mysteries self-defended, the mysteries that *can* not be revealed. Fools can only profane them. The dull can neither penetrate the secretum nor divulge it to others." When Pound wrote that he learned how to "make NO compromise with the public" from Yeats, he meant to refer to the audience of his art. But the public soon became the public at large. At Stone Cottage, an apparently apolitical discussion of symbolism nurtured the social attitudes of the secret society of modernism.

3

Symbolism in Its Profounder Sense

During the summer following their first winter in Stone Cottage, Pound composed an essay titled "Imagism" to expand upon his earlier formulation of the doctrine of the Image. Before the manifesto appeared in the September 1914 issue of the *Fortnightly Review*, he changed the title to "Vorticism," explaining in a letter to Harriet Monroe that "Vorticism" was "the generic term now used on all branches of the new art, sculpture, painting, poetry." For Pound's purposes, Vorticism was Imagism writ large. But when he adopted the Vorticist nameplate he became part of a movement clearly associated with Lewis and Gaudier-Brzeska and even more clearly divorced from Yeats; while the Imagist manifestoes retained an aura of Pre-Raphaelite aestheticism, Lewis's Vorticist essays proclaimed the movement of the machine age. Yet at the same time, Yeats continued to shape Pound's personal conception of the Vorticist aesthetic (just as Pater appeared as a proto-Vorticist in Pound's contribution to *Blast*). Pound's remarks on symbolism in the "Vorticism" essay not only betray his debts to Yeats but also make a concealed reference to the material he and Yeats had studied at Stone Cottage.

Pound writes in "Vorticism" that "one does not want to be called a symbolist, because symbolism has usually been associated with mushy technique." Yet he also states that to hold a "belief in a sort of permanent metaphor is, as I understand it, 'symbolism' in its profounder sense. It is not necessarily a belief in a permanent world, but it is a belief in that direction." Given the enigmatic style of this essay, it is not easy to determine what Pound means by " 'symbolism' in its profounder sense." A letter Pound wrote during his stay at Stone Cottage provides the key. Dorothy Shakespear wrote to Pound asking him to explain "symbolism" to her; Pound replied with another question:

> What *do* you mean by symbolism? Do you mean real symbolism, Cabala, genesis of symbols, rise of picture language, etc. or the aesthetic symbolism of Villiers de l'Isle Adam, & that Arthur Symons wrote a book about—the literwary movement? At any rate begin on the "*Comte de Gabalis*", anonymous & should be in catalogue under "Comte de Gabalis." Then you might try the Grimoire of Pope Honorius (IIIrd I think).
>   There's a dictionary of symbols, but I think it immoral. I mean that I think a superficial acquaintance with the sort of shallow, conventional, or attributed meaning of a lot of symbols *weakens*— damnably, the power of receiving an energized symbol. I mean a symbol appearing in a vision has a certain richness & power of energizing joy—whereas if the supposed meaning of a symbol is familiar it has no more force, or interest of power of suggestion than any other word, or than a synonym in some other language.
>   Then there are those Egyptian language books, but O. S. [Olivia Shakespear] has 'em so they're no use. . . . Ennemoser's History of Magic may have something in it—Then there are "Les Symbolists"—french from Mallarmé, de l'Isle Adam, etc. to De Gourmont, which is another story.

The texts Pound recommends to Dorothy Shakespear were among those Yeats was studying in order to write his notes for Lady Gregory's *Visions and Beliefs in the West of Ireland*. For Pound, these esoteric writings formed part of a tradition of symbolism distinct from "literwary" symbolists, and the esoteric tradition is what he means by " 'symbolism' in its profounder sense." Postponing for a moment an investigation of Pound's reading list of occult works, we can now see why Pound writes in "Vorticism" that this kind of symbolism is "not necessarily a belief in a permanent world, but it is a belief in that direction." As Pound's earlier letter to Dorothy Shakespear about "intellectual vision" suggested, he believed that true symbolism depends upon the artist's visionary power: "a symbol appearing in a vision has a certain richness & power of energizing

joy" that a conventional "literwary" symbol does not, he now tells
Dorothy Shakespear; the "literwary" symbol has lost its power to
embody the divine or permanent world. Pound continues this critique
of literary symbolism in "Vorticism" when he writes that "almost
anyone can realize that to use a symbol *with an ascribed or intended
meaning* is, usually, to produce very bad art. We all remember
crowns, and crosses, and rainbows, and what not in atrociously mum-
bled colour." These symbols have become so conventional that one
might find them in an "immoral" dictionary of symbolism. "The
symbolists dealt in 'association,'" Pound argues, "that is, in a sort of
allusion, almost of allegory. They degraded the symbol to the status
of a word. They made it a form of metonomy. One can be grossly
'symbolic,' for example, by using the term 'cross' to mean 'trial.'" As
the literary symbols become codified, they lose the energizing power
granted to them by the individual artist's vision, and they are "degraded . . . to the status of a word" that has no magical power.

Pound wants to differentiate Imagism from this debased literary
symbolism and align it with "'symbolism' in its profounder sense."
As "Ikon" suggests by its concern with the afterlife, the Image is not
the simple word on the page, not a representation of the natural
world: "The image is the word beyond formulated language," Pound
writes in "Vorticism," and the Imagist poem is an attempt to embody the transcendental Image in words. "Heather" and "His Vision
of a Certain Lady Post Mortem" are not unique among Pound's
Imagist poems in being inspired by the method of "intellectual
vision" that Pound learned from Yeats. In September 1912 he wrote
to Dorothy Shakespear that he "had last night a most gorgeous
dream about the marriage in Cana of Galilee, it began in symbolical
patterns on a rug and ended in a wedding dance to exceed the Rus-
sians both in grace, splendour & legerity—convincingly naive and
oriental!!" Pound eventually made this dream-vision into "Dance
Figure, for the Marriage in Cana in Galilee," which he included in
"Contemporania," his first published group of Imagist Poems. The
poem begins:

> Dark eyed,
> O woman of my dreams,
> Ivory sandaled,
> There is none like thee among the dancers.
> None with swift feet.

Pound's "Contemporania," published in the April 1913 issue of *Poetry*, also included "In a Station of the Metro." In "Vorticism" Pound tells the now well-known story of the visionary experience that led to this poem. He wanted not simply to describe his vision of one "beautiful face, and then another and another" but find an equation for it that "seemed . . . worthy, or as lovely as that sudden emotion." In his quest for this "word beyond formulated language" Pound finally settled on an equation that has become the Image of Imagist poems.

> The apparition of these faces in the crowd:
> Petals, on a wet, black bough.

This "one image poem" is Pound's textbook example of " 'symbolism' in its profounder sense."

Like Pound, Yeats valued symbols that do not have a fixed meaning, symbols that are infinitely suggestive and suggestive of the infinite. The most powerful symbols, he wrote in "The Symbolism of Poetry" (1900), "call down among us certain disembodied powers, whose footsteps over our hearts we call emotions." Yeats presents two lines, misquoted from a song by Burns, as "perfectly symbolical":

> The white moon is setting behind the white wave
> And Time is setting with me, O!

Here, in the pages of "The Symbolism of Poetry" is the prototype of Pound's most famous Imagist poem. Like "In a Station of the Metro" these two lines achieve what Pound calls a "one image poem" in which "one idea [is] set on top of another." Yeats writes that Burns's lines "evoke an emotion which cannot be evoked by any other arrangement of colours and sounds and forms."

The early Yeats was not the only source of Pound's special understanding of symbolism, but the winters Pound spent studying the occult reinforced his belief in the esoteric aspects of the symbol. The occult literature he read during the winter of 1913–14 actually helped him to focus his ideas about Imagism and make more explicit the doctrine of the Image he had hinted at in "Ikon." The statements about Imagism in the "Vorticism" essay, written just after his first winter with Yeats, are much more assured than the vague definitions given in "Imagisme," written just before it. Pound's earlier definition of the Image as "an intellectual and emotional complex in an instant of time" which gives "that sense of freedom from time limits" only hints at the visionary quality that in "Vorticism" becomes more explicit. And while the 1913 list of "Dont's" concentrates on the stylistic aspects of the Imagist aesthetic, Pound could write in "Vorticism" that Imagism "has been known chiefly as a stylistic movement, as a movement of criticism rather than of creation" and move on to discuss the creative, visionary process that gives birth to the Imagist poem. The growth of Imagism depended on Pound's reading of Montfaucon's *Comte de Gabalis*, Kirk's *The Secret Commonwealth*, and Ennemoser's *History of Magic*.

The first text on Pound's syllabus of esoteric works on symbolism, *Le Comte de Gabalis, ou entretiens sur les sciences secrètes* (1670) by the Abbé de Montfaucon de Villars, had made another appearance in English literary history: it provided Pope with the Sylphs and Salamanders of his enlarged (1717) edition of *The Rape of the Lock*. In his dedication to Mrs. Arabella Fermer he describes *Le Comte* as a book "which both in its Title and Size is so like a *Novel*, that many of the Fair Sex have read it for one by mistake." Yeats read the book at Stone Cottage in his effort to correlate Lady Gregory's folklore with the literature of the occult, and he shared the book with Pound. On January 6, 1914, a week before Dorothy Shakespear asked Pound for some help with symbolism, Pound had already written to her that he and Yeats had "been reading The Comte de Gabalis—a charming and spritely book about Sylphes & Salamanders, you must read it when the Eagle lends it to O.S. [Olivia Shakespear] as I suppose he will sooner or later—tho' he borrowed it from somebody else. I have half a mind to translate only it seems too delicate to give to a prophane english vulgo." As important as *Le Comte de Gabalis* turned out to be for Pound, he did not translate it; however, he did persuade Dorothy Shakespear's mother Olivia to translate the book, and he published the translation in the *Egoist*. The five dialogues of *Le Comte de Gabalis* appeared in five issues of the *Egoist* from March 16th to June 1st, running concurrently with A *Portrait of the Artist as a Young Man*. Both books were sacred texts of the Order of the Brothers Minor.

※※

Olivia Shakespear, through whom Pound and Yeats first met, played an indispensable role in both their lives. Yeats originally met her

Olivia Shakespear, c. 1915.

through her cousin, Lionel Johnson, in June 1894, the same month in which she published her first novel, *Love on a Mortal Lease*. By August, Olivia Shakespear had virtually completed a novella, *Beauty's Hour* (published two years later in the *Savoy*), to which Yeats had contributed suggestions for the library of her character Dr. Trefusis: "I think you have chosen wisely in making Dr. Trefusis read the mystics rather than the purely magical books I suggested. *The Morning Redness* by Jacob Boehme is a great book beautifully named, which might do, and *The Obscure Night of the Soul* by St. John of the Cross is among the most perfectly named things in the world." Olivia Shakespear also had Dr. Trefusis read the *Grimoire of Pope Honorius*, one of the books Pound suggested Dorothy Shakespear read in his letter about " 'symbolism' in its profounder sense." As Olivia Shakespear knew, however, there was little that was authentic about this little book of black magic, falsely attributed to Pope Honorius III; in *Beauty's Hour* Dr. Trefusis speaks of Honorius as a "most absorbing old imposter."

In 1896–97 Yeats and Olivia Shakespear had a brief love affair.

She is the "Diana Vernon" of Yeats's memoirs, where he described how he found his rooms in Woburn Buildings when he and Olivia Shakespear decided they should "live together":

> . . . Diana Vernon tried to get a separation from the husband who had for her, she believed, aversion or indifference. "He ceased to pay court to me from the day of our marriage," she had said. He was deeply distressed and became ill, and she gave up the project and said to me, "It will be kinder to deceive him." Our senses were engaged now, and though we spoke of parting it was but to declare it impossible. I took my present rooms at Woburn Buildings and furnished them very meagerly with such cheap furniture as I could throw away without regret as I grew more prosperous. She came with me to make every purchase, and I remember an embarrassed conversation in the presence of some Tottenham Court [Road] shop man upon the width of the bed—every inch increased the expense.

Their love affair ended early in 1897 when Yeats was once again overcome by his obsession for Maud Gonne. He lamented the fading of his love for Olivia Shakespear in "The Lover Mourns for the Loss of Love," one of the poems from *The Wind Among the Reeds* which Pound admired for being made "of a single sentence, with no word out of natural order."

> Pale brows, still hands and dim hair,
> I had a beautiful friend
> And dreamed that the old despair
> Would end in love in the end:
> She looked in my heart one day
> And saw your image was there;
> She has gone weeping away.

When Olivia Shakespear died in 1938 Yeats wrote that "For more than forty years she has been the centre of my life in London and during all that time we have never had a quarrel, sadness sometimes but never a difference." One common interest that sustained them was the literature and practices of the occult. In a letter of 1895 Yeats offered her advice about her own visionary experiences: "The vision is correct in one thing and the rest is merely the opening of a vision. I do not tell you what is right, or the exact nature of the symbol you have used, because I will make the vision complete itself when I see you, and it is best that it do all the explaining. You had better not try and go on with the vision yourself." Yeats's advice is consistent with his and Pound's feelings about symbolism: the symbol that appears in a vision is better left unexplained. Yeats's and Olivia Shakespear's mutual interest in the esoteric continued to the end of their lives; Yeats's letters to her from the Twenties and Thirties are filled with the results of the research he undertook as he wrote and rewrote A Vision.

When Pound first arrived in London, Olivia Shakespear became his guide to a complicated literary society. Early in 1909 he wrote that she had invited him to meet Yeats "in a room all full of white magic where Uncle Hilary lives." Uncle Hilary was a small statue of the Buddha in the Shakespear home, but it also became the title of Olivia Shakespear's sixth and final novel, published in 1910. Pound quickly became Olivia Shakespear's confidant, especially as it became clear that her daughter Dorothy was falling in love with him. Perhaps thinking back to her own frustrated love affair with a fickle poet, Olivia Shakespear wrote Pound this startlingly frank letter in 1912:

> You told me you were prepared to see less of Dorothy this winter. I don't know if you wd rather leave it to me to say I don't think it advisable she should see so much of you etc. or whether you wd rather do it in your own way—I suppose I cd trust you to do it? I don't want to put the onus of it on your shoulders if you don't want me to—on the other hand, it seems to be a sort of surgical operation with her before she can say anything to me about you & of course, we *might* have a row over the business—for I don't intend to give way about it—She has never mentioned you to me, & I don't know if she still considers herself engaged to you— but as she obviously can't marry you, she must be made [to] realize that she can't go on as though you were her accepted lover—it's hardly *decent!* . . .
>
> If you had £ 500 a year I should be delighted for *you* to marry her (no nonsense about waiting 5 years etc.) but as you haven't, I'm obliged to say all this—as her mother I can't see it any other way—I've seen too much of girls wasting their lives on men who can't marry them, & they generally end up being more or less compromised demivierges. I only *hope* you have not talked about her to your friends. I trusted, perhaps wrongly, to your honour in the matter—but I know that Mme. Hueffer, for one, knows you have an affair with somebody.

Despite this opposition, Pound did marry Dorothy Shakespear in the summer of 1914, and his mother-in-law remained a close friend. Fluent in French and Italian, Olivia Shakespear introduced Pound to the works of various late nineteenth-century poets and philosophers. In 1915 Pound persuaded her to review D. H. Lawrence's poetry in the special Imagist number of the *Egoist*. She ended her essay by suggesting that Lawrence would be a great writer if he added "two qualities" to his work: "I mean the quality of 'strangeness,' which some one has declared to be a necessary part of beauty, and that of 'distinction'—so difficult to analyse, which is perhaps the indirect expression of a philosophy of life which rejects everything but essentials."

Olivia Shakespear would certainly have seen at least the first of these qualities in *Le Comte de Gabalis*, and it was probably her intimate knowledge of French combined with her interest in the occult that prompted Pound to encourage her to translate the book. Like Sinistari's *De Daemonialitate* (the book Pound asked his father to send to Stone Cottage for Yeats), Montfaucon's *Le Comte de Gabalis* explains the existence of a race of creatures that are neither human nor divine; in 1886 an English translation of *Le Comte* was published with an appendix from Sinistrari's work. Although these two books treat similar material, they nevertheless differ greatly in scope and design. *De Daemonialitate* (though like the *Grimoire of Pope Honorius*, a nineteenth-century forgery posing as an older book) is a rigorously argued "proof" of the existence of these creatures; it documents many accounts of their antics and cites numerous Biblical passages to show that commerce with these creatures is not sinful. *Le Comte de Gabalis*, on the other hand, is a Rosicrucian romance complete with a wonderfully naive narrator, creatures called Sylphs, Gnomes, Nymphs, and Salamanders, who inhabit the four elements, and sordid tales of their sexual relations with Adam and Noah.

Le Comte is not the work of serious scholarship that Ennemoser's *History of Magic* is; as Pope suggested, the book could be "mistaken" for a novel. The eternal pedagogue, Pound suggested that Dorothy Shakespear begin her investigation of esoteric symbolism with *Le Comte* to whet her appetite before moving on to the more rigorous but less spritely work of Ennemoser. He probably persuaded Olivia Shakespear to translate the book for the same reason. Although *Le Comte de Gabalis* was not useful for Yeats's scholarly annotations to Lady Gregory's *Visions and Beliefs* (he does not refer to the work in his notes), it did provide a pleasant and diverting approach to the doctrine of symbolism in its profounder sense.

A certain mystery surrounds Olivia Shakespear's translations. Although she published her novels under her own name and signed her review of "The Poetry of D. H. Lawrence" with "O. Shakespear," she signed her translation of *Le Comte de Gabalis* with "M. de V.-M.," the initials of the author, the Abbé de Montfaucon de Villars. Furthermore, in the pages of the *Egoist*, *Le Comte de Gabalis* is given a new title: "Memoirs of a Charming Person." While Pound suggested in a private letter that one should begin an investigation of symbolism with *Le Comte*, the title chosen for its public appearance seems to be designed to disguise its occult trappings and emphasize its "charming and spritely" character.

Yet Pound was sometimes eager to jump to the defense of those trappings. When Henry Bryan Binns wrote the *Egoist* to object to "the Cabalistic extravaganza now appearing" in its pages, Pound replied, "I trust no one will take Mr. Binns too seriously. Mr. Binns evidently believes in a general djinn like Jehovah having droits du Seigneur over all his female connections. . . . Mr. Binns objects to M. De Gabalis, permit me to object to Mr. Binns." Pound believed that the ethnocentricity of Christian monotheism was at the root of the disease of Western culture, and he approved of anything that undermined its power. Early in 1914, when Dorothy Shakespear's father objected to Pound's unwillingness to be married in the Church of England, Pound wrote to him,

> I have some religion. What you say about a priest's benediction is sound enough but I count myself much more a priest than I do some sceptic who is merely being paid for public pretense of something he has probably never considered. . . .
>
> I think, seriously, that the spiritual powers are affronted when a person who takes his religion seriously complies with a ceremony which has fallen into decay. I can not find any trace of Christ's having spoken against the greek gods. . . .
>
> I should no more give up my faith in Christ than I should give up my faith in Helios or my respect for the teachings of Confucius. . . .
>
> The whole sanity of classic religion was in their recognition that different men have different gods and that there are many sorts of orthodox piety.

Pound took his religion seriously, and, as the priest of his own church, sought the riches of many religious traditions, ancient and modern, orthodox and occult.

Pound's attraction to *Le Comte de Gabalis* and esoteric literature in general is explained further by "The New Sculpture," the account of lectures that he, Wyndham Lewis, and T. E. Hulme delivered at the Quest Society just after Pound returned to London after his first winter with Yeats. As I have said, this essay was Pound's proclamation of his new-found anti-humanism: he laments the fact that the "artist has been for so long a humanist" and has had to "lead and persuade [humanity] to save it from itself." Pound goes on to explain that the solution to this problem lies in the new spiritualist emphasis of modern art.

> Humanism has . . . taken refuge in the arts.
>   The introduction of Djinns, tribal gods, fetiches, etc. into the arts is therefore a happy presage. . . .
>   We turn back, we artists, to the powers of the air, to the djinns who were our allies aforetime, to the spirits of our ancestors. It is by them that we have ruled and shall rule, and by their connivance that we shall mount again into our hierarchy. . . .
>   Modern civilization has bred a race with brains like those of rabbits and we who are the heirs of the witch-doctor and the voodoo, we artists who have been so long the despised are about to take over control.

Introducing elements from spiritualism and the occult into the arts accomplishes three things for Pound: it enhances the artist's own visionary powers; it places the modern artist firmly in the aristocratic tradition of the divinely inspired bard; and, most important, it provides the artist with an esoteric language and practice that distinguishes him from the rest of humanity.

Le Comte de Gabalis gave Pound access to what he called in "The New Sculpture" the aristocratic tradition of "the witch-doctor and the voodoo." Like the work of Sinistrari and Kirk, *Le Comte* is about the "Djinns, tribal gods, fetiches, etc." that Pound wants to restore to the arts. Over the course of five "conversations" the narrator explains how the Count de Gabalis, a Cabalist and Sage of the Secret Sciences, came to tell him of "the existence of an order of beings between God and man, to whom everything can be attributed which is super-human, but less than divine." To give an example of the kind of dialogue that characterizes *Le Comte*, I shall quote Olivia Shakespear's translation at length: "When you are one of Us," explains the Count,

". . . you will discover, by the help of occult drugs, that living in the elements are most charming people, cut off from us by the sin of Adam: you may think the air was made for birds and flies, the water for whales, and the earth for moles, and that fire is of no use at all. The air is really full of multitudes of beings, proud but friendly; fond of science, subtile-minded, and the sworn foes of the silly and ignorant; their wives and daughters are beautiful like Amazons."

"What," cried I, "do you mean to say these hobgoblins are married!"

"You needn't be alarmed," said he. "All this is only teaching from the ancient Cabala. You must put away all you have ever learnt, or you may have to acknowledge your own obstinacy, when you have had more experience. Let me tell you the rivers and seas also are full of Undines and Nymphs; very few of them males, of great beauty. The earth is full of little Gnomes, who look after treasure, and mines, and jewels; they are friendly too, ingenious, and easy to control: they have little wives, but pleasing, with curious habits."

He went on to tell me about the Salamanders, and when I disclaimed any wish to know such ugly creatures, he defended them ardently; saying that as they are made of the purest element, fire, they are all the more beautiful, besides being interesting in their minds, and attitudes towards life. They have, he said, laws and customs like ourselves, but their great grief is that they are mortal, though they live for many centuries. The Sages, it appears, interceded with God Himself on their behalf, and it was revealed to them that Sylphs, Gnomes, Nymphs and Salamanders were all capable of gaining an immortal soul by mating with a man, particularly if he were a Sage; whilst the males of these beings had the same advantages through marrying our daughters.

Le Comte de Gabalis is not only about the existence of these "elemental" people but about the necessity of having sexual relations with them. The Count explains that "If Adam had not grossly violated the command given him to have no relations with Eve, but had been satisfied with the Nymphs and Sylphs, the world would never have been shamefully peopled with imperfect creatures—almost monsters, compared with the children of the Philosophers."

The Count then documents the many church fathers who conceived children with the "elementals," and he tells the narrator that he must choose a Sylph, Gnome, Nymph, or Salamander for his bride.

Le Comte de Gabalis is an amusing book, with artfully turned exchanges between the mysterious Count and the incredulous narrator; the narrator learns that "There was no use . . . in trying to reason with a Cabalist." Pound's attraction to a book about spirit-sexuality is not so absurd as it may seem when we recall that "Psychology and Troubadours" focuses on the influx of pagan sexual mysticism into Christian thought: when we examine Medieval mysticism, writes Pound, "we find sex." For Pound, however, the subject matter of *Le Comte* is not so important as the attitude which the book projects toward its subject matter. Pound insisted, as we have seen, on the superiority of a symbol that appears in a vision because he felt that a symbol should never be explained: "I think a superficial acquaintance with the sort of shallow, conventional, or attributed meaning of a lot of symbols *weakens*—damnably, the power of receiving an energized symbol." By the time Pound made this statement to Dorothy Shakespear, he had held this view of symbolism for several years. In a note to his prose poem "Malrin," written while he was teaching at Wabash College in 1907, Pound said that "To give concrete for a symbol, to explain a parable, is for me always a limiting, a restricting." These sanctions are central to the snatches of Cabalistic doctrine presented in the fanciful conversations of *Le Comte de Gabalis*. Although Olivia Shakespear does not include it in her translation, the French text begins with an epigraph from Tertullian: "Quod tanto impendio absconditur etiam solummodo demonstrare destruere est" [when a thing is hidden away with so much pain, merely to reveal it is to destroy it]. When the narrator objects to the Count's assertion that Adam's sin was that he had sexual relations with Eve instead of the elementals (" 'Then,' cried I, 'you think Adam's sin didn't lie in eating the apple?' "), the Count replies, "Are you among those who take the story of the apple literally? . . . Do you not know that Holy Writ uses metaphorical language to express what could not otherwise be decently said? But the Sages have understood the mystery, and know that if Adam had had relations only with Sylphs, Gnomes, Nymphs or Salamanders, the world would have been filled with a wonderfully strong, wise race."

This brief lesson in the interpretation of symbols contains the central tenet of Pound's understanding of esoteric symbolism: knowledge worth having can be expressed only in symbols that are unfamiliar and obscure. When the narrator of *Le Comte* objects that the oracles through which the "elementals" speak are too obscure to be understood, the Count replies, "As for the obscurity to which you object, isn't truth generally concealed by darkness—and isn't Holy Writ itself so obscure as to put off the haughty and presumptuous, and to guide the humble?" To explain a symbol is to destroy its ability to embody what Pound called the divine or permanent world; knowledge that could be understood by the uninitiated masses would not be knowledge at all.

This attitude toward symbolism is mentioned only briefly in *Le Comte de Gabalis*, but it is central to most of the esoteric literature Pound was reading at Stone Cottage. In his *History of Magic* (1854), Joseph Ennemoser maintains that mythological symbols are not arbitrary fictions but originate in primitive man's attempts to use figurative language to explain visionary experiences he does not understand. Pound would have agreed with this theory; in "Psychology and Troubadours" he wrote that "Greek myth arose when someone having passed through delightful psychic experience tried to communicate it to others." For the individual who undergoes this delightful psychic experience, Pound and Ennemoser agree, the resulting symbol is perfectly clear and intelligible, Ennemoser quotes Georg Friedrich Creuzer, the German classical philologist, to explain why these symbols become opaque: while the Greeks understood that art could intelligibly express the infinite, they also knew that "an expression of higher knowledge of the secret doctrine" as "an embodied enigma" could be even more powerful: "Therein especially consists the temple symbolism of Greece and Rome. When the clearness of the scene is wholly annihilated, and only the astonishment remains, so that a certain religious instruction is implied, the symbolism is still more enigmatical, and the key to the mystery is in many cases lost." Those who possess the "secret doctrine" possess the key to the mysteries of its symbolism and establish themselves as priests—divinely inspired interpreters to whom the uninitiated public must turn for knowledge. At the beginning of *Le Comte de Gabalis* the narrator says that he has heard that the Count "is dead of an apoplexy. The curious will not fail to say that such a death is usual for one who has failed to keep the secrets of the Sages." It is imperative that the highest knowledge be veiled.

This attitude permeates the literature of the occult and justifies its obscurity. It also characterizes the sacred texts of literary modernism. In his initial editorial statement for the *Little Review* (1917) Pound surveyed his work with the *Egoist* and recalled Olivia Shakespear's translation: "I do not think it can be too often pointed out that during the last four years *The Egoist* has published serially in the face of no inconsiderable difficulties, the only translation of Remy de Gourmont's *Chevaux de Diomedes;* the best translation of le Comte de Gabalis; Mr. Joyce's masterpiece, A *Portrait of the Artist as a Young Man,* and is now publishing Mr. Lewis's novel *Tarr.*" Pound sets Olivia Shakespear's work among prestigious company here, and the juxtaposition is suggestive: in their readings in the esoteric and the occult, Pound and Yeats found a justification for the anti-democratic attitudes of literary modernism. *Four Plays for Dancers* (1921) and *Three Cantos* (1917), the works directly influenced by their studies at Stone Cottage, are allusive and obscure for the same reason that occult literature conceals its secret knowledge in a language that only a small circle of initiates can understand: to explain their work to the public would be to destroy its beauty and undermine their priest-like status. In *'Noh' or Accomplishment* Pound wrote that "The art of allusion, or this love of allusion in art, is at the root of the Noh. These plays, or eclogues, were made only for the few; for the nobles; for those trained to catch the allusion." Yeats remembered that with the help of Pound's translations of the Noh plays he "invented a form of drama, distinguished, indirect, and symbolic, and having no need of mob or Press to pay its way— an aristocratic form." He wanted to create "an unpopular theatre and an audience like a *secret society."* Pound was not joking when at the end of "The New Sculpture" he wrote that "the public will do well to resent these 'new' kinds of art."

It is finally not so much the subject matter as the attitude of occult literature that was most important for the modernist literature of Yeats and Pound. Both poets cultivated a poetry of cabalisic obscurity and wrote their own keys to elucidation. To show how his poems represent "states of consciousness," in "The Wisdom of Poetry" (1912) Pound compared his poems to analytic equations (it was an analogy he had used in *The Spirit of Romance* to explain the symbolism of the *Paradiso* and would use again in "Vorticism" to explain " 'symbolism' in its profounder sense") :

What the analytical geometer does for space and form, the poet does for the states of consciousness. Let us therefore consider the nature of the formulae of analytics.

By the signs $a^2 + b^2 = c^2$, I imply the circle. By $(a - r)^2 + (b - r)^2 = (c - r)^2$, I imply the circle and its mode of birth. I am led from the consideration of the particular circles formed by my ink well and my table-rim, to the contemplation of the circle absolute, its law; the circle free in all space, unbounded, loosed from the accidents of time and place. Is the formula nothing, or is it cabala and the sign of unintelligible magic? The engineer, understanding and translating to the many, builds for the uninitiated bridges and devices. He speaks their language. For the initiated the signs are a door into eternity and into the boundless ether.

For the uninitiated, Pound's imagist poems may be technical and emotional masterpieces, but for the initiated they are allegorical expressions of Pound's spiritual and political values. To quote the Comte de Gabalis, they employ "metaphorical language to express what could not otherwise be decently said." Yeats knew what he was doing when in "A Packet for Ezra Pound" (1929; later printed as a preface to the revised version of A *Vision*) he quoted Pound's "The Return" to illustrate his belief that "every two thousand and odd years something happens in the world to make one [side of the balance] sacred, the other secular; one wise, the other foolish; one fair, the other foul; one divine, the other devilish."

> See, they return; ah, see the tentative
> Movements, the slow feet,
> The trouble in the pace and the uncertain
> Wavering!
>
> See, they return, one, and by one,
> With fear, as half-awakened;
> As if the snow should hesitate
> And murmur in the wind,
> and half turn back;
> These were the "Wing'd-with-Awe,"
> Inviolable.
>
> Gods of the wingèd shoe!
> With them the silver hounds,
> sniffing the trace of air!

Haie! Haie!
> These were the swift to harry;
These the keen-scented;
These were the souls of blood.

Slow on the leash,
> pallid the leash-men!

T. S. Eliot also understood the coded message of "The Return" when he alluded to the poem in the final movement of "Little Gidding":

> We die with the dying:
> See, they depart, and we go with them.
> We are born with the dead:
> See, they return, and bring us with them.

And even Pound himself provided a gloss on the poem in a passage in Canto 113 which makes the movement toward the boundless ether explicit:

> The hells move in cycles,
> > No man can see his own end.
> The Gods have not returned. "They have never left us."
> > They have not returned.
> Cloud's processional and the air moves with their living.

Like *Le Comte de Gabalis*, "The Return" is about the ancient spiritual presences which Pound wants to restore to his work in order to resurrect "the aristocracy of the arts." The poem also announces (as Yeats wrote) "some change of style," but for the initiated members of the secret society of modernism, the poem is a manifesto of a new artistic, social, and political order.

Pound's often cryptic poems concealed revolutionary intentions, a politicization of symbolism for which he recognized historical precedent. Yeats's essay "What is Popular Poetry?" in *Ideas of Good and Evil* offered one such precedent: "I learned from the people themselves, before I learned it from any book, that they cannot separate the idea of an art or a craft from the idea of a cult with ancient technicalities and mysteries. They can hardly separate mere learning from witchcraft, and are fond of words and verses that keep half their secret to themselves." Pound made this insight his own: "The people have never objected to obscurity in ballads," he remarked in one of the Bastien von Helmholtz essays written at Stone Cottage: "The bitterest and most poignant songs have been often written in cypher—of necessity. It is not for nothing that Verdi's name was cheered hysterically after his operas; was cheered for its half secret anagram V.E.R.D.I., Vittorio Emanuele Re d'Italia, cheered in cities where in Verdi's obscure, but not quite sufficiently obscure, chorus 'Liberta' had been changed by the censors to 'Lealta.'" Victor Emmanuel became king of a united and liberated Italy in 1861; Verdi's two most political operas, *I Lombardi alla prima crociata* (1843) and *Ernani* (1844), provoked public demonstrations against Austrian rule and brought Verdi into direct conflict with the authorities. Pound's choice of these Italians as his predecessors is especially revealing; although he railed against the stupidity of the public and intended his poetry to be misunderstood, he paradoxically continued to think of himself as an artist who worked for the common good of the people. Pound did not write popular operas, however, but unpopular poems designed to nourish an aristocratic "state of mind"; the commoners, having no other choice, he reasoned, would follow.

Although this political dimension never left Pound's poetry, his early conception of symbolism was sometimes forsaken. In the *Pisan Cantos* he disparaged Yeatsian symbolism, forgetting that he himself was once one of its strongest advocates:

> Le Paradis n'est pas artificiel
> and Uncle William dawdling around Notre Dame
> in search of whatever
> paused to admire the symbol
> with Notre Dame standing inside it
> Where in St. Etienne
> or why not Dei Miracoli:
> mermaids, that carving.

In this passage from Canto 83, Pound criticizes Yeats for searching for some inner reality to which the objects of the outer world correspond. In Canto 76 Pound clarifies his reasons for preferring Santa Maria dei Miracoli, the quattrocento Church in Venice, to Yeats's Notre Dame:

> and Tullio Romano carved the sirenes
> as the old custode says: so that since
> then no one has been able to carve them
> for the jewel box, Santa Maria Dei Miracoli.

In contrast to the Gothic cathedral, the quattrocento carvings have a natural precision; as Pound phrases it in Canto 82, they consist of the *res* rather than *verba*.

This duality, one of Pound's later cardinal principles, has been invoked to justify the procedures of *The Cantos* as a whole. Yet Pound did himself and his interpreters an injustice by offering such a seductive oversimplification of his aesthetic. Pound thought about symbolism in different ways at different points in his life, and his comments about symbolism in the *Pisan Cantos* do not explain the theory of "'symbolism' in its profounder sense" that he developed in his London years. Like a Gothic cathedral (rather than Santa Maria dei Miracoli), *The Cantos* are built out of different and sometimes contradictory styles, different conceptions of the relationship of *res* and *verba*. In Canto 113, the same fragment in which Pound quotes his own "The Return," he also admits that he has returned to the profounder conception of symbolism that he articulated with Yeats's help in his youth. These lines reverse Pound's critique of Yeats in Canto 83:

> That the body is inside the soul—
>   the lifting and folding brightness
>   the darkness shattered,
>   the fragment.
> That Yeats noted the symbol over that portico
>   (Paris).

As Pound attempted to write paradise in his old age, he realised once again that symbolism was the only mode available to him. He begins this passage in Canto 113 by invoking the Plotinian notion that the body of man is enveloped in its soul, then recognizes the wisdom of Yeats's perception of the symbol containing Notre Dame. The sentiment is not far from Yeats's own in the essay on "The Necessity of Symbolism," written with Edwin Ellis for their 1893 edition of *The Works of William Blake, Poetic, Symbolic, and Critical*. The individual body of man is not evil, said Yeats: "It becomes evil in the true sense of the word only when man invents a philosophy from reasoning upon it, asserts that its limited life is alone real. . . . Having denied the existence of that for which his bodily life exists, man begins an unceasing preoccupation with his own bodily life, neglecting to regard it as a symbol." Yeats saw the symbol, and so Pound places him not among the ignorant in Canto 113 but among those who "do not surrender perception."

> "but that kind of ignorance" said the old priest to Yeats
>   (in a railway train) "is spreading every day from the schools"
>   to say nothing of other varieties.

The first winter at Stone Cottage came to an early end when Yeats sailed for America on the Lusitania on January 28, 1914; their stay the next two winters would last until the first week of March. Yeats had written and polished his material for his lecture tour in Sussex, dictating the final product to Pound. On March 1st, *Poetry* magazine gave a banquet in Yeats's honor, and in his after-dinner speech Yeats offered what must have seemed to be the ultimate compliment to Pound: he compared their collaboration to the meetings of the Rhymers' Club.

> We young writers rebelled against . . . rhetoric; there was too much of it and to a great extent it was meaningless. When I went to London I found a group of young lyric writers who were also against rhetoric. We formed the Rhymers' Club; we used to meet and read our poems to one another, and we tried to rid them of rhetoric. . . .
> We rebelled against rhetoric, and now there is a group of younger poets who dare to call us rhetorical. When I returned to London from Ireland, I had a young man go over all my work with me to eliminate the abstract. This was an American poet, Ezra Pound. Much of his work is experimental; his work will come slowly, he will make many an experiment before he comes into his own. I should like to read to you two poems of permanent value, "The Ballad of the Goodly Fere" and "The Return." This last is, I think, the most beautiful poem that has been written in the free form, one of the few in which I find real organic rhythm.

Yeats photographed by Arnold Genthe in 1914 for the limited edition of *Nine Poems* printed for John Quinn.

During the third week in March Yeats traveled to New York, visiting his father and John Quinn. His father wrote to his sister that he noticed in Yeats "a subtle change, a something assured, a quiet importance." This confidence—more than lessons in abstraction—was what Pound helped to give the older poet. When they met in 1909, Yeats had just experienced what he called a "breakdown"; he was depressed over the death of Synge and the state of his own poetry. By the end of the first winter at Stone Cottage, the assured man of letters had emerged, confident that even the most adventurous of *les jeunes* considered him the greatest living poet.

Yeats's father also wrote that Yeats was hurrying to return to England in time for Pound's wedding: "[Pound] is to marry Mrs. Shakespear's daughter. She is beautiful and well off and has the most charming manners. . . . Both are clever, and I fancy Ezra is a nice fellow. As Willie remarks, when rich and fashionable people bring up a daughter to be intellectual, naturally she will turn away from the 'curled darlings' of her own class and fall in love with intellect which is mostly to wed with poverty as well. I hope it will turn out that Ezra Pound is not an *uncomfortable* man of genius." Pound had been trying to overcome the Shakespear family's objections to his poverty for several years, and he had made his final proposal to Dorothy Shakespear in a brief note written just after he returned from Stone Cottage: "I perceive that this week will be unduly elongated. I think you'd better perhaps marry me and live in one room more than the dryad [Hilda Doolittle]." Neither Pound nor any of the Shakespears informed Yeats of the wedding plans before he left for the United States. On March 7th, Dorothy Shakespear told Pound that her mother had "heard from W.B.Y. who seems to quite approve of us." Pound replied that he did not "see how you've heard from W.B.Y. unless O. S. [Olivia Shakespear] wrote him before I did. He appears to be puffing me in the Abyssinian backwaters." In Chicago, a large city in the middle of Abyssinia, Yeats was puffing Pound, and on March 8th he wrote to his protégé from Pittsburgh: "You will have a beautiful & clever wife & that is what few men get." The letter Yeats wrote to Lady Gregory was more frank: "Yesterday I got a note from Ezra Pound announcing his marriage to Dorothy Shakespear at the end of April. Everybody had thought it was broken off especially as Ezra had written quite a number of satiric poems on his bethrothed, one comparing his engagement to a bath in which the hot-water tap was broken. He is never to be let know that I knew of the engagement. He is at present at war with the girl's father who says they must be married in church while Ezra demands a registry office."

"The Bath Tub" was actually written in 1912 when Pound's relationship with Dorothy Shakespear was free of internal tensions. The poem's address to a "much praised but-not-altogether-satisfactory lady" seemed more appropriate in 1913 when Dorothy Shakespear told Pound she could not marry him after his attempt to dictate the guest list for Walter Rummel's piano recital in honor of Rabindranath Tagore. Pound responded to her rejection with three lines of Imagist concision surrounded by a page of white space.

> you can not.
> you can not.
> you can not.

A reconciliation followed quickly, and once they were formally engaged after Pound returned from Stone Cottage, the tensions in their relationship (as Yeats suggested) were external: Henry Hope Shakespear preferred a church wedding, but Pound told him that he would find himself "much more in the presence of the aerial and divine powers in taking a formal legal oath." Despite his faith in his own power to communicate with the deities, Pound eventually acquiesced to his father-in-law's wishes, and after the wedding, he and his wife spent part of their honeymoon at Stone Cottage. They paid a visit to Wilfrid Scawen Blunt at Newbuildings Place; many years later Dorothy Pound remembered that Blunt drank champagne mixed with water and took them for a tour of his estate in a wagon. Yeats had given the couple a sum of money for their wedding gift, and Pound wrote to thank him from Stone Cottage, explaining that he was using the money to purchase a clavichord from Arnold Dolmetsch: "Thanks, [for] your wedding present which is being sent to Dolmitsch. we hope it will flower into deathless music—at least into an image of more gracious & stately times."

Before he and his new wife retreated to Stone Cottage, Pound planned the contents of the May issue of *Poetry* magazine; the issue was a record of his winter with Yeats. It included *Nishikigi* (Yeats's favorite of the Noh plays Pound had translated from Fenollosa's notes), twelve poems which would appear in Yeats's *Responsibilities* (including "When Helen Lived," which Yeats had read at the dinner for Blunt), and "The Later Yeats," Pound's review of *Responsi-bilities*.

Pound began the review by answering those younger writers who questioned his desire to spend two months alone in the middle of the country with a poet twenty years his senior:

> I live, so far as possible, among that more intelligently active segment of the race which is concerned with today and tomorrow; and, in consequence of this, whenever I mention Mr Yeats I am apt to be assailed with questions: "Will Mr Yeats do anything more?", "Is Yeats in the movement?", "How *can* the chap go on writing this sort of thing?"
>
> And to these inquiries I can only say that Mr Yeats' vitality is quite unimpaired, and that I dare say he'll do a good deal; and that up to date no one has shown any disposition to supersede him as the best poet in England.

Yeats remained the greatest living poet in Pound's eyes because he continued to develop. To those readers of Yeats (like Pound himself) who grew to love *The Wind Among the Reeds*, Pound said that "*Romantic Ireland's Dead and Gone* is no better than Red Hanrahan's song about Ireland, but it is harder. . . . I've not a word against the glamour as it appears in Yeats' early poems, but we have had so many other pseudo-glamours and glamourlets and mists and fogs since the nineties that one is about ready for hard light." Pound was probably thinking of himself when he wrote these sentences; he began his poetic career by imitating Yeats's glamour, then remade his style as the master transformed his own. As if to reprimand himself, Pound quoted the final line of Yeats's "To a Poet, who would have me Praise certain Bad Poets, Imitators of His and Mine"—and as if to stress his privileged position among Yeats's imitators, he quoted the line not as it appeared in *The Green Helmet and Other Poems* but from an alternate version which Yeats must have read to Pound from his diary: "Tell me, do the wolf-dogs praise their fleas?"

Even as Yeats remade himself as a poet, the aspect of his verse that Pound admired most was what he called the "constant element"—what did not change: "*The Grey Rock* is, I admit, obscure, but it outweighs this by a curious nobility, a nobility which is, to me at least, the very core of Mr Yeats' production, the constant element of his writing." Nobility: Pound saw it especially clearly in Yeats's deification of the dead Rhymers in "The Grey Rock," and he had seen it at Stone Cottage in "Notoriety" and "Pardon, old fathers," the poems written in response to George Moore. By returning to Stone Cottage with Yeats, Pound continued to be a part of an aristocracy of the arts that could claim the Rhymers' Club as its ancestor. He would spend the summer of 1914 nursing a Vorticist renaissance in the arts, but a war would break out, companions would die, and Pound would return to Stone Cottage for another meeting of the Brothers Minor, the only society small and secret enough to keep alive his version of the older poet's noble dream.

II

4

War Poets
by the Waste Moor

When the first issue of *Blast*, the journal of the Great English Vortex, appeared early in the summer of 1914, Pound took the opportunity to satirize his own desire to establish the "Order of the Brothers Minor." His poem "Fratres Minores" was considered too ribald for even so disreputable a venue as *Blast*, and before the journal was distributed, the publisher demanded that the first and last two lines of the poem be blotted out with heavy black lines.

> With minds still hovering above their testicles
> Certain poets here and in France
> Still sigh over established and natural fact
> Long since fully discussed by Ovid.
> They howl. They complain in delicate and exhausted metres
> That the twitching of three abdominal nerves
> Is incapable of producing a lasting Nirvana.

In condemning these members of the Brothers Minor, Pound had elevated himself to some higher order, for he wrote that *Blast* was "a magazine one can appear in without a feeling of degradation—without feeling that one is slumming among mentalities of a loathsomely lower order."

Pound devoted a great deal of energy to the Vorticist movement during the summer of 1914, for he saw it as a large-scale effort to re-establish the aristocracy of the arts. In his first Vorticist pronounce-ment, "The New Sculpture," written under Yeats's heavy influence, he had declared that "the war between [the artist] and the world is a war without truce." But Pound's war with his audience was soon over-shadowed by a greater conflict. On June 28, 1914, exactly one week after *Blast* was published, the Archduke Franz Ferdinand was assas-sinated. Within months Pound discovered that it was impossible to maintain a secret society of the arts during wartime.

Even after Britain declared war on Germany on August 4th, how-ever, Pound was unable to foresee the prolonged suffering of the next five years. In November he described the war effort to Harriet Mon-roe in a supercilious tone that he would abandon after the deaths of several of his most admired colleagues:

> Ricketts has made the one mot of the war, the last flare of the 90's: "What depresses me most is the horrible fact that they can't *all* of them be beaten." It looks only clever and superficial, but one can not tell how true it is. This war is possibly a conflict between two forces almost equally detestable. Atavism and the loathsome spirit of mediocrity cloaked in graft. One does not know; the thing is too involved. I wonder if England will spend the next ten years in internal squabble *after* Germany is beaten. It's all very well to see the troops flocking from the four corners of Empire. It is a very fine sight. But, but, but, civilization, after the battle is over and everybody begins to call each other thieves and liars *inside* the Em-pire. They took ten years after the Boer War to come to. One won-ders if the war is only a stop gap. Only a symptom of the real dis-ease.

Like most Englishmen, Pound had little doubt that the war would end quickly and that the British would be the victors. Yet even as he wrote that the war effort seemed "a very fine sight," he had already begun to feel the energy of the Great English Vortex being drained away by the conflict on the continent. Pound came to England, as he wrote in 1908, in search of his "own kind," comrades who "have some breath for beauty and the arts." To build an artistic commu-nity was Pound's highest ideal, and the war dashed his efforts. During the autumn of 1914 he honed his adaptations of Fenollosa's transla-tions of eighth-century Chinese poetry, in the process expressing his grief for the passing of the Vortex. In his adaptation of Li Po's "Exile's Letter," as Ronald Bush has noted, "Pound exaggerated Li Po's nostalgia for a past when poets were joined in fellowship." He introduced plural pronouns into the following lines, transforming what had been praise for a close friend into a lament for the passing of the Brothers Minor.

> And with them, and with you especially
> There was nothing at cross purpose,
> And they made nothing of sea-crossing or of mountain-crossing.
> If only they could be of that fellowship,
> And we all spoke out our hearts and minds, and without regret.

But Pound did more than lament his loss; he realized that his future productivity and poetic career were at stake, and he decided he must manufacture an artistic fellowship if it would not arise naturally. He sent Harriet Monroe the prospectus for his proposed College of the Arts, calling it "a scheme to enable things to keep on here in spite of the war-strain and (what will be more dangerous) the war back-wash and post bellum slump." Recalling the ideals presented in Yeats's "To a Wealthy Man" Pound wrote in the "Preliminary Announcement of the College of the Arts" that he aimed "at an intellectual status no lower than that attained by the courts of the Italian Renaissance." He wanted his College of the Arts to serve London as Yeats had hoped that Hugh Lane's picture gallery would elevate Dublin into an artistic center: "It has been noted by certain authors that London is the capital of the world, and 'Art is a matter of capitals.' At present many American students who would have sought Vienna or Prague or some continental city are disturbed by war. To these The College of the Arts offers a temporary refuge and a permanent centre." Although Pound assembled a notable faculty (Dolmetsch, Gaudier-Brzeska, Lewis), his dream of the College of the Arts was never realized. Just a few weeks after the fighting began he wrote to Harriet Monroe that "the war is eating up all everybody's subconscious energy. One does nothing but buy newspapers." At the same time Yeats wrote to Lady Gregory that outside his own private world, "people do nothing but read newspapers and talk each other into a fright!" While the modernist war against the English middle-class had run out of ammunition, the war across the channel had only begun.

Yeats felt that over time the war might help to shape the middle-class "mob" into the kind of audience he and Pound wanted for their work. The day after war was declared he wrote that he wondered "how the war will affect the minds of what audience it leaves us. Nietzsche was fond of foretelling wars for the possession of the earth that were to restore the tragic mind, & banish the mass mind which he hated." Like Pound, Yeats could forecast positive consequences for the war because at this very early stage in the fighting he had no conception of the protracted agonies which the next five years would bring. By the end of August 1914 he saw that the war would do nothing as dramatic or useful as restore a "tragic" mind to modern Europe; he told Lady Gregory about Richard Aldington's attempt to enlist: "owing to the wildness of his appearance, instead of being taken as a recruit he was arrested as a spy. His emotion made him incoherent and he was shut up in a barrack-room of some kind for a while." Another friend of Yeats's was sent off to the trenches at Antwerp without having been taught how to fire his rifle. The war soon appeared to be a singularly unamusing comedy of errors, and Yeats confessed to John Quinn that he tried not to think about it but only sometimes succeeded: "It seems impossible to believe that someday it will be over, & that Sparta & Athens, Prussia & Paris will ever visit one another."

Pound too was trying not to think of the war and not succeeding; at the end of November he wrote his father that the war was "losing interest" and he had "stopped taking in the paper." But like Yeats, he could not ignore the fighting. Both poets became deeply affected by the war, especially as they witnessed its effects on their close friends. Yet at the same time, they resisted these emotions, trying to maintain an aristocratic indifference to a war that seemed to recall the world of Sparta and Athens less and less as it dragged on.

Yeats wondered if citizens from rival nations would ever visit one another again. This worry was a personal one, for both he and Pound were unable to travel to the continent. Pound lamented his cultural isolation in *Three Cantos* (1917), asserting his ability to travel mentally if not physically: "I walk Verona. (I am here in England.) / I can see Can Grande. (Can see whom you will.)" Yeats also settled for imagined journeys. He had planned to travel to Austria in August 1914 but the trip was cancelled when the war was declared. A few months later he wrote John Quinn that he had been awake much of the night reading Bram Stoker's *Dracula*—not because he valued the work highly; indeed, it interested him no more than any other sensational story. Yeats read the book because his cancelled trip to Austria would have featured a night in the real Dracula castle, which had been haunted for generations. On the way to the castle Yeats was to have visited another haunted house, but its present owner was fighting, perhaps killed, and now, Yeats told Quinn, the house's "priceless imp has no one to haunt."

Yeats mentioned to Quinn that his evening of reading had strained his eyes and given him a headache as if he had drunk too much claret. One reason he looked forward to a second winter at Stone Cottage was that he would have the benefit of Pound's eyes. At the end of October 1914 Yeats wrote to Lady Gregory that he had heard that Pound and his wife were thinking of going to the cottage with him: "I hope they will. Here I cannot get any routine. One day I work too little & the next day too much & I always overuse my sight." In late December both Ezra and Dorothy Pound did return to Sussex with Yeats. Once they were occupying the cottage, Dorothy Pound designed a Vorticist cover for a new edition of her husband's *Ripostes*. Yeats watched her work and wrote that she looked "as if her face was made out of Dresden China. I look at her in perpetual wonder. It is so hard to believe she is real; yet she spends all her daylight hours drawing the most monstrous cubist pictures."

Dorothy Pound's cubist drawings, one of which would appear in the 1915 issue of *Blast*, were remnants of the London vortex which the war had dissipated. Yeats's eyesight and Pound's debilitated finances were not the only reasons for returning to Stone Cottage. Once Pound realized that he could not transform London into an artistic center, immune from the pressures of the war, it became clear to him that the only way to preserve the aristocracy of the arts in wartime was to sequester himself with Yeats. If the Great English Vortex and the College of the Arts were dead, an even more exclusive secret society could reconvene in the privacy of Stone Cottage. When Pound and Yeats returned to Ashdown Forest, they resumed their esoteric studies, left newspapers behind, and tried to assume a lofty indifference to the forces that were rearranging the lines of European geography.

Throughout his life Yeats would maintain this indifference more successfully than Pound. When he compiled the *Oxford Book of Modern Verse* in 1936, he excluded the popular poems of Wilfred Owen, invoking Arnold's preface to *Poems* (1853) to justify the omission:

I have a distaste for certain poems written in the midst of the great war. . . . The writers of these poems were invariably officers of exceptional courage and capacity, one a man constantly selected for dangerous work, all, I think, had the Military Cross; their letters are vivid and humorous, they were not without joy—for all skill is joyfull—but felt bound, in the words of the best known, to plead the suffering of their men. In poems that had for a time considerable fame, written in the first person, they made that suffering their own. I have rejected these poems for the same reason that made Arnold withdraw his *Empedocles on Etna* from circulation; passive suffering is not a theme for poetry.

Dorothy Shakespear's "Aldeburgh Boats," 1914.

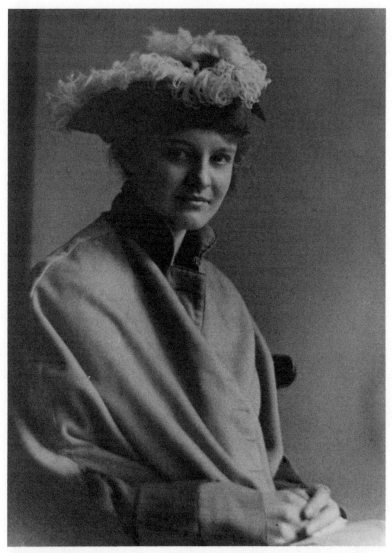

Dorothy Shakespear in 1915. She "looks as if her face was made out of Dresden China," wrote Yeats, "yet she spends all her daylight hours drawing the most monstrous cubist pictures."

He concluded that if "war is necessary, or necessary in our time and place, it is best to forget its suffering as we do the discomfort of fever." Yeats was speaking from his own experience in this preface, for he was far from immune to the fever of wartime. After sequestering themselves at Stone Cottage, Pound and Yeats paradoxically found themselves in closer contact with the realities of the war. Both poets wrote war poems during their tenure in Sussex (some of which have never been published), and these poems offer a new perspective on the Great War's crucial role in the rise of literary modernism.

Almost all of the modernist masterpieces reveal the effect of a wartime consciousness. *The Waste Land, A Draft of XVI Cantos,* and *The Tower* each present a civilian's perspective on the long-range psychological impact of war. The novels of Lawrence and Woolf are similarly marked by the nearly palpable yet peculiarly inexpressible sense of loss that clung to England after the armistice. In *Mrs. Dalloway* Woolf wrote that "Those five years—1918 to 1923—had been . . . somehow very important. People looked different. Newspapers seemed different." In the "Time Passes" section of *To the Lighthouse* (where the duration of the war and the death of Andrew Ramsey are reduced to two brief sentences), Woolf remarked that "The war, people said, had revived their interest in poetry." Indeed it had. After Britain's ultimatum to Germany ran out at midnight, a war poem by Henry Newbolt appeared in the London *Times* on the morning of August 5, 1914—probably before the first shots were fired. The poems would continue to fill the newspapers and weeklies as long as the fighting continued.

Although the longer works of Pound and Yeats produced in the years following the armistice treat the war in the oblique manner of the novels of Woolf or Lawrence, both poets held a certain contempt for the poems that treated the experience of war directly and filled the daily papers. They wanted to avoid the hysteria that had taken hold of even so fine a mind as Henry James's. Shortly after war was declared, James attended a luncheon given by Edith Wharton. When he arrived, he burst into the room, "his great eyes ablaze": " 'My hands, I must wash them!' he cried. 'My hands are dripping with blood. All the way from Chelsea to Grosvenor Place I have been bayoneting, my dear Edith, and hurling bombs and ravishing and raping. It is my day-dream to squat down with King George of England, with the President of the French Republic and the Czar of Russia on the

Emperor William's belly, until we squeeze out of it the last irrevocable drops of bitter retribution.' "

Pound in particular found this kind of rabid patriotism offensive. His first exposure to the very idea of war poetry came just before his return to Stone Cottage. In the September 1914 issue of *Poetry*, a group of anonymous donors offered a prize of one hundred dollars for the best war or peace poem "based on the present European situation." The volume of submissions was so large that Harriet Monroe devoted the entire November issue of *Poetry* to war verse. "Phases," a sequence of poems by an unknown poet from New York named Wallace Stevens, surfaced from the mass of submissions and made it into print. Unlike Stevens's later sequence of war poems, "Lettres d'un Soldat" (1917–18), written after the actual horror of the war had become known (and based upon the letters of Eugène Emmanuel Lemercier, a French painter killed in April 1915), Stevens's early sequence of poems were cast in a rhetoric borrowed from Kipling and Housman:

> Death's nobility again
> Beautified the simplest men.
> Fallen Winkle felt the pride
> Of Agamemnon
> When he died.
>
> What could London's
> Work and waste
> Give him—
> To that salty, sacrificial taste?
> What could London's
> Sorrow bring—
> To that short, triumphant sting?

Stevens's poems were among the best in a jingoist collection filled with Kipling's imperialism and Housman's soldiers dying young. The prize for the best poem was awarded to Louise Driscoll's "The Metal Checks"—causing Pound to refer to the whole incident as "the war-poem scandal." When he first read the announcement for the competition he wrote Harriet Monroe that he was "VERY glad" she had nothing to do with the prize:

After trying for two years to make the point that poetry is an art, it is rather disheartening to have the magazine burst out with a high school folly, a prize for a poem "In Occasion." GOGDD DAMMMMM! Poet laureates making birthday odes! Maeterlinck doing columns in the Daily Mail. Even he has the grace to say that those who aren't carrying rifles ought to keep quiet.

Who is going to write "Of Nelson and the North" or "Mein Kaiser verfangen" until one knows where is what and etc. etc. The beastly offer is like that parvenu who offered a million for a new national anthem. These things are not written because somebody offers two months board. If Louvain won't make a man write, 100 dollars damn well won't either.

In any case, no one is going to grind out a masterpiece on two weeks notice.

The idea of writing a poem to order offended Pound's sense of the higher function of the arts, and he wondered if anyone who had not actually fought would be able to write a convincing war poem. Pound himself had considered writing a "planh for Louvain" (a medieval Belgian town destroyed in the first days of the fighting) but decided that as a civilian he was not equipped to do so; he feared that his own attempt at a war poem would be no better than Stevens's. Contemplating his own thwarted effort, he asked Harriet Monroe, "Is, in heaven's name, IS a war poem, as a work of art in any way different or more meritorious than any other poem?"

This question would trouble Pound for the duration of the war, and all of his writings about the war can be seen as attempts to find an answer. When his poem "Abu Salammamm—A Song of Empire" appeared in the August 1914 issue of *Poetry*, Pound was confronted by this dilemma in a very real way: although he had written the poem before the fighting broke out, he worried that it might now be interpreted as a jocular treatment of what had suddenly become a serious situation.

> Great is King George the Fifth;
> For his army is legion,
> His army is a thousand and forty-eight soldiers
>   with red cloths about their buttocks,
> And they have red faces like bricks.
> Great is the King of England and greatly to be feared,
> For he has chained me to this fountain;
> He provides me with women and drinks.

After "Abu Salammamm" was published, Pound wrote Harriet Monroe that he was sorry it "appeared just at the outbreak of hostilities but I think a formal apology would possibly only draw attention to what will probably be overlooked in the present excitement." After August 4, 1914, Pound suddenly recognized that almost any poem became a war poem when it entered the domain of the reader. He confronted this problem again in 1915 when he published "Our Contemporaries," a satire of Rupert Brooke, in the war issue of *Blast,* only to discover that Brooke was killed in action while the magazine was in press. Pound protested that the poem was merely "a complaint against a literary method" and that it "was written months before his death." Still, he could not prevent the events of the war from intruding upon the pure impulse of lyric poetry. He was writing war poetry whether he wanted to or not.

When Pound first saw the announcement of the war-poem prize in *Poetry* he did finally write, as he had intended, a "planh for Louvain," but the poem turned out to be less a poem about war than a poem about the possibility of writing war poetry. He sent these lines, titled "War Verse," to Harriet Monroe, instructing her that they were "not submitted to the war verse competition" and were to be printed anonymously. "War Verse" was, however, never printed at all.

> O two-penny poets, be still!—
> For you have nine years out of every ten
> To go gunning for glory—
>   with pop-guns;
> Be still, give the soldiers their turn,
> And do not be trying to scrape your two-penny glory
> From the ruins of Louvain,
> And from the smouldering Liège,
> From Leman and Brialmont.

This, Pound's first poem written in conscious response to the war, is addressed as much to himself as to the would-be war poets who filled *Poetry* magazine: although Pound felt the impulse to address the European conflict in verse, he worried that without any firsthand experience of the war, his poetry would seem facile and opportunistic, the emotion literary and false.

To find the real emotions of war, Pound turned to translation. Around the same time that he wrote "War Verse" he was working

with Fenollosa's Chinese translations, and he found that the work of
Li Po expressed the wartime emotions he himself did not have the
experience to know. A few months before Pound published the translations in *Cathay* (April 1915) he wrote an article on "Webster
Ford" (the pseudonym of Edgar Lee Masters) which appeared in the
January 1st issue of the *Egoist*. In contrast to the poems of Li Po, he
felt that Masters's early work was already dated.

> Good poetry is always the same; the changes are superficial. We
> have the real poem in nature. The real poet thinking the real poem
> absorbs the *decor* almost unconsciously. In the fourth century B.C.
> he writes:—
>
> > "quivers ornamented with fish-skin";
>
> in the twentieth of our era, he writes:—
>
> > "khaki, with a leather strap for his map-case."
>
> But the real poem is the same. Of course there are very few poems.
> You have to go back to Rihoku [Li Po] to find a man telling the
> truth about warfare:—
>
> > "Lice swarm like ants over our accoutrements,
> > Our mind is on getting forward the feather-silk banners.
> > Hard fighting gets no reward.
> > Loyalty is hard to explain.
> > Who will be sorry for General Rishogu, the swift-moving,
> > Whose white head is lost for this province!"

Pound did not see any contemporary poets telling the truth about
war, but he found convincing emotions in the ancient verse of Li Po.
The lines Pound quotes are from his draft of "South-folk in Cold
Country," the final poem in *Cathay*. (Pound would tighten the second line to read "Mind and spirit drive on the feathery banners.")
When Pound sent *Cathay* to Gaudier-Brzeska, the vorticist sculptor
who was stationed in the trenches, Gaudier wrote that the "poems
depict our situation in a wonderful way." The poems also pleased
civilians. In April 1915 Yeats gave a copy of *Cathay* to Mabel Beardsley, who soon asked him to tell Pound that he had undoubtedly discovered the right way to translate Chinese verse. Yeats forwarded her
praise to Pound, adding his own praise for the volume: "I think you
are going to have a great success."

By the time Pound's early version of Li Po's "South-folk in Cold

Country" appeared in his essay on "Webster Ford," he and Yeats
had settled back into Stone Cottage; the complete volume of *Cathay*
had already gone to press and Pound was correcting the proofs. Although he and Yeats had returned to Sussex to perform such literary
tasks and escape London's wartime frenzy, neither poet was immune
from the fever, and each continued to watch the war's progress closely.
In January 1915 Yeats read in the *Times* that an American cargo ship
had struck a German mine. "I don't suppose Wilson has guts enough
to send over the navy," Pound wrote to his father. "Besides I don't
know that a German conquest would do any real harm." Pound was
still able to treat the war lightly; the fighting remained a distant reality. Yeats, on the other hand, began to sense the tragedy to come. He
wrote to Lady Gregory from Stone Cottage:

> I wonder if history will ever know at what man's door to lay the
> crime of this inexplicable war. I suppose, like most wars it is at
> root a bagman's war, a sacrifice of the best for the worst. I feel
> strangely enough most for the young Germans who are now being
> killed. These spectacled, dreamy faces, or so I picture them, re-
> mind me more of men that I have known than the strong-bodied
> young English football players who pass my door at Woburn Build-
> ings daily, marching in their khaki, or the positive-minded young
> Frenchmen.

Letters from Gaudier-Brzeska helped both Yeats and Pound to picture the daily life of the soldier; letters from Maud Gonne (who was
nursing the wounded) reminded them of how those lives came to an
end. Pound wrote his parents that Gaudier had "been promoted to
corporal, has less hard work, has been 25 days without [a] dry place
to sleep or time to wash; now however [he is] back out of [the] front
line for two weeks rest." Maud Gonne told Yeats that she was "nursing the wounded from 6 in the morning till 8 at night & trying in material work to drown the sorrow & disappointment of it all—& in my
heart is growing up a wild hatred of the war machine which is grind-
ing the life out of these great natures & reducing their population to
a helpless slavery & ruin, among all the wounded I have nursed I have
only met one man who spoke with real enthusiasm of returning to the
front."

Pound and Yeats soon had an even more immediate experience of
the battlefield—far more immediate than if they had remained in
London taking in the papers and watching soldiers pass by on the

street. "The country is full of armed men," Pound told Harriet Monroe. "Last week we were under military orders that no light should show after 5 o clock. . . . Last night W.B.Y. and I issued into the moonlit garden [at] about midnight and fenced for some time, awaiting military intervention, which did not arrive. What the local police would make of it, remains yet to be seen." While Pound and Yeats honed their fencing skills, British soldiers were holding maneuvers on the heath before Stone Cottage. Pound wrote his mother that a "Regiment came over the hill the other day and drank up our cider." Early in February, when he and Yeats watched a "whole battery of artillery deployed for our benefit on the heath before Stone Cottage," the poets were offered firsthand experience of the smoke and noise that shook the French countryside across the channel. Pound mused that "That is about as near as we'll get to the war zone, I reckon."

This experience provoked both Pound and Yeats to write war poems. At the time of the British troops' maneuvers on the waste moor, Yeats received a request from Edith Wharton for a poem to be included in *The Book of the Homeless*, an anthology of war literature published to raise money for the Belgian refugees. On February 6th Yeats wrote "A Reason for Keeping Silent" (retitled "On Being Asked for a War Poem" when reprinted in *The Wild Swans at Coole*). In *The Book of the Homeless* the poem appeared in a slightly different form:

> I think it better that at times like these
> We poets keep our mouths shut, for in truth
> We have no gift to set a statesman right;
> He's had enough of meddling who can please
> A young girl in the indolence of her youth
> Or an old man upon a winter's night.

Like Pound in "War Verse," Yeats felt that a poet should confine himself to traditional lyric subjects, leaving the war to soldiers and statesmen. When he sent the poem to Henry James a few months later he added that it "is the only thing I have written of the war or will write, so I hope it may not seem unfitting."

"A Reason for Keeping Silent" actually turned out to be the first of several war poems Yeats would write, and it codified the remote attitude that both he and Pound would continue to project in their comments about the war. Pound was impressed with Yeats's poem and sent it to Harriet Monroe several years later, telling her that she could not publish it but adding that "this anyhow is worth having." Twelve days after Yeats composed the poem, he read Pound a war poem that Sturge Moore had published in the London *Times*. Pound's interest in war poetry was increasing. He clipped Moore's "Tocsin to Men at Arms" from the paper and sent it to Harriet Monroe, commenting, "we may as well quote this scrap of Sturge Moore in the notes [to *Poetry* magazine]. I admit it sounded much finer when Yeats boomed it out over the breakfast table than it does now. Still most of the war verse has been such slop, and we ought to have taken a little (*not* much) more notice of more than we have. *mea* culpa."

Moore's poem, on the heels of Yeats's "A Reason for Keeping Silent," inspired Pound to try his hand at another war poem. Having witnessed the artillery fire on the heath, he had acquired a bit of the direct experience of the war he felt he needed. Pound must have run upstairs to write his own poem the morning Yeats boomed Moore's poem across the breakfast table, for he sent it to H. L. Mencken the same day, explaining he had done it that morning. "I think it has some guts, but am perhaps still blinded by the fury in which I wrote it, and still confuse the cause with the result." Pound titled this attempt at a war poem "1915: February," finding precedent in Yeats's "September 1913." The poem, like "War Verse," has remained unpublished until now.

> The smeared, leather-coated, leather-greaved engineer
> Walks in front of his traction-engine
> Like some figure out of the sagas,
> Like Grettir or like Skarpheddin,
> With a sort of majestical swagger.
> And his machine lumbers after him
> Like some mythological beast,
> Like Grendel bewitched and in chains,
> But his ill luck will make me no sagas,
> Nor will you crack the riddle of his skull,
> O you over-educated, over-refined literati!
> Nor yet you, store-bred realists,
> You multipliers of novels!
> He goes, and I go.
> He stays and I stay.
> He is mankind and I am the arts.

We are outlaws.
This war is not our war,
Neither side is on our side:
A vicious mediaevalism,
A belly-fat commerce,
Neither is on our side:
Whores, apes, rhetoricians,
Flagellants! in a year
Black as the *dies irae*.
We have about us only the unseen country road,
The unseen twigs, breaking their tips with blossom.

Pound was not completely satisfied with "1915: February." His sense that he was confusing the cause of the war with the result matched his sense that the war itself might be only "a symptom of the real disease." Because of his doubts, Pound did not attempt to publish the poem immediately, but waited until May to send it to Harriet Monroe. Even then he hesitated:

> I do not like my damn poem, it is too rhetorical, it contains too much that is not presentation. Please send it back, I don't know whether I've another copy. It may make part of a sequence. I want to put down real war emotion, not the froth, the conventional "what-is-to-be-expected-of-all-patriotic-poets-in-war-time," horrors of blood, etc.
>   The war is still like a great cataclysm in nature, but I now think, despite my contempt for certain policies of the british empire, the struggle at Ypres is the struggle for free life and free thought.

Pound's sense of the urgency of the war was increasing rapidly; only three months before he had written from Stone Cottage, "I don't know that a German conquest would do any real harm." Yet his new identification of the war's importance only made his task as a war poet more difficult, and he continued to doubt his ability to set down "real war emotion" in the way that Li Po did so well. On the manuscript of "1915: February" Pound bracketed the first eight lines, writing "presentation marred by 2 inescapable comparisons" in the margin. The comparisons to Grettir and Skarpheddin (drawn from the Norse sagas Pound was reading to Yeats in the evening) were not fully integrated into the poem. Pound bracketed the following seventeen lines and wrote "damn'd talk" beside them. Only the last two

lines—really a perfect Imagist poem that might have been written by
Li Po—pleased Pound completely:

> We have about us only the unseen country road,
> The unseen twigs, breaking their tips with blossom.

Despite Pound's reservations, "1915: February" is a crucial poem
in his development, a pivot point between the aestheticism of his
Imagist work and the social engagement of *Hugh Selwyn Mauberley*.
The poem is also interesting because of the way it enacts the attitude
toward war and poetry that Yeats expressed in "A Reason for Keeping Silent." The central section of the poem is "damn'd talk," full of
rhetorical excess, but it shows what happens to poetry when a poet is
forced to address a topic better left to statesmen. If the poet were left
alone, isolated from the war which is not his war, then he could gaze
peacefully at "the unseen country road, / The unseen twigs" outside
the windows of Stone Cottage and write nothing but the pure Imagist poem.

A few days before he was killed on June 5, 1915, Gaudier-Brzeska
wrote to Olivia Shakespear, "To-day is magnificent, a fresh wind,
clear sun and larks singing cheerfully. The shells do not disturb the
songsters. In the Champagne woods the nightingales took no notice
of the fight either. They solemnly proclaim man's foolery and sacrilege
of nature. I respect their disdain." Pound respected it too. In 1917 he
would write that the "real artists who have been plunged into the
present inferno have written simply and without rhetoric, without
any glorification of war. Gaudier-Brzeska wrote back from the front
that the nightingales were still singing despite the bombardment."
T. S. Eliot, whose direct comments about the Great War were few,
captured nature's aristocratic disdain for warfare in the final lines of
"Sweeney Among the Nightingales," a poem which in this context
emerges as a commentary on the homecoming of war heroes, ancient
and modern.

> The host with someone indistinct
> Converses at the door apart,
> The nightingales are singing near
> The Convent of the Sacred Heart,
>
> And sang within the bloody wood
> When Agamemnon cried aloud,

> And let their liquid siftings fall
> To stain the stiff dishonoured shroud.

Yeats would remark that these lines comprise the single moment in Eliot's early work which speaks "in the great manner" of English poetry; they fulfill the prescriptions of "A Reason for Keeping Silent." Like Yeats, like the nightingales, Pound wanted to maintain a lofty indifference to the war, but the fighting intruded even upon the inner sanctum of art he shared with Yeats in Ashdown Forest, pushing him from the private contemplation of the Image to the impure rhetoric of the war-obsessed London he had left behind. For Pound, the war was what the Hugh Lane controversy, the Parnell dispute, and the furor over *The Playboy of the Western World* were to Yeats: one of the "public controversies [that] have stirred my imagination."

The war also caused Pound to reconsider the anti-humanism he had been espousing over the last year. During their first winter at Stone Cottage, George Moore's attack on Yeats had provoked Pound to declare his war on humanity: "The artist has been for so long a humanist," he wrote in "The New Sculpture," adding that "the war between [the artist] and humanity is a war without truce." During his second winter at Stone Cottage, the Great War caused him to be reconciled with humanity—if only temporarily. In "1915: February" Pound aligns himself with the "leather-greaved engineer" working in the fields:

> He goes, and I go.
> He stays and I stay.
> He is mankind and I am the arts.
> We are outlaws.
> This war is not our war,
> Neither side is on our side.

Confronted with what he perceived as the enormous stupidity of world leaders, Pound discovered that he had more in common with the people he had previously scorned. "1915: February" reveals Pound in a wartime mood similar to that of Thomas Hardy, a poet whom he rarely resembles. In "In Time of 'The Breaking of Nations' " (1915) Hardy looks across a field to a farmer and, like Pound gazing at the engineer, discovers a permanence in the lives of ordinary people which uncovers the ultimate irrelevance of the war.

I

Only a man harrowing the clods
   In a slow silent walk
With an old horse that stumbles and nods
   Half asleep as they stalk.

II

Only thin smoke without flame
   From the heaps of couch-grass;
Yet this will go onward the same
   Though Dynasties pass.

III

Yonder a maid and her wight
   Come whispering by:
War's annals will fade into night
   Ere their story die.

Pound felt much more conflict over his humanism than Hardy, however, and though he was temporarily reconciled with the farmers and maids of Ashdown Forest, he continued to have second thoughts about revealing "1915: February" to the audience to which the poem reached out. He became more and more "convinced that [the war] is civilization against barbarism and atavism and that it is everyone's place to turn in and end it." Pound himself tried to enlist only to find that the British army would not accept American citizens: he berated Wilson for keeping the United States out of the war. "The war 1915 poem was all right," he told Harriet Monroe in the autumn of 1915, "but I've since volunteered and been refused on account of being a citizen of a dishonoured nation, so the true loftiness of the artist don't any longer apply." Yet in December he wrote Monroe, "You can also print my poem on the arts & humanity being out of the war, exiles if you like." But early in 1916 he changed his mind again and insisted that "the one about the traction engine and neutrality is NOT to be used."

In the meantime, Poünd did publish another poem about the war. The March 1915 issue of *Poetry* included "The Coming of War: Actaeon."

An image of Lethe,
   and the fields

> Full of faint light
> > but golden,
> Gray cliffs,
> > and beneath them
> A sea
> Harsher than granite,
> > unstill, never ceasing;
> High forms
> > with the movement of gods,
> Perilous aspect;
> > And one said:
> "This is Actaeon."
> > Actaeon of golden greaves!
> Over fair meadows,
> Over the cool face of that field,
> Unstill, ever moving
> Hosts of an ancient people
> The silent cortège.

Unlike "1915: February" this poem offers a purely Imagistic presentation of the war; the mythic elements are more successfully integrated. "The Coming of War: Actaeon" is also Pound's first treatment of the battalion of British troops holding maneuvers on the heath before Stone Cottage. Now the "leather-greaved engineer" of "1915: February" appears as "Actaeon of golden greaves." In Pound's imagination, the soldiers became their mythic counterparts in the Norse sagas, a host "of an ancient people" moving "Over fair meadows, / Over the cool face of that field." In "The Coming of War: Actaeon" Pound was able to pull his experience of the war into the private world of the Image.

The poem consequently offers yet another answer to the question Pound first asked about war poetry: "Is a war poem, as a work of art in any way different or more meritorious than any other poem?" In "The Coming of War: Actaeon" Pound was able to treat the war without any of the rhetorical excess of "1915: February," unifying his lyric impulse and political fervor. Yet the sacrifice was a large one. "The Coming of War: Actaeon" addresses the war only by mythologizing it out of its place in history and ignoring the brutality of the actual experience. The sense of "a year / Black as the *dies irae*" in "1915: February" is missing. Pound had achieved the detachment

Yeats encouraged in "A Reason for Keeping Silent" but sacrificed the intensity of political engagement.

Pound tried to rectify this problem in a poem written at around the same time that "The Coming of War: Actaeon" was published. Having translated an eighth-century Chinese war poet, Pound now "translated" a twentieth-century British war poet. "Poem: Abbreviated from the Conversation of Mr. T.E.H." appeared in Pound's *Catholic Anthology* (November 1915) under Hulme's signature; in 1920 Pound reprinted it in *Umbra* as his own poem.

> Over the flat slope of St. Eloi
> A wide wall of sandbags.
> Night,
> In the silence desultory men
> Pottering over small fires, cleaning their mess-tins:
> To and fro, from the lines,
> Men walk as on Piccadilly,
> Making paths in the dark,
> Through scattered dead horses,
> Over a dead Belgian's belly.
>
> The Germans have rockets. The English have no rockets.
> Behind the lines, cannon, hidden lying back miles.
> Before the line, chaos:
>
> My mind is a corridor. The minds about me are corridors.
> Nothing suggests itself. There is nothing to do but keep on.

Pound probably performed the actual act of writing this poem, taking "real war emotion" from the details Hulme spoke of when he was on leave from the trenches. Several of the poem's images are repeated in Hulme's wartime diary. He describes "the ground between the trenches, a bank which is practically never seen by anyone in the daylight, as it is only safe to move through it at dark. It's full of dead things, dead animals here & there, dead unburied animals, skeletons of horses destroyed by shell fire. It's curious to think of it later on in the war, when it will again be seen in the daylight." At night, Hulme noted, the troops move over this terrain "always in the same direction [and] make definite paths." In daylight, one of Hulme's comrades "discovered that one of these paths that we walk over led right over the chest of a dead peasant (Belgian)."

As these details were incorporated into "Poem: Abbreviated from the Conversation of Mr. T.E.H.," Pound stirred them together with the emotions he found in eighth-century Chinese war poetry, and then presented his twentieth-century war poem in the diction he had perfected for Li Po. In the Hulme poem Pound writes that "There is nothing to do but keep on"; in "South-folk in Cold Country" we learn that "Emotion is born out of habit," that "Hard fight gets no reward" yet "Loyalty is hard to explain." The details of Hulme's wartime experience are made even more horrific by Pound's comparison of the soldiers walking through their wasteland to civilians walking in Piccadilly. "I see crowds of people, walking round in a ring," Madame Sosostris would intone in *The Waste Land*. And Pound would present the same wartime living dead in Canto 7:

> Life to make mock of motion:
> For the husks move, before me, move,
> The words rattle: shells given out by shells.

Pound's paraphrase of Hulme finally gave him a successful blending of the lyric impulse and "war emotion," but the relationship of these two modes continued to trouble Pound for many years. *Homage to Sextus Propertius* (1917) circles around this question, and "Near Perigord" (1915), one of the first of Pound's "poems including history," takes it as its subject. The accumulating tragedy of the war weighed heavily on Pound as he wrote this poem. When he sent it to Harriet Monroe on June 28, 1915, he sent also news of Gaudier-Brzeska's death:

> He was killed at Neuville St Vaast, early this month, but the news is just in.
> This is the heaviest loss in personnel the arts have suffered by the war, it is not the case of a beautiful youth who had perhaps done his best work. Brzeska was five years younger than Brooke, but he was a man full of vigorous genius, and there is no one to replace him. Also he had seen months of fighting and had been twice promoted for daring. There is probably no artist fighting with any of the armies who might not have been better spared.
> Finis.

Pound's meditations on artists and fighting did not end here. The intricate design of "Near Perigord" has so preoccupied its readers that the urgency of its subject matter has gone unnoticed: throughout the poem Pound examines Bertran de Born's canzon, "Dompa pois de me no'us cal," attempting to determine whether the poem was inspired by love or war:

> Is it a love poem? Did he sing of war?
> Is it an intrigue to run subtly out,
> Born of a jongleur's tongue, freely to pass
> Up and about and in and out of the land,
> Mark him a craftsman and a strategist?
>
> . . . .
>
> Maent, Maent, and yet again Maent,
> Or war and broken heaumes and politics?

In his canzon, Bertran takes the best parts of several ladies to make a "borrowed lady" of incomparable beauty. Pound wonders if his intention was to praise the lady Maent, his lost love, or to bring the husbands of all the ladies he mentions in the poem into conflict. Can war, the poem asks, be the subject of lyric poetry? Pound's concerted effort to begin *The Cantos*, his epic, during the later years of the war reveals that he himself felt he had to leave songs of love behind.

"Near Perigord" ends with the question of Bertran's intentions unanswered; but what is most important about the poem is that the questions worried Pound. The question bothered Yeats too, and the poems he wrote about the war after his time at Stone Cottage reveal a similar struggle to unify a lyric impulse with political fervor. Yeats kept his vow of silence until the conflict hit so close to home it hurt him into song. On May 7, 1915, Hugh Lane went down with the Lusitania, and with him went all Yeats's hopes for a Dublin art gallery. A few years later, on January 23, 1918, Lady Gregory's son Robert was shot down over Italy. Yeats began his first elegy for the young man soon afterwards, writing to Lady Gregory in February, "I am trying a poem in manner like one that Spenser wrote for Sir Philip Sidney." "Shepherd and Goatherd" is modeled on Spenser's *Astrophel* and Virgil's fifth eclogue, but like Stevens's "Phases" or Pound's "1915: February," the poem fails (in Pound's words) to "put down real war emotion": "He stayed for a while," sings Yeats's shepherd, but the shepherd and his companions

Had scarcely accustomed our eyes
To his shape at the rinsing-pool
Among the evening shadows,
When he vanished from ears and eyes.
I might have wished on the day
He came, but man is a fool.

Only when the poem approaches Yeats's personal concerns with apparitions and the afterlife does the verse come alive:

They say that on your barren mountain ridge
You have measured out the road that the soul treads
When it has vanished from our natural eyes;
That you have talked with apparitions.

Yeats probably chose to cast his elegy for Robert Gregory in the artificial pastoral form because he doubted his ability to convey the real emotion of the tragedy. Yet he knew right away that the poem was inadequate. In June he began working on "In Memory of Major Robert Gregory," imitating a stanza form of Cowley's, and he published the poem in the August number of the *English Review* with this note: "Major Robert Gregory, R.F.C., M.C., Legion of Honour, was killed in action on the Italian Front, January 23, 1918." The poem is one of Yeats's most famous achievements, but, like "The Coming of War: Actaeon," "In Memory of Major Robert Gregory" addresses the war only by mythologizing the loss out of its place in history. By incorporating Gregory's death into his private mythology of "companions of my youth" who "cannot sup with us / Beside a fire of turf in th' ancient tower," Yeats evaded the brutal reality of the war.

In "An Irish Airman Foresees his Death" (1918) Yeats would present the war from Gregory's own point of view ("In balance with this life, this death"), but not until the beginning of the Anglo-Irish war was Yeats provoked to write his most devastating evaluation of the loss. At Stone Cottage in 1915 Yeats wrote "A Reason for Keeping Silent" (instead of simply keeping silent) because the poem was to be published in a book to benefit Belgium, a small nation overrun by imperialists. After the Easter Rebellion, Yeats came to feel that England "treated Ireland as Germany treated Belgium," and in "Sixteen Dead Men" (written in 1917 but not published until 1920

when the Great War was over and the Anglo-Irish war had begun)
Yeats was no longer preaching silence:

> You say that we should still the land
> Till Germany's overcome;
> But who is there to argue that
> Now Pearse is deaf and dumb?

As the Black and Tan's retaliations against the Irish Republican
Army brought the war to Yeats's doorstep, he could not contain
what Pound called "real war emotion" in a pastoral cadence or private
mythology. "Reprisals" (written in 1921) remained unpublished during Yeats's lifetime because Lady Gregory feared that it would offend
her son's widow. In this poem, Robert Gregory's life is no longer in
balance with his death; Yeats tells the young man's ghost that "second
thoughts" have come upon the cause that they imagined "such a fine
affair":

> Half-drunk or whole-mad soldiery
> Are murdering your tenants there.
> Men that revere your father yet
> Are shot at on the open plain.
> Where may new-married women sit
> And suckle children now? Armed men
> May murder them in passing by
> Nor law nor parliament take heed.
> Then close your ears with dust and lie
> Among the other cheated dead.

"Reprisals" was based on events that actually took place outside
Yeats's door in Ireland. In "Nineteen Hundred and Nineteen" (originally titled "Thoughts Upon the Present State of the World") Yeats
invoked this nightmare scene once again: "drunken soldiery / Can
leave the mother, murdered at her door." The tone of these poems
is very much like that of those Yeats excluded from the *Oxford
Book of Modern Verse*. When Yeats places Robert Gregory among
"the other cheated dead" and expresses his "second thoughts" about
the war they believed was undertaken with noble aspirations, he exhibits the same disillusionment with patriotism and heroism that
one finds in the war poems of Owen or Sassoon.

Pound too was capable of writing verse which reveals a sensibility very close to those poets who saw action. In *Hugh Selwyn Mauberley* (1920) he fulfilled his desire to set down "real war emotion." Much like Owen in "Dulce et Decorum Est," Pound turns the famous lines from Horace to horrifyingly ironic effect:

> Died some, pro patria,
>   non "dulce" non "et decor" . . .
> walked eye-deep in hell
> believing in old men's lies, then unbelieving
> came home, home to a lie,
> home to many deceits,
> home to old lies and new infamy;
> usury age-old and age-thick
> and liars in public places.

Both *Mauberley* and "Reprisals" were written after the armistice and were probably influenced by the enormous amount of war poetry produced since 1914. The poems Pound and Yeats wrote at Stone Cottage during the winter of 1914–15 present their more idiosyncratic responses to the war. As the years passed, however, the hostility expressed in *Mauberley* and "Reprisals" became part of a larger sense of postwar loss and betrayal. Pound lost Gaudier-Brzeska and T. E. Hulme in the trenches, but he also considered the deaths of Henry James and Remy de Gourmont to be "crimes of the war" though they died as civilians:

> de Gourmont was only fifty-seven, and if he had not been worried to death, if he had not been grieved to death by the cessation of all that has been "life" as he understood it, there was no reason why we should not have had more of his work and his company.
> He is as much "dead of the war" as if he had died in the trenches, and he left with almost the same words on his lips. "Nothing is being done in Paris, nothing can be done, *faute de combattants*." There was an elegy on current writing by him in the *Mercure*. It was almost the same tone in which Gaudier-Brzeska wrote to me a few days before he was shot at Neuville St. Vaast: "Is anything of importance or even of interest going on in the world—I mean the 'artistic London?' "

Very little was happening in "artistic London," especially after the College of the Arts had collapsed and Pound retreated to Sussex.

For Pound, the war destroyed not only individuals but the possibility of culture. He believed, largely because of Remy de Gourmont's influence, that civilization was the product of individual sensibilities.

> The soul starts with itself, builds out perfection.
> Confucius, Dante.
>   Or the best man killed in France,
> Struck by a Prussian bullet at St Vaast
> With just enough cut stone left here behind him.

As these lines from a very early draft for Canto 4 make clear, Pound saw that the war had destroyed the prospects for a second Renaissance as it destroyed Gaudier or Gourmont. As Pound revised his drafts for Canto 4, all reference to the war disappeared; only the melancholic sense of waste remained. Similarly, Yeats's "The Second Coming" (1920) began with explicit references to the Russian Revolution and the First World War ("The falcon cannot hear the falconer / The Germans are [   ] now to Russia come"), but in revision the poem's apocalypse became mythical rather than historical. Not until Canto 16 (1925), a group elegy for those who fought and died in the Great War, would Pound specify the cause of the emotions that was latent in the earlier cantos.

> And Henri Gaudier went to it,
>   and they killed him,
> And killed a good deal of sculpture,
> And ole T.E.H. he went to it,
> With a lot of books from the library,
> London Library, and a shell buried 'em in a dug-out,
> And the Library expressed its annoyance.
>   And a bullet hit him on the elbow
> And he read Kant in the Hospital, in Wimbledon,
> in the original,
> And the hospital staff didn't like it.

Pound knew that the obliteration of the possibility of a London vortex was only one small part of the loss incurred by Western culture; a more drastic remedy than a College of the Arts was in order. In 1949 Pound told Wyndham Lewis that it was Gaudier's death that prompted his first "serious curiosity" in politics and economics.

The brief biography Pound composed for his *Selected Poems* (1949) explains that in 1918 he "began investigation of causes of war, to oppose same." Pound continued this investigation for the rest of his life. All of his fanatical interests in social and economic programs grew from his desire to save civilization from this postwar decline. His years in prewar London became a prelapsarian era in his mind, and once the second World War had passed and Pound was incarcerated at Pisa, he recalled them as the last high point of Western culture. Even then he feared the achievement would be lost: "remember that I have remembered," he intoned in the *Pisan Cantos*.

> Romains, Vildrac and Chennevière and the rest of them
> before the world was given over to wars
> Quand vous serez bien vieille
>   remember that I have remembered,
> mia pargoletta,
>   and pass on the tradition
> there can be honesty of mind
>   without overwhelming talent
> I have perhaps seen a waning of that tradition.

When Pound first arrived in London as a young man he came to know "the tradition of the dead" by meeting people "whose minds have been enriched by contact with men of genius." Through Arthur Galton he came to know Arnold. Ford Madox Ford gave him second-hand knowledge of the Pre-Raphaelites. And most of all, Yeats passed on memories of Johnson, Dowson, Wilde, and Symons, the writers Pound admired most in his youth. Now, in old age, after two world wars, Pound became a bearded Tiresias himself. "Remember that I have remembered," he warned, fearing that no one listened.

After the Great War the rest of Pound's career was in some sense inevitable. And in less obvious ways, the direction of Yeats's later work was also shaped by the war. When he sent "A Reason for Keeping Silent" to Henry James, he commented that he would "keep the neighbourhood of the seven sleepers of Ephesus, hoping to catch their comfortable snores till bloody frivolity is over." Yeats would continue to use the metaphor of the seven sleepers of Ephesus to describe the origin of his visionary system: the intricate world of *A Vision* (written between 1917 and 1925 and revised for many years thereafter) was built as a conscious alternative to the world shaken by the Great

War. In "On a Picture of a Black Centaur by Edmund Dulac" (written in 1920) Yeats offered an allegory for the origin of his esoterica.

> What wholesome sun has ripened is wholesome food to eat,
> And that alone; yet I, being driven half insane
> Because of some green wing, gathered old mummy wheat
> In the mad abstract dark and ground it grain by grain
> And after baked it slowly in an oven; but now
> I bring full-flavoured wine out of a barrel found
> Where seven Ephesian topers slept and never knew
> When Alexander's empire passed, they slept so sound.

Traditionally, the seven sleepers are said to have slept through the Roman persecution of the Christians to awaken in the Christian age. Yeats distorts the legend and has them sleep through the fall of Alexander's empire so that we may compare their era with the period of "bloody frivolity" initiated by the Great War. Like the seven sleepers, Yeats has slept through the crumbling of a civilization, but he has spent that long dream producing A Vision, a book that reveals the historical cycles that explain the rise and fall of empires. In the first version of A Vision (1925) Yeats made the connection between the wars of Alexander and the wars of the twentieth century even clearer when he wrote that "at Phase 22 [there is] always war, and as this war is always a defeat for those who have conquered, we have repeated the wars of Alexander." According to Yeats's system, the time of the war and the writing of A Vision correspond to phase 22 of the millennium which began in 1050 A.D. In a draft of this passage in A Vision Yeats wrote even more explicitly that "We have in our great war repeated the wars of Alexander." In Yeats's mind, he had repeated the task of the seven sleepers, emerging from the dream to find the old gods dead, the new world waiting for its sacred book.

That Pound's A Draft of XVI Cantos (1925) is as much a poem about the war as The Waste Land (1922) is now a critical commonplace; Yeats's A Vision (1925) should be included in their company. When the book was published in its first edition, Yeats was reluctant to claim authorship and constructed what he later called "an unnatural story of an Arabian traveller" as a narrative frame for the volume, explaining that A Vision was based on writings by Giraldus and Kusta Ben Luka which had been delivered to Yeats by Owen Aherne and Michael Robartes (characters from Yeats's early stories).

In the "Introduction by Owen Aherne," Yeats's character explains that after years of separation he met Michael Robartes in the spring of 1917 in the National Gallery in London. Robartes gazed at a "story of Griselda pictured in a number of episodes, the sort of thing he had admired thirty years ago." Yeats locates Robartes and Aherne and A Vision itself in the troubled years of the Great War:

> [Aherne] drew him [Robartes] from the picture with difficulty, because his indignation that the authorities of the gallery had not thought it was worth saving from the German bombs had heightened his admiration for all pictures of that type and his need for its expression. "The old painters," he said, "painted women with whom they would if they could have spent the night or a life, battles they would if they could have fought in, and all manner of desirable houses and places, but now all is changed, and God knows why anybody paints anything. But why should we complain, things move by mathematical necessity, all changes can be dated by gyre and cone, and pricked beforehand upon the Calendar."

As Robartes explains, the historical gyres of A Vision are designed to give order to a world destroyed by German bombs and to give consolation by showing that an earlier age of grace and nobility is destined to return. Although the Great War is not mentioned in A Vision, it overshadows the entire work.

Pound's early cantos take on the war more directly, but he shares Yeats's desire to forge a new order for a postwar world. He agreed with Yeats that "order is the conspiracy of a few," and though his later esoterica dealt with social credit rather than spooks, he too constructed a vast system to order history—one as idiosyncratic and schematic as Yeats's, despite Pound's effort to give his work the illusion of unadulterated fact. Both poets were nostalgic for a time of aristocratic artists and a social elite that nourished the arts. Such things lay on the other side of the abyss that the Great War opened in modern history. For Pound, Stone Cottage—the small piece of the aristocratic dream that he himself remembered—lay on the far side of the abyss. In "Blood and the Moon" Yeats proclaimed that he had created his system "In mockery of a time / Half dead at the top." Halfway through The Cantos Pound remarked,

> "half dead at the top"
> My dear William B. Y. your ½ was too moderate.

5

Poems Cold and Passionate
as the Dawn

When Pound and Yeats wrote war poems at Stone Cottage, their goal was nobility—not only of attitude but of diction too. For Pound, the struggle to find an idiom for modern poetry became inextricably entwined with the struggle to set down "real war emotion." So at the same time that he thought deeply about the war in France, he continued his own attack on American poets who neglected their craft. The day after he wrote "1915: February" he wrote "Morning on the Farm: An Impression à la Vachel Lindsay." Like the war poem, this parody was never published. Coming so soon after what Pound himself called the "damned rhetoric" of "1915: February," these concluding lines of the parody seem as much directed at Pound's own lack of nobility as they are at Lindsay's flaccid diction.

> I wish I was in a boat at sea
> Where all the wobbling waves
> That wetted galley slaves
> And indian braves
> With bright imag'ry
> Were tumbling and rumbling
> On the rocky shore
> I want some more
> HASH!

When Pound sent this effusion to Harriet Monroe, asking her to keep it to herself, he explained that "Mr. Lindsay is doubtless very spirited, but really any body can do it if they set out, just to gobble wobble gobble without saying or meaning anything in particular. . . . One can pour out irrelevancies as this scrap is dumped out, speed only limited by the medium, i.e. the speed in which one can drive a pencil across paper." Pound added that his parody had taken him one minute, fifty-eight seconds to write and came with the author's "guarantee to keep it up at the same rate eight hours per day as long as the demand holds out." And yet despite this smugness, Pound was at the same time worried that his own poem about the war was an irrelevancy itself.

Pound could not have considered Lindsay's verse to be completely without merit; in 1913, when Yeats refused *Poetry* magazine's first annual Guarantors' prize, Pound had suggested that the money be split between Aldington and Lindsay before Yeats persuaded Harriet Monroe to give it to the other member of the Brothers Minor. Yeats found some merit in Lindsay's work too. Just after the first winter at Stone Cottage, when he spoke at a *Poetry* magazine banquet held in Chicago in his honor, Yeats praised Lindsay's verse as being stripped bare of ornament; it has an earnest simplicity, a strange beauty, and you know Bacon said, 'There is no excellent beauty without strangeness.' "

This comment seems more like a description of the kind of poetry Pound and Yeats wanted to write themselves. A poet such as Lindsay haunted Pound as the image of what he might have become if he had remained in America. He mailed his Lindsay parody to Monroe not only to condemn Lindsay's verse but to differentiate the itinerant poet's method from his own. Amy Lowell was issuing a new Imagist anthology, and Pound was on the defensive. In criticizing poets such as Lindsay and Lowell, Pound confined himself to their flaccid diction. Yet the vehemence of his attacks on Lowell reveal that something far closer to Pound than the "direct treatment of the thing" was at stake. On January 5, 1915 he wrote to Monroe from Stone Cottage that Lowell "deliberately tries [to] dilute the meaning" of Imagism: "we do NOT say that one thing *is* another. Fame is fame, it is *not* fickle fish slithering about on something or other." Pound's choice of the word *fame* as his example is revealing, for it was not so much his program for poetic diction that Amy Lowell threatened as his place as the leader of the Imagist movement. In several long letters written from Stone Cottage, Pound continued to justify his own position as the ringleader of *les jeunes*:

> In the Imagist book I made it possible for a few poets who were not over-producing to reach an audience. That delicate operation was managed by the most rigorous suppression of what I considered faults.
>
> Obviously such a method and movement are incompatible with effusion, with flooding magazines with all sorts of wish-wash and imitation and the near-good. If I had acceded to A. L.'s [Amy Lowell's] proposal to turn "Imagism" into a democratic beergarden, I should have undone what little good I had managed to do by setting up a critical standard.
>
> My problem is to keep alive a certain group of advancing poets, to set the arts in their rightful place as the acknowledged guide and lamp of civilization.

Pound's dispute with Lowell over the rights to the Imagist name hinged on Pound's desire to maintain the artist as the acknowledged legislator of the world. Consequently, it was Lowell's decision to give equal representation to each poet in her *Some Imagist Poets* rather than her dilution of the Imagist idiom that bothered Pound most of all. For Pound, the legislation of the arts had to take the form of a dictatorship, not a democracy, and Imagism had to retain its status as a secret society—not a "democratic beer-garden"—if it were to continue to be the guide and lamp of civilization.

The tone of Pound's letter to Harriet Monroe is oddly extravagant; the pressure of the Great War was already pushing him to extremes, and he began to feel that a great deal more than perpetuating an aesthetic rested upon the compilation of an anthology. Properly edited, an anthology could begin to counteract the war's threat to the progress of civilization. Or so Pound thought, and in opposition to Lowell's *Some Imagist Poets* he put together his own *Catholic Anthology*. "I should not call it an Imagist anthology," he wrote to Monroe from Stone Cottage, "but should select from the newer schools,—stuff on modern subjects, mostly *vers libre*." The inclusion of T. S. Eliot's work in the anthology was especially important to Pound. He had first sent "Prufrock" to Monroe soon after he met Eliot on September 22, 1914, and he was still trying to persuade her to publish the poem when he wrote from Stone Cottage: " 'Mr. Prufrock' does not 'go off at the end.' It is a portrait of failure, or of a char-

Dorothy Shakespear's artwork for the cover of Pound's *Catholic Anthology*, 1915.

acter which fails, and it would be false art to make it end on a note of triumph."

Pound did not know how long it would take the editor of *Poetry* to publish "Prufrock," and in the meantime he realized that *Blast* was the only magazine daring enough to print Eliot's "modern" verse. But the poems Eliot sent Lewis for the second issue of *Blast* were (like Pound's "Fratres Minores" in the first issue) too ribald even for the journal of the Vorticist "men at war." "Eliot has sent me Bullshit & the Ballad for Big Louise," Lewis wrote to Pound at Stone Cottage. "They are excellent bits of scholarly ribaldry. I am longing to print them in *Blast*; but stick to my naif determination to have no 'Words ending in -Uck, -Unt and -Ugger.' " Pound replied that "Eliot will consent to leaving blanks for the offending words." And because Lewis had asked if there was anything at Stone Cottage to be blasted "except Yeates [sic]," Pound added that "Yeats says there is no one for you to work on here except the Vicar" who had paid an unwelcome visit to the cottage. Pound concluded his note to Lewis with "Salutations to the brethren," asserting his camaraderie with the young Vorticist gang, but at the same time emphasizing his exclusive membership in an order impervious to blasts from wars either artistic or political.

Eliot sent a copy of his "Portrait of a Lady" to Stone Cottage, and thanked Pound for introductions to both Lewis and Dolmetsch. He had not yet met Yeats but looked forward to doing so. Writing from Oxford, he explained to Pound that he would "not be in town again until March. I hope Mr. Yeats will still be there." He also told Pound that there was no chance of his scatalogical poems appearing in *Blast*; deleting the offensive words was not an option. Lewis's "Puritanical Principles seem to bar my way to Publicity," said Eliot.

> I fear that King Bolo and his Big Black Kween will never burst into print. I understand that Priapism, Narcissism etc are not approved of, and even so innocent a rhyme as
>
> > . . . pulled her stockings off
> > With a frightful cry of "Hauptbahnhof!"
>
> is considered decadent.

Instead of King Bolo, Eliot's "Preludes" and "Rhapsody on a Windy Night" appeared in *Blast* in July 1915; by then "Prufrock" had appeared in the June issue of *Poetry*. Pound placed "Portrait of a Lady" in the September issue of Alfred Kreymborg's *Others*. And when his own *Catholic Anthology* appeared in November, it contained not only "Prufrock" and "Portrait" but also "The Boston Evening Transcript," "Hysteria," and "Miss Helen Slingsby" (later "Aunt Helen"). Pound later commented that he had compiled his anthology "for the sake of printing sixteen pages of Eliot." This remark is slightly disingenuous, however, for while he was confined to Stone Cottage during war time, Pound felt that his own reputation and the future of the arts rode on the *Catholic Anthology*. He discussed the problem with Yeats, who agreed to give Pound a new poem for the anthology. *Catholic Anthology* may include sixteen pages of Eliot, but the volume begins with Yeats's "The Scholars," a sign to Amy Lowell that Pound's circle was no "democratic beer-garden" but a secret society of the arts that included the greatest living poet. When Pound compiled another anthology titled *Profile* in 1932, he recalled that the *Catholic Anthology* "appeared as it were under Yeats' *patronato*, at least it started with a poem in his then newer manner, which might be regarded as a turning point from the twilit to his more stony and later phase." Pound began his anthology with the poet who had made his modern poetry possible.

"The Scholars" appeared in *Catholic Anthology* in a form substantially different from that in which it would finally appear in later editions of Yeats's work. In the first stanza of both versions Yeats presents the "bald heads" of scholars who weigh down poems written by young men "in love's despair" with pointlessly learned annotation. In the final version of the poem Yeats begins the second stanza with "All shuffle there; all cough in ink" and concludes that the scholars merely "think what other people think" and "know the man their neighbour knows." In the version of the poem published in Pound's anthology, Yeats's indictment of the bald heads found a slightly rougher expression.

> They'll cough in the ink to the world's end;
> Wear out the carpet with their shoes
> Earning respect; have no strange friend;
> If they have sinned nobody knows:
> Lord, what would they say
> Should their Catullus walk that way!

Pound had published Yeats's poems in the past to establish the reputation of *Poetry* magazine, but his use of "The Scholars" to elevate the contents of the *Catholic Anthology* marked a new stage in his relationship with the older poet. Although Pound tinkered with the poems Yeats published in *Poetry* in 1912, it would be rash to say that they (or any of the other poems Yeats eventually published in *Responsibilities*) reveal much of Pound's influence; Yeats had been pushing for his stonier idiom long before the younger poet attempted to enhance his own reputation by boasting that he had bullied Yeats into making a few minor changes in his verse. "The Scholars," on the other hand, is a poem marked by Yeats's close association with Pound. Pound had been ranting against the stale scholarship of the philologists ever since he had arrived in London, and in 1911 he had unveiled his "New Method" in scholarship in *I Gather the Limbs of Osiris*. Pound offered a parable to illustrate the deadening effect of the old method of scholarship:

> If a man owned mines in South Africa he would know that his labourers dug up a good deal of mud and an occasional jewel, looking rather like the mud about it. If he shipped all the mud and uncut stones northward and dumped them in one heap on the shore of Iceland, in some inaccessible spot, we should not consider him commercially sound. In my own department of scholarship I should say the operations are rather of this complexion. There are many fine things discovered, edited, and buried. Much very dull "literature" is treated in like manner. They are dumped in one museum and certain learned men rejoice in the treasure. They also complain of a lack of public interest in their operations.

Pound felt that scholarship was worthless unless it was combined with a creative interest in the past; the artist must bring the past to life in his work in the same way that Odysseus revives the ghost of Tiresias in Canto 1. To revive the ghost of Catullus, a possibility Yeats suggests in the final lines of "The Scholars," was one of Pound's greatest dreams. In "Prologomena" (1912) he wrote that "I would much rather lie on what is left of Catullus' parlour floor and speculate the azure beneath it and the hills off to Salo and Riva with their forgotten gods moving unhindered amongst them, than discuss any processes and theories of art whatsoever." Pound and Yeats probably discussed the "New Method" of scholarship at Stone

Cottage, especially when they read Maurice Bourgeois's biography of Synge (a book which Yeats complained was filled with nothing but "facts"). While the two poets were together at Stone Cottage Pound wrote to Harriet Monroe that "Scholarship is but a hand-maid to the arts"; he had previously told her that "the arts, INCLUD-ING poetry and literature, should be taught by artists, by practicing artists, not by sterile professors." When Pound began the Catholic Anthology with Yeats's "The Scholars," he was giving higher sanction to some of his own most treasured ideas.

The Catholic Anthology was a conspicuous riposte to Amy Lowell's Some Imagist Poets, but Pound also worked to preserve the secret doctrine of the Image more surreptitiously. During the previous winter he had worked with Yeats to redefine the bourgeoisie as a "state of mind"; that made the truly aristocratic "state of mind" even more exclusive because one could not be born into it—the initiation rights were mysterious. Eliot would mystify the idea of tradition in the same way by maintaining that it could not be "inherited" but was attainable only through "great labour." To save Imagism from inferior poets who simply borrowed the term, Pound redefined it not as a school of poetry that arose in London in 1913 but as a "state of mind" that only the best poets of the past and present had reached. Fenollosa's essay on "The Chinese Written Character," which Pound edited during the winter of 1914-15, helped him to see Imagism as a trans-historical tendency in poetry rather than an exclusively "modern" technique. "The best poetry," said Fenollosa, "deals not only with natural images but with lofty thoughts, spiritual suggestions and obscure relations." As Pound's "Ikon" makes clear, his Imagist poems were designed to express these lofty spiritual realities. And he now saw more clearly that the poetry made with Chinese ideograms had been Imagist centuries before the term was coined. In "Imagisme and England" (published in February 1915) Pound stated that Imagist poetry "is as old and as distinct" as lyric poetry "but until recently no one had named it. We now call it Imagist, [but] it is not a new invention, it is a critical discrimination."

Throughout "Imagisme and England" Pound draws his historical examples of Imagism from the poets he was reading to Yeats during the evenings of their second winter together: Wordsworth, Browning, and Morris. Pound also mentions his usual touchstones—Catullus, "The Seafarer," Shakespeare's "the morn in russet mantle clad," and Fenollosa on the ideogram—but this anecdote about Morris probably came from Yeats, late one evening after Pound had finished reading one of the Victorian poet's translations of the Icelandic sagas: "They say that when they wished to make William Morris forget his gout they praised Milton to him. His rage was based on his firm conviction that Milton was a d——d rhetorician and that 'a good poet *makes pictures.*'" From Wordsworth Pound chose the famous passage in the first book of *The Prelude* about the young boy "stealing a boat and rowing out on to a dark lake, and then getting very frightened and rowing back breathless. It is an image." Although Yeats believed that he had "shocked" his companion by bringing seven volumes of Wordsworth to Stone Cottage—and although Pound needled Yeats by saying that their visit from the local vicar had been brought on "by reading Wordsworth"—Pound actually enjoyed the reading. He found the doctrine of the Image not only in *The Prelude* and Morris's sagas, but also in Browning's *Sordello* and poems by Swinburne and Lionel Johnson. Pound quoted these lines in "Imagisme and England" to show that Imagism was not simply fodder for anthologies but the mainstay of the noble tradition of English verse. With the exception of Browning (Yeats allowed Pound to read *Sordello* aloud in order "to raise his spirits"), the version of the tradition Pound invoked was the one Yeats thought of as his private ancestry.

In addition to Morris and Wordsworth, Pound was also reading Charles Doughty's *Travels in Arabia Deserta* (1888) to Yeats, and the book provided Pound with a method to organize his memories of his 1912 walking tour through southern France into a poem. His "Provincia Deserta" (first published in the March 1915 issue of *Poetry*) borrows not only from the title of Doughty's work but from Doughty's concern with spiritual presences lurking in the Arabian landscape. Over the course of his tale about his wanderings through the Middle East, Doughty explains the nature of the Arabian version of the kind of creatures Pound and Yeats read about in *Le Comte de Gabalis:* "There was a certain *muderris* or studied man in Medina. . . . One night when the great learned man was going to rest, he heard a friend's voice in the street bidding him come down quickly; so he took his mantle and went forth. His friend said then, "Come with me I pray thee."—When they were past the wall of the town, the learned man perceived that this man was a jin in his friend's likeness! Some more gathered to them, and he saw well that all these were jân."

Like the Abbé de Montfaucon de Villars's *Le Comte de Gabalis,*

Arabia Deserta offered Pound the "Djinns, tribal gods, fetiches, etc"
that he wanted to restore to modern art. But in "Provincia Deserta"
he put these spirits in the service of his historical sense. Pound describes himself walking through Provence "thinking of old days" until the ghosts of the past appear to him as living presences:

> I have walked
> > into Perigord,
> I have seen the torch-flames, high-leaping,
> Painting the front of that church;
> Heard, under the dark, whirling laughter.

After invoking the presence of Richard the Lionhearted, Arnaut de
Mareuil, and Bertran de Born, Pound then resurrects the troubadours
Peire and Austors de Maensac, working a reference to Yeats's "No
Second Troy" into the story of these two brothers' decision to split
their political and artistic duties:

> I have thought of the second Troy,
> Some little prized place in Auvergnat:
> Two men tossing a coin, one keeping a castle,
> One set on the highway to sing.
> > He sang a woman.

The coin tossing precipitated a second Troy because Peire "won the
lady" to whom he sang and "Stole her away for himself, kept her
against armed force." Pound's reference to Yeats's mythologizing of
Maud Gonne in "No Second Troy" is a coy response to an aging
courtly lover; equipped with his historical sense, Pound saw that there
had been many Troys to burn.

At the conclusion of "Provincia Deserta," Pound pulls away from
the ghostly presence of these troubadours, allowing them to recede
back into the landscape:

> Pieire de Maensac is gone.
> I have walked over these roads;
> I have thought of them living.

"Provincia Deserta" was an important poem for Pound because it established one of the means of "including history" in his poetry that

would carry him through the early *Cantos*, a poem which begins with Odysseus reviving the ghost of Tiresias to uncover the secrets of the past and future. Like "Provincia Deserta," each of Pound's first *Three Cantos* (1917) would be organized around some sacred place infused with spirits supernatural and historical.

Pound put his reading of *Arabia Deserta* to use immediately, but Yeats waited a few years before he incorporated aspects of Doughty's descriptions of Arabia in *A Vision: An explanation of life founded upon the writings of Giraldus and upon certain doctrines attributed to Kusta Ben Luka* (1925). Doughty supplied most of the details in the fictional narrative frame which explains the supposed Middle Eastern origins of Yeats's esoterica. In his poem "The Gift of Harun Al-Rashid" (first published in 1924 and then reprinted in the 1925 version of *A Vision*) Yeats told the narrative in such a way that it became a straightforward allegory for his discovery of his wife's automatic writing. In *A Vision* Yeats tells us that before Michael Robartes gave him the "Giraldus" manuscript that we are about to read in Yeats's elaborated version, Robartes spent several years among the Judwali Arabs, finding confirmation of the manuscript in the teachings of Kusta Ben Luka. In "The Gift of Harun Al-Rashid," Kusta Ben Luka himself tells us of the origins of his teachings in the strange events that occurred after his marriage:

> Upon a moonless night
> I sat where I could watch her sleeping form,
> And wrote by candle-light; but her form moved,
> And fearing that my light disturbed her sleep
> I rose that I might screen it with a cloth.
> I heard her voice, 'Turn that I may expound
> What's bowed your shoulder and made pale your cheek';
> And saw her sitting upright on the bed;
> Or was it she that spoke or some great Djinn?
> I say that a Djinn spoke.

Like Pound, Yeats was fascinated by Doughty's accounts of the Arabian djinn and their ability to possess human minds. Kusta Ben Luka's wife speaks truths "without father," "Self-born, high-born, and solitary truths." A dozen nights later, she not only speaks in her sleep but rises and runs into the desert to inscribe great geometric designs in the sand. Yeats explained them in a note: " 'All those gyres and cubes and midnight things' refers to the geometrical forms which Robartes describes the Judwali Arabs as making upon the sand for the instruction of their young people, & which, according to tradition, were drawn or described in sleep by the wife of Kusta-ben-Luka."

In the mythology Yeats built around his work, such were the "origins" of the diagrams of A Vision. The Judwali tribe is Yeats's own invention, but Doughty's *Arabia Deserta* does explain the Arab practices of "sand-divination" which involved great figures drawn in the desert. Yet *Arabia Deserta* was more important for Pound's poetry and Yeats's esoterica than these minor borrowings can suggest. Pound did not necessarily need to read Doughty to write "Provincia Deserta"; the "spirit of the place" is a topos common enough in English poetry. Yeats could have found the practices of "sand-divination" in the tales of the *Arabian Nights*. But Doughty left his mark on both poets. Pound and Yeats were fascinated by Doughty's account of the djinn, but the studied convolution of Doughty's prose, the very difficulty of his book, cast a greater shadow over the poets' work. Pound wrote that "the number of people who can read Doughty's 'Arabia Deserta' is decently and respectfully limited; so much so that the readers of that work tend to form an almost secret society, a cellule, at least, of an actual, if almost imperceptible aristocracy." A *Vision* and *The Cantos*, so different from each other, are designed to do the same thing. Both texts are esoteric enough to define their own readership and create a secret society of readers who understand the codes. The increasingly obscure poems Pound wrote during and after his winters at Stone Cottage not only address the problem of forming an elite but were designed to forge that imperceptible aristocracy through the process of reading.

Yeats was a more prolific poet than Pound during their second winter. On January 31, 1915, Pound wrote to Harriet Monroe that "Yeats has sent five poems to his agent with note that they should be submitted to you; there are three here (in his desk) which will be sent either direct or through the agent." The three poems in Yeats's desk were his new trilogy of poems about Maud Gonne ("Her Praise," "The People," and "His Phoenix"), written at Stone Cottage during the month of January. The five other poems Pound mentioned appeared with the Maud Gonne poems in the February 1916 issue of *Poetry*: "The Dawn," "On Woman," "The Fisherman," "The Hawk," and "Memory," most of which were written during the summer of 1914.

Yeats's thoughts returned to Maud Gonne at Stone Cottage because he was in the process of writing his autobiography. Just before returning to Ashdown Forest he had completed a draft of *Reveries Over Childhood and Youth*, and although he probably did not begin writing the portion of the manuscript devoted to Maud Gonne for at least another several months, his poems reveal that memories of the one he would call the most beautiful woman in the world weighed upon him heavily. Pound was particularly interested to see what new developments Yeats's poems about Maud Gonne would bring because for several years he had been tracking Yeats's career through his changing perspective on his unrequited love. In 1910, when Yeats left behind the dreamy love poems of *The Wind Among the Reeds* for good and wrote his tougher poems about Maud Gonne ("No Second Troy" and "Reconciliation"), Pound felt that he and Yeats were joined "in one movement with *aims* very nearly identical." But as time went on, Pound grew dissatisfied with the Yeats of "No Second Troy" just as he had grown impatient with the Yeats of *The Wind Among the Reeds*. The December 1912 issue of *Poetry* included Yeats's "The Realists," "The Mountain Tomb," "To a Child Dancing Upon the Shore" (later "To a Child Dancing in the Wind"), "Love and the Bird" (later "A Memory of Youth"), and "Fallen Majesty," a new poem about Maud Gonne. In these lines Yeats recognizes that Maud Gonne no longer appears as she did in the Nineties when "crowds gathered" around her. But instead of confronting a diminished present, Yeats sings the majesty of "what's gone":

> The lineaments, a heart that laughter has made sweet,
> These, these remain, but I record what's gone. A crowd
> Will gather, and not know it walks the very street
> Whereon a thing once walked that seemed a burning cloud.

Pound confessed to Harriet Monroe that he did not think these poems represented "W.B.Y. at his best, but the prestige of the name is worth a lot." Pound made several minor revisions of Yeats's wording and punctuation in these poems (Yeats thought of them, as I have said, as "misprints"), but Pound was more bothered by what he perceived as Yeats's lack of development: " 'Fallen Majesty' is just where he was two years ago," he told Harriet Monroe; " 'The Realists' is . . . tending toward the new phase." Pound felt that his mentor was stagnating. "Fallen Majesty" simply repeated "No Second

Troy" in its celebration of Maud Gonne as she had appeared to Yeats
in his youth. "The Realists," on the other hand, a poem that avoided
nostalgic reminiscence and stressed the sobering effect of passing
years, seemed to hint at something new.

> What can books of men that wive
> In a dragon-guarded land,
> Paintings of the dolphin-drawn
> Sea-nymphs in their pearly wagons
> Do, but awake a hope to live
> That had gone
> With the dragons?

These lines pleased Pound because of Yeats's tough-minded refusal
to dwell in an unproductive fantasy of his personal past. The relative
lack of this quality in Yeats's love poetry was thrown into relief for
Pound after he began reading Joyce's prose in 1914. In " 'Dubliners'
and Mr. James Joyce" (1914) Pound revealed that he was surprised
that Joyce was Irish: "One is so tired of the Irish or 'Celtic' imagination (or 'phantasy' as I think they now call it) flopping about. Mr
Joyce does not flop about. He defines. He is not an institution for the
promotion of Irish peasant industries. He accepts an international
standard of prose writing and lives up to it."

Pound's desire to purge Yeats's work of its dreamy nostalgia and
push it towards the precision of Joyce's "realism" led him to write
"In Exitum Cuiusdam," a riposte to Yeats's "The Lover Pleads with
his Friend for Old Friends." In this poem from *The Wind Among
the Reeds* Yeats instructs Maud Gonne to

> think about old friends the most:
> Time's bitter flood will rise,
> Your beauty perish and be lost
> For all eyes but these eyes.

In "In Exitum Cuiusdam," first published in *Ripostes* (October 1912),
Pound offered a brash rejoinder to these nostalgic lines.

> "Time's bitter flood"! Oh, that's all very well,
> But where's the old friend hasn't fallen off,
> Or slacked his hand-grip when you first gripped fame?

It is important to notice that Pound rebuts the Yeats of *The Wind Among the Reeds* in these lines, not the Yeats of "Adam's Curse" or "The Realists." Pound knew that the tougher language of the later Yeats had paved the way and made his own more brashly "realistic" verse possible. But the later Yeats was not tough enough for the later Pound, and by the time he returned to Stone Cottage for his second winter with Yeats, Pound was looking for more of the unclouded precision he had found in Joyce and glimpsed in "The Realists." Parts of the new trilogy of poems Yeats wrote about Maud Gonne at Stone Cottage measured up to these standards. The poems are quite specific in their references to Yeats's living conditions with Pound and his wife. In "Her Praise" Yeats describes himself pacing about the confines of the cottage, mulling over the most beautiful women in the world:

> She is foremost of those that I would hear praised.
> I have gone about the house, gone up and down
> As a man does who has published a new book,
> Or a young girl dressed out in her new gown,
> And though I have turned the talk by hook or crook
> Until her praise should be the uppermost theme,
> A woman spoke of some new tale she had read,
> A man confusedly in a half dream
> As though some other name ran in his head.

Neither Dorothy nor Ezra Pound would listen to his praise of Maud Gonne. So Yeats resolved to leave their company and "talk no more of books or the long war" that raged in miniature on the heath, and venture out into the forest to seek fit audience: he would find "Some beggar sheltering from the wind, and there / Manage the talk until her name come round." Among the poor, says Yeats, "both old and young gave her praise."

Yeats continued to celebrate Maud Gonne as she once was, but he realized that the people willing to indulge his obsession with the old days were few. Pound confessed in print that he had grown tired of Yeats's fixation on Maud Gonne. In "The Non-Existence of Ireland," published in the *Egoist* while the poets were still in Sussex, Pound remarked, "I cannot remember quarrelling with any Irishman whatsoever. I usually enjoy their conversation, until they become aged and glue their eyes resolutely upon some single date in the past." In his eyes, Yeats had become an aged Irishman writing poems about a woman he had loved twenty years ago. Lady Gregory still tried to persuade Yeats to marry; she even brought aristocratic young ladies (including the daughter of the prime minister) to Stone Cottage for Yeats's approval. But Yeats's memories of the past were more powerful than his desires in the present. At Stone Cottage by the waste moor, Yeats was living (as Beckett would put it in *Waiting for Godot*) a "million years ago, in the nineties."

The aged Irishman did not let the young American's criticism of his infatuation with Maud Gonne go unanswered. Richard Ellmann has suggested that Yeats began the third stanza of "His Phoenix," the second of the poems he wrote at Stone Cottage, with a list of Pound's former girlfriends.

> There's Margaret and Marjorie and Dorothy and Nan,
> A Daphne and a Mary who live in privacy;
> One's had her fill of lovers, another's had but one,
> Another boasts, 'I pick and choose and have but two or three.'

"His Phoenix" marks the appearance of a new playfulness in Yeats's treatment of Maud Gonne. He begins by asserting that her dignity stands far above any of Pound's modern lovers, but he is finally unable to maintain this idealized vision of his past and must entertain the possibility that another young woman could be as beautiful as his phoenix: "who can say but some young belle may walk and talk men wild / Who is my beauty's equal." As he had suggested in "The Realists" several years before, he has forsaken the hope to live in a world "That had gone / With the dragons." When Yeats published "His Phoenix" in *The Wild Swans at Coole* he placed it within a suite of poems about Maud Gonne that makes the change in his attitude more explicit. In his early verse Yeats had imagined her as an old woman; in "Broken Dreams" he now faces the fact that she has actually grown old:

> There is grey in your hair.
> Young men no longer suddenly catch their breath
> When you are passing.

Yeats's new realism allowed Pound to feel once more that he and his older colleague were joined "in one movement." "The People,"

Pound's favorite of the Maud Gonne poems composed at Stone Cottage, grew out of a quatrain that Yeats wrote after her marriage to John MacBride in 1903.

> My dear is angry that of late
> I cry all base blood down
> As though she had not taught me hate
> By kisses to a clown.

Yeats never published these lines, and, by 1915, after George Moore's mockery of his aristocratic pretensions, both his desire to condemn the bourgeois "state of mind" and his self-conscious feelings of hypocrisy as he did so were much stronger. "The People" begins with a spiteful condemnation of the "mob" that balked at *The Playboy of the Western World* and rejected Hugh Lane's paintings.

> 'What have I earned for all that work,' I said,
> 'For all that I have done at my own charge?
> The daily spite of this unmannerly town,
> Where who has served the most is most defamed,
> The reputation of his lifetime lost
> Between the night and morning.

As he had done in "To a Wealthy Man," Yeats moves on in "The People" to hold up the Renaissance courts of Ferrara and Urbino as his ideal; their noblemen talked "the stately midnight through" and ignored the people rather than pandering to their desires. Instead of worrying about the public's response to his work—instead of writing letters to the *Times* when the Liverpool police shut down the Abbey players—Yeats wants to live in some more noble time, indulging in "the one substantial right / My trade allows: chosen my company, / And chosen what scenery had pleased me best." At the same time, the memory of Maud Gonne's rebuke of this arrogance rings in Yeats's ears: despite the "drunkards, pilferers of public funds, / All the dishonest crowd I had driven away," she says, "never have I, now nor any time, / Complained of the people." Yeats attempts to justify his complaint but finally admits that his "heart leaped at her words."

"The People" ends with Yeats divided between his aristocratic ideal and his awareness of its unattractive lack of generosity. Pound was less uncertain about these matters. Unlike Maud Gonne he cheered Yeats's rejection of the people and elaborated the elitist side of Yeats's sensibility in one of his own poems. "Villanelle: The Psychological Hour" was written as a companion poem to Yeats's "The People" just as "The Fault of It" was written as a descant to "Reconciliation," and "In Exitum Cuiusdam" as a commentary on "The Lover Pleads with his Friend for Old Friends." Pound portrays a neurotic artist who looks to his audience for approval; he waits for visitors who do not call:

> Two friends: a breath of the forest . . .
> Friends? Are people less friends
>   because one has just, at last, found them?
> Twice they promised to come.
>
> *"Between the night and morning?"*
>
> *Beauty would drink of my mind.*
> Youth would awhile forget
>   my youth is gone from me.

These lines do not conform to the traditional shape of the villanelle in any way; instead of relying on the intricate repetitions of the form, Pound wrote a poem which embodies a compulsive mind caught in its own web of repetition. Except for one couplet which is repeated literally (*"Beauty is so rare a thing / So few drink of my fountain"*), the most important repetition is of a line which exists outside the villanelle: *"Between the night and morning"* is a quotation from Yeats's "The People." The older poet complained of "this unmannerly town, / Where who has served the most is most defamed, / The reputation of his lifetime lost / Between the night and morning." Like Yeats's "The People," Pound's "Villanelle" is about the artist's right to choose his own company. But unlike Yeats, Pound is not conscious of a second voice rebuking his dismissal of the people. He is more desperately concerned with differentiating his art from the "common" world of Amy Lowell and Vachel Lindsay.

The allusion to Yeats helps to make "Villanelle: The Psychological Hour" the kind of work Pound considered *Arabia Deserta* to be: the poem demands that its readers be part of "an almost secret society, a cellule, at least, of an actual, if almost imperceptible aristocracy." Without knowledge of Yeats's "The People" the point of Pound's poem is all but imperceptible, for "The People" tells us

that the poet should not worry about his fickle friends and the reputation that could be lost "between the night and morning." Pound
would perfect this method of allusion in his longer poems; without
knowledge of the numerous texts to which *The Cantos* refer, our experience of the poem is thin. Despite his promulgation of the "New
Method" in scholarship, Pound's work often demands the kind of
source-hunting philological scholarship in which he himself was trained
at the University of Pennsylvania. But Pound mystified that mode of
scholarship—as Amy Lowell pointed out when she answered Pound's
rejection of her work in *A Critical Fable* (1922). Speaking as one
excluded from the secret society of modernism, she points out that
"such men seldom bother their wits / With outsiders at all, whether
fits or misfits." Her diatribe against Pound and his followers culminates in a parody of the conversation between Peire and Austors de
Maensac which Pound first presented in "Near Perigord" and later
recast in Canto 5:

> There is Pierre de Maensac, and Pierre won the singing—
> Where or how I can't guess, but Pound sets his fame ringing
> Because he was *dreitz hom* (whatever that is)
> And had De Tierci's wife; what happened to his
> We don't know, in fact we know nothing quite clearly,
> For Pound always treats his ghosts cavalierly.

Lowell was a good deal more generous to Pound than he had been to
her; she remembered that "he preserved fledgling poets from extinction" and conceded that "his worse is / Much better than most people's good." But her diagnosis of Pound's obscurity as a means of
alienating "outsiders" is particularly appropriate to "Villanelle: The
Psychological Hour." When Pound first published it in December
1915, the secret society of readers capable of identifying the allusion
to Yeats's "The People" would have been very small: Yeats's poem
was not published for another two months. These were not poems
written for the people at large.

But more than either of these, the poem that best epitomizes their
conception of their audience is Yeats's "The Fisherman," one of the
five poems that appeared in *Poetry* along with the trilogy of Maud
Gonne poems. If "The Fisherman" had ended with these lines, it
would have been a poem that shared the defeated tone of the "Poems
Written in Discouragement" in *Responsibilities*. Yeats explains that

he once tried to write for the Irish people who rejected Hugh Lane
and John Synge ("The living men that I hate") as well as Synge
himself ("The dead man that I loved") and a host of others:

> The craven man in his seat,
> The insolent unreproved,
> And no knave brought to book
> Who has won a drunken cheer,
> The witty man and his joke
> Aimed at the commonest ear,
> The clever man who cries
> The catch-cries of the clown,
> The beating down of the wise
> And great Art beaten down.

With these lines, "The Fisherman" comes as far as Yeats was able
to go in "To a Wealthy Man"; when he wrote for the Irish people,
Yeats was doomed to rejection and failure. Pound was probably expressing Yeats's opinion more openly when he wrote in his 1915 essay on Vorticism that "I have even seen a paper from Belfast which
brands J. M. Synge as a 'decadent.' Is such a country fit for Home
Rule?" This essay appeared in the New Age in January 1915 while
the poets were living in Sussex. In February Pound published his essay on "The Non-Existence of Ireland," where he asserts that because
of the Irish people's rejection of Joyce, Synge, and Lane, Ireland
"ceased, quite simply, to exist"; the people had denied the only vital
part of their heritage. Yeats comes to the same conclusion in "The
Fisherman," then in the second half of the poem moves beyond discouragement and great art beaten down to imagine an audience. For
Yeats as for Pound, Ireland had in some sense ceased to exist.

> Maybe a twelvemonth since
> Suddenly I began,
> In scorn of this audience,
> Imagining a man,
> And his sun-freckled face,
> And grey Connemara cloth,
> Climbing up to a place
> Where stone is dark under froth,
> And the down-turn of his wrist

> When the flies drop in the stream;
> A man who does not exist,
> A man who is but a dream;
> And cried, 'Before I am old
> I shall have written him one
> Poem maybe as cold
> And passionate as the dawn.'

Yeats's fisherman was not completely imagined; in his "General Introduction for my Work" (1937), Yeats recalled, "I once boasted, copying the phrase from a letter of my father's, that I would write a poem 'cold and passionate as the dawn.'" Yeats still counted his father as well as Pound as part of his audience. But many years would pass before Yeats could define his inner circle with such confidence. When "The Fisherman" was written during the summer of 1914, between the first and second winters at the cottage, Yeats remained defensive. More than any other poem, "The Fisherman" reveals the motives behind Pound's and Yeats's repeated sojourns to Ashdown Forest; when the poem was finally published Pound called it "one of the best things [Yeats] has done of late." The two poets secluded themselves in Sussex to imagine an audience to replace the American and Irish people who had rejected their own potential for a second renaissance—and to write the poems that would summon an audience to replace those people.

Pound did not turn his back on Ireland after he declared that it had "ceased to exist." Despite his doubts about the Irish people, he had complete confidence in the Irish aristocracy of the arts. In 1918 he wrote that "the best English poetry and the best English drama might seem to come out of Ireland. I have no partiality for the Celt, but, without bias, I am unable to discover among the works of the last thirty years any English product to match the body of work produced by Synge, Yeats, Colum and James Joyce." For Pound, the keynote of that Irish tradition—and the keynote of Yeats's oeuvre itself—was that certain nobility, a willingness to face an unappreciative public, a refusal to acquiesce to their demands. Pound inherited these values from Yeats himself, and as he watched the older poet transform the dead Rhymers into the "tragic generation," mythologizing their stoic refusal to condescend to their age, Pound absorbed the vocabulary he would use to deify his own companions. His was the next tragic generation.

6

Tragic Generations

Late in his life Yeats called "the images of thirty years" to his side and remembered that he, John Synge, and Lady Gregory

> alone in modern times had brought
> Everything down to that sole test again,
> Dream of the noble and the beggar-man.

During the years from 1913 to 1916, Yeats's own life was nearly divided between these two sides of the dream. In winter he lived with Pound, a citizen of a country that had no nobility, in a tiny cottage on the edge of the manor of Duddlesworth. In summer, he resided at Coole Park, Lady Gregory's estate in the midst of the Seven Woods. Yeats was no more born an aristocrat than Pound, yet Coole Park played a part in his personal mythology of his own life that Stone Cottage did not. In the *Pisan Cantos*, in contrast, Stone Cottage figures largely—but as part of a noble dream. Pound could even recall Yeats's idealization of Coole Park and conclude:

> old William was right in contending
> that the crumbling of a fine house
> profits no one
> (Celtic or otherwise).

Pound was thinking of houses of both stone and descendants when he wrote these lines. During the years he knew Yeats best, the older poet was deeply concerned with both. Soon after Pound and Yeats met in 1909, Yeats returned to Ireland to spend the summer at Coole. On August 7th he wrote some notes ("Subject for poem") in his diary: "How should the world gain if this house failed, even though a hundred little houses were the better for it. . . . ? How should the world be better if the wren's nest flourish and the eagle's house is scattered?" These remarks were soon transformed into "Upon a House Shaken by the Land Agitation," in which Yeats assumed the lofty gaze of the eagle's lidless eye:

> How should the world be luckier if this house,
> Where passion and precision have been one
> Time out of mind, became too ruinous
> To breed the lidless eye that loves the sun?
> And the sweet laughing eagle thoughts that grow
> Where wings have memory of wings, and all
> That comes of the best knit to the best?

During the years of his new responsibilities in London's literary culture, the eagle became one of Yeats's favorite emblems. After 1910, when he became a founding member of the Academic Committee of the Royal Society of Literature, Yeats sometimes used the letterhead of the Royal Societies Club; its telegraphic address was "Aquilae, London." Pound probably sympathized with the note Yeats published with "Upon a House Shaken by the Land Agitation" in December 1910: "This house has enriched my soul out of measure because here life moves within restraint through gracious forms. Here there has been no compelled labour, no poverty-thwarted impulse." Pound had come to London, after all, to inherit the noble dream of the Rhymers' Club. Yet the young American from Hailey, Idaho also saw the humor in Yeats's aristocratic pretensions. It was at this time that Pound began to call the older poet the "Eagle" in his private correspondence. In January 1913 when Yeats shared a portion of "Upon a Dying Lady" with Pound, the young critic told Dorothy Shakespear that the "Eagle has done two more poems to Mabel Beardsley, and I object to his having rimed 'mother' immediately with 'brother' and I wish he wouldn't ask me for criticism except when we're alone. *One* of [the] lyrics is rather nice, but he cant ex-

pect me to like stale riming, even if he does say its an imitation
of an Elizabethan form. Elizifbeefan. . . . Its just moulting eagle."
Yeats promptly cut the lines in question, which contained not only
"stale riming" but a paean to the aristocratic tradition of the house
of Beardsley.

> Although she has turned away
> The pretty waxen faces
> And hid their silk and laces
> For Mass was said to-day
> She has not begun denying
> Now that she is but dying
> The pleasures she loved well
> The strong milk of her mother
> The valour of her brother
> Are in her body still
> She will not die weeping
> May God be with her sleeping.

In criticizing these lines, Pound was returning a lesson he had learned
from Yeats. In *The Spirit of Romance* (1910) Pound had written,
"Yeats gives me to understand that there comes a time in the career
of a great poet when he ceases to take pleasure in riming 'mountain'
with 'fountain' and 'beauty' with 'duty.'" When Dorothy Shakespear wrote back to Pound, responding to his criticism of Yeats's
poem, she said, "The Eagle has been inspired." The inspiration had
been mutual. Pound would publish "Upon a Dying Lady" in the
Little Review (August 1917) after Mabel Beardsley finally died in
1916. In the *Pisan Cantos* he would remember that "Mabel's red
head was a fine sight / worthy of his minstrelsy."

During the first winter at Stone Cottage Pound came to appreci-
ate Yeats's acquiline sensibility. After George Moore's attack on
Yeats prompted Pound to make his extravagant counterattack in
"The Bourgeois," Pound began to see a more valuable stoicism
in Yeats's aristocratic pretensions. Moore had repeated a story about
Yeats told to him by AE (George Russell): "on one occasion when
Yeats was crooning over AE's fire he had said that if he had his
rights he would be Duke of Ormonde, and . . . AE had answered,
'In any case, Willie, you are overlooking your father,'—a detestable
remark to make to a poet in search of an ancestry, and the addition,

'Yeats, we both belong to the lower middle classes,' was in equally
bad taste." Yeats was distantly related to the Ormonde family (his
great-great-grandfather, Benjamin Yeats, had married Mary Butler,
one of the Irish Ormondes), and at the time of Moore's attack, Pound
suggested that Yeats "get himself proclaimed Duke of Ormonde—
as that should be the final extinction of g.m. [George Moore]."

Instead, Yeats began to plan his autobiographies, which he described to his sister as "some sort of an 'apologia' for the Yeats family." As a prologue to the rehearsal of his ancestry in *Reveries Over
Childhood and Youth* (1915) Yeats first composed the "Introductory Rhymes" ("Pardon, old fathers") to *Responsibilities*. On January 3, 1914, he told Lady Gregory that the poem was very carefully
accurate and that it would turn the tables on the enemy. But Yeats
did not know his ancestry as well as he thought. The version of the
poem that he finished during his first winter at Stone Cottage and
published in the first edition of *Responsibilities* included these lines.

> you that did not weigh the cost,
> Old Butlers when you took to horse and stood
> Beside the brackish waters of the Boyne,
> Till your bad master blenched and all was lost.

When he reprinted "Pardon, old fathers" in the 1920s, Yeats rewrote the passage, having learned that his Butler ancestors had
fought on the side of Holland's William of Orange, not Britain's
James II, at the battle of the Boyne (1690):

> A Butler or an Armstrong that withstood
> Beside the brackish waters of the Boyne
> James and his Irish when the Dutchman crossed.

Along with "Notoriety," "Pardon, old fathers" was the last of the
poems in *Responsibilities* to be written. Yeats originally planned to
open the volume with "A Coat," the little poem which announces
his rejection of "old mythologies" for new responsibilities, but "Pardon, old fathers" replaced it as the program piece. Two epigraphs
preceded the poem to his ancestors. The source of the first ("In
dreams begins responsibility") is given as an "old play" but is in fact
from Nietzsche. The second must have been chosen with Pound's
help. It comes from the Confucian analects, which Pound read at
Stone Cottage in Pauthier's French translation:

How am I fallen from myself, for a long time now
I have not seen the Prince of Chang in my dreams.

Khoung-fou-tseu

"Khoung-fou-tseu" is Pauthier's transliteration of the name we usually
spell "Confucius," and the epigraph is translated from Pauthier's
French. Both Pound and Yeats almost certainly had read the phrase
in English prior to their stay at Stone Cottage, however, for their
friend Allen Upward had printed it in his own translation in "Sayings of K'ung the Master" in the *Egoist* (November 1, 1913): "For
a long time I have not dreamed, as I was wont to do, that I saw the
Duke of Chow."

Confucius admired the Duke of Chou (as the name is commonly
transliterated), the founder of the Chou dynasty, because he established the ancient rites of ancestor worship; consequently, Yeats
quoted Confucius as a preface to his own exhortation of his personal
and cultural heritage. Pound admired the Duke of Chou for the same
reason. Early in 1918, after the first *Three Cantos* were published,
he wrote, "I desire to go on with my long poem; and like the Duke
of Chang [Chou], I desire to hear the music of a lost dynasty." The
music resurfaced in the final version of Canto 3, in which Pound
mentions "the gray steps [that] lead up under the cedars." As Confucius tells us, the gray steps lead up to the ancestral temple dedicated to the Duke of Chou. Pound's reference to them in the original (1917) version of Canto 1 was more elaborate.

> (Confucius later taught the world good manners,
> Started with himself, built out perfection.)
>   With Egypt!
> Daub out in blue of scarabs, and with that greeny turquoise?
> Or with China, O *Virgilio mio*, and gray gradual steps
> Lead up beneath flat sprays of heavy cedars,
> Temple of teak wood, and the gilt-brown arches
> Triple in tier, banners woven by wall.

After this passage was scuttled, Pound worked the same narrative
into Canto 13: as Confucius walks past "the dynastic temple" of
the Duke of Chou "and into the cedar grove," he says: "If a man
have not order within him / He can not spread order about him."
For Pound, a leader cannot have order within him unless he remains
aware of his ancestry. Yeats had made the same point in "Upon a

House Shaken by the Land Agitation" when he idealized Coole Park as a nesting ground for eagles where "wings have memory of wings." He wrote in his diary entry for the poem that Coole gives "to a far people beneficent rule; and still under its roof living intellect is sweetened by old memories of its descents from far off." At Stone Cottage, both poets would see that this precept itself had an ancient precedent in the Duke of Chou.

The Duke of Chou presides over Yeats's autobiography as he presides over *The Cantos* and *Responsibilities*, for, like those works, *Reveries Over Childhood and Youth* was meant to preserve the music of a better tradition. Yeats began them soon after he wrote "Pardon, old fathers." By the end of August 1914 he was deeply involved in the work, telling Mabel Beardsley that he had never written anything so exciting. He completed a draft on Christmas, as he explained in a letter to his father the following day: "Yesterday I finished my memoirs; I have brought them down to our return to London in 1886 or 1887. After that there would be too many living people to consider and they would have besides to be written in a different way. While I was immature I was a different person and I can stand apart and judge. Later on, I should always, I feel, write of other people. I dare say I shall return to the subject but only in fragments."

On December 31st, four days after he wrote this letter, Yeats went to Sussex to begin his second winter with Pound. He told his father that "Ezra Pound and his wife are staying with me, we have four rooms of a cottage on the edge of a heath and our back is to the woods." He did not mention that he continued to work on *Reveries Over Childhood and Youth*, though he did—and with Pound's assistance. Yeats told Mabel Beardsley on January 15th that he was still patching his memoirs. He dictated from the manuscript he had completed on Christmas day, adding new material, and Pound typed the finished product for the printer. At the same time, Pound wrote his parents that he was reading Yeats the autobiography of Herbert of Cherbury. It is likely that this seventeenth-century life provided a model for *Reveries Over Childhood and Youth* as Yeats and Pound collaborated to produce its final form. In 1925 Yeats would call Dante's *Convivio* the first "modern autobiography," a signpost for an age in which an author "imposes his own personality upon a system and a phantasmagoria hitherto impersonal." In 1915 Yeats looked for the same precedent in one of the first English autobiographies.

Edward Herbert, Baron of Cherbury (1583–1648), brother of the poets Thomas and George Herbert, portrayed himself in his autobiography as a flamboyant adventurer, but what attracted Yeats was Herbert's reverence for his family tree. Herbert begins the book by rehearsing the lives of his ancestors, then relates the events of his own life so that they might serve as an example for his progeny:

> Certainly it will be found much better for men to guide themselves by such observations as their father, grandfather, and great-grandfather might have delivered to them, than by those vulgar rules and examples, which cannot in all points so exactly agree unto them.
>
> Therefore, whether their life were private, and contained only precepts necessary to treat with their children, servants, tenants, kinsmen, and neighbours, or employed abroad in the university, or study of the law, or in the court, or in the camp, their heirs might have benefited themselves more by them than by any else; for which reason I have thought fit to relate to my posterity those passages of my life which I conceive may best declare me, and be most useful to them.

Herbert's wishes were fulfilled, for although his autobiography remained unknown until it was published by Horace Walpole in 1764, Walpole dedicated it to Herbert's living relative: "Herbert Arthur Herbert, Earl of Powis, Viscount Ludlow, Lord Herbert of Cherbury, Baron Powis and Ludlow, and Treasurer of his Majesty's Household." Walpole explained how the autobiography would enhance the noble reputation of the Herbert family line: "Hitherto Lord Herbert has been little known but as an author. I much mistake, if hereafter he is not considered as one of the most extraordinary characters which this country has produced. Men of the proudest blood shall not blush to distinguish themselves in letters as well as arms, when they learn what excellence Lord Herbert attained in both. Your Lordship's lineage at least will have a pattern before their eyes to excite their emulation."

The reasons for Yeats's interest in Herbert's autobiography are clear: in composing his own memoirs he wanted to refute George Moore's claims and like the Duke of Chou reveal the true nobility of his own ancestry. Like Herbert, he begins the story of his life by documenting the history of his family. His Aunt Mary serves as his Tiresias, telling him the secrets of the dead:

She was full of family history; all her dinner-knives were pointed like daggers through much cleaning, and there was a little James the First cream-jug with the Yeats motto and crest, and on her dining-room mantlepiece a beautiful silver cup that had belonged to my great-great-grandfather, who had married a certain Mary Butler. It had upon it the Butler crest and had been already old at the date 1534, when the initials of some bride and bridegroom were engraved under the lip. All its history for generations was rolled up inside it upon a piece of paper yellow with age, until some caller took the paper to light his pipe.

Despite this accidental loss of the Yeats genealogy, Mary Yeats remembered the stories of her ancestors. Yeats reports them in his autobiography, once again stressing his distant relation to the aristocratic Ormonde family. His lineage, like Herbert's, is presented as one worthy of emulation.

When Yeats described his autobiography to his sister as "some sort of an 'apologia' for the Yeats family" he added that he wanted it "to lead up to a selection of our father's letters." The letters, Yeats reasoned, would refute George Moore's charge that he had overlooked his father in claiming an aristocratic ancestry; like the bourgeoisie, the aristocracy was more a "state of mind" than an accident of birth for Yeats, and his father's letters would reveal the nobility of his family in its finest form. Yeats had been planning to publish J. B. Yeats's letters even before Moore's attack; in December 1913 he wrote his sister that he planned to make the selection himself. After the attack, he realised that it would be better to have Pound edit the collection. "I am handing the letters over to Ezra Pound," Yeats wrote to his father, "who is to make a first small volume of selections for Lollie's [Yeats's sister] press, I thought he would make the selection better than I should. I am almost too familiar with the thought, and also that his approval, representing as he does the most aggressive contemporary school of the young, would be of greater value than my approval, which would seem perhaps but family feeling."

Pound did edit the letters, welcoming the chance to contribute to Yeats's fight against George Moore. He had met J. B. Yeats in New York when he returned to America for a visit in 1910. At the time the elder Yeats "very much" liked Pound's "look and air, and the few things he said." A few years later Pound would tell John Quinn that he had "a very clear recollection of Yeats père on an elephant (at Coney Island), smiling like Elijah in the beatific vision, and of you plugging away in the shooting gallery." The memory remained with him at Pisa:

> his, William's, old "da" at Coney Island perched on an elephant
> beaming like the prophet Isaiah
>   and J. Q. as it were aged 8 (Mr John Quinn)
> at the target.

After *Passages From the Letters of John Butler Yeats* was published in 1917, Pound (unlike the younger Yeats) was not worried about objectivity. He not only edited the collection but reviewed it for *Poetry* magazine: "I make no excuse for reviewing this small book which I myself have edited. I have been through the matter more often than any other critic or reviewer is likely to go through it, and I am in at least that degree more fit to praise it. . . . I know of no modern book which contains so much good sense about poetry." T. S. Eliot agreed. In his review of the letters he proclaimed that "Mr. Yeats understands poetry better than any one I have ever known who was not a poet." W. B. Yeats's original purpose in publishing his father's letters was to reveal his family's aristocratic "state of mind," and, like Pound, Eliot valued the elder Yeats's sensibility. He called J. B. Yeats "a highly civilized man" and approved of his dictum that "Democracy *devours* its poets and artists."

In the interval between collecting the letters and their publication in 1917, Yeats continued to write his own history of his aristocratic family and friends. After his January 1915 letter to Mabel Beardsley saying that he was polishing *Reveries Over Childhood and Youth* with Pound's help, Yeats's next known remark about his autobiography appears in a letter dated "*circa* November-December 1915": "I am going on with the book," he told his father, "but the rest shall be for my own eye alone." The next portion of his memoirs, which took his life through the Nineties, contained not only memories of the tragic generation but also some intimate details about his sexual awakening and his love affairs, consummated and unconsummated, with Olivia Shakespear and Maud Gonne. Much of this material would be revealed in *The Trembling of the Veil* (1922), but a good deal remained locked, as we now know, in the manuscript marked "Private. A first rough draft of Memoirs made in 1916–17 and containing much that is not for publication now if ever." As Curtis

Bradford has demonstrated, Yeats probably began this draft in 1915; I would add that he was probably planning the material as early as January 1915 while at Stone Cottage with Pound: the three poems he wrote that month about Maud Gonne show that Yeats was already giving a good deal of thought to his life after his childhood and youth. By the summer of 1915 Yeats must have had a fairly large portion of the manuscript completed; in August Pound was planning the contents of a new magazine and told John Quinn that it was "too late for the *first* batch" of Yeats's memoirs because it had already been published, but, he continued, "I suppose we can have some of the next period." The next period was the Nineties, and Pound knew that Yeats had begun writing.

Throughout 1915, then, Yeats was deeply involved in his memories of the Nineties. Pound's interest in the material extended beyond his duties as an editor; although he was tired of Yeats's adulation of Maud Gonne, he had delighted in anecdotes about the Rhymers from the time he met Yeats in 1909. Yeats would not publish his recollections until *The Trembling of the Veil* began to appear in the *London Mercury* and the *Dial* in 1922, but Pound left Stone Cottage with many of the same stories Yeats would tell in "The Tragic Generation" chapters. Pound himself told the stories in his review of Victor Plarr's *Ernest Dowson* (1915), his own introduction to the *Poetical Works of Lionel Johnson* (1915), and finally in *Hugh Selwyn Mauberley* (1920)—long before Yeats published the canonical version of the Nineties in *The Trembling of the Veil*. In the process, Pound assumed an eagle's lofty gaze.

In "How I Began" (1913) Pound remembered that when he first arrived in London he not only met "living artists" but came "in touch with the tradition of the dead. . . . I have enjoyed meeting Victorians and Pre-Raphaelites and men of the nineties through their friends." Yeats became Pound's personal guide through a poet's underworld. And, like Yeats, Pound held a strong belief in the literary and emotional value of the anecdote. He had a capacious memory for them, which the *Pisan Cantos* is the final fruition of—a poetic sequence structured by an anecdotal sensibility. In his early years Pound became more knowledgeable about the Rhymers than some of the remaining Rhymers themselves. Victor Plarr (whom Pound would cast as "Monsieur Verog" in his own tale about the Rhymers in *Hugh Selwyn Mauberley*) wrote in his book on Dowson (1915) that "Young Mr Ezra Pound, to whom Dowson is a kind of classical myth, just as the ancients are a myth to us all, tells me a story, told him in turn by a good recorder, of how Dowson went to see poor Wilde in Dieppe after the *débâcle,* and how he endeavoured to reform his morality by diverting it at least into a natural channel. It is at best a smoking-room anecdote, not fit for exact repetition." The "good recorder" from whom Pound learned this tale was probably Yeats, who had in turn probably learned it from Arthur Symons. In *The Trembling of the Veil* Yeats presented a more candid version of this smoking-room anecdote:

> Wilde had arrived in Dieppe, and Dowson pressed upon him the necessity of acquiring "a more wholesome taste." They emptied their pockets on to the café table, and though there was not much, there was enough if both heaps were put into one. Meanwhile the news had spread, and they set out accompanied by a cheering crowd. Arrived at their destination, Dowson and the crowd remained outside, and presently Wilde returned. He said in a low voice to Dowson, "The first these ten years, and it will be the last. It was like cold mutton"—always, as Henley had said, "a scholar and a gentleman" he now remembered that the Elizabethan dramatists used the words "Cold mutton"—and then aloud so that the crowd might hear him, "But tell it in England, for it will entirely restore my character."

When Pound reviewed Plarr's book in the April 1915 issue of *Poetry* he made no mention of the fact that he himself had contributed to it. He wrote that the "first chapters are perhaps the best account of Ernest Dowson that has been written" but lamented that Plarr "does not give 'the whole Dowson.'" Tacitly asserting himself as a more knowledgeable scholar of the Nineties than Plarr himself, Pound then relates another anecdote with which Plarr was unfamiliar: "Certain people will rather remember the beautiful story of the French magistrate who had condemned Dowson for assaulting the local baker. Someone rushed into the court protesting that Dowson was a distinguished writer. 'What, what, Monsieur Dowson, a distinguished English litterateur! Release M. Dowson—at once! Imprison the baker.'" Pound must have learned this tale from Yeats during the previous winter, while the older poet was drafting his memoirs of the Nineties. Yeats explained in the first draft of this portion of his autobiography that the tale was told to him by Arthur Symons: while Dowson was living in Normandy, Symons received a telegram from him saying " 'Sell my ring and send money: arrested.'

There was a ring he had left with Symons for such an occasion. He had got drunk and fought the village baker. His money proved unnecessary, for the French magistrate on being told by some sympathetic villager that he had 'an illustrious English poet' before him had said, 'Quite right, I will imprison the baker.' "

Pound treasured Yeats's anecdotes about the Rhymers, but he absorbed Yeats's attitude toward his dead companions even more deeply. In Yeats's 1910 lecture on "Friends of my Youth" Pound had heard Yeats's first and tentative transformation of the Rhymers into the "tragic generation." Pound saw this idealization even more vividly when "The Grey Rock" appeared in *Poetry* magazine in 1913.

> You had to face your ends when young—
> 'Twas wine or women, or some curse—
> But never made a poorer song
> That you might have a heavier purse,
> Nor gave loud service to a cause
> That you might have a troop of friends.
> You kept the Muses' sterner laws,
> And unrepenting faced your ends,
> And therefore earned the right—and yet
> Dowson and Johnson most I praise—
> To troop with those the world's forgot,
> And copy their proud steady gaze.

For Yeats, the Rhymers met their sordid ends for noble reasons. They refused to break the muses' higher laws and pander to the exigencies of public taste or personal gain; they wrote a passionate lyric poetry in an age fed on protracted Tennysonian rumblings. Yeats recognizes that Johnson and Dowson died with their potential unfulfilled, but he commands them to assume the "proud steady gaze" of their noble predecessors because they faced their ends without compromise or derision.

Throughout "The Grey Rock" Yeats interweaves his narrative of the Rhymers with an Irish legend, using the heroic tale as an implicit commentary on the Rhymers' tragic fate. The poem seems to anticipate the methods of some later modernist poems in its juxtaposition of narratives mythic and modern. Yet when Pound reviewed *Responsibilities* in 1914 this structural aspect of the poem did not seem as important to him as the attitudes which Yeats ascribed to the Rhymers. Pound even complained that "The Grey Rock" was "obscure," but (as I have noted) he concluded that the poem "outweighs this by a curious nobility, a nobility which is, to me at least, the very core of Mr Yeats' production, the constant element of his writing."

Pound saw in "The Grey Rock" the same aristocratic sensibility that he knew from "Upon a House Shaken by the Land Agitation." The eagle's gaze was something he now took quite seriously. And as he watched the energy of his own generation dissipated by the war, Pound wondered if he too would be the lone survivor of a tragic generation. Pound modeled his own sense of the noble artist, fighting against the demands of his age, on Yeats's mythology of the Nineties. In the 1915 draft of his autobiography Yeats wrote that in Johnson,

> more than all others one can study the tragedy of that generation. When the soul turns from practical ends and becomes contemplative, when it ceases to be a wheel spun by the whole machine, it is responsible for itself, an unendurable burden. Not yet ready for the impression of the divine will, it floats in the unnatural emptiness between the natural and the supernatural orders. Johnson had refused rather than failed to live, and when an autopsy followed his accidental death during intoxication it was found that in him the man's brain was united to a body where the other organs were undeveloped, the body of a child.

In *Hugh Selwyn Mauberley* Pound not only relates the tale of Johnson's macabre death and autopsy but reiterates Yeats's sense that the tragedy of the Rhymers grew from their aristocratic refusal to condescend to the world of practical experience. Pound casts Victor Plarr as "Monsieur Verog," and describes him as "out of step with the decade, / Detached from his contemporaries, / Neglected by the young." There was no place for him in the past and there continues to be no place in the present. Yet his memory provides access to "the tradition of the dead"; he is a link in what Pound called the "apostolic succession," and for the few who will listen, he recreates the noble dream of the Rhymers. As he tells it, their story is as simple as the line spoken by La Pia in the fifth canto of the *Purgatorio*, which Pound quotes as his title: "Siena made me; Maremma unmade me":

For two hours he talked of Galliffet;
Of Dowson; of the Rhymers' Club;
Told me how Johnson (Lionel) died
by falling from a high stool in a pub . . .

But showed no trace of alcohol
At the autopsy, privately performed—
Tissue preserved—the pure mind
Arose toward Newman as the whiskey warmed.

Dowson found harlots cheaper than hotels;
Headlam for uplift; Image impartially imbued
With raptures for Bacchus, Terpsichore and the Church.
So spoke the author of "The Dorian Mood,"

M. Verog, out of step with the decade,
Detached from his contemporaries,
Neglected by the young,
Because of these reveries.

In Pound's analysis, the Rhymers suffered from too much of the very thing that made lyric poetry worth reading; Johnson and Dowson escaped too far into what Yeats's father called "the delirium of beauty and ecstasy" and lived lives of passion pursued to debilitating excess. Yet like Yeats, Pound saw not only a cautionary tale but also a stoic nobility in their sordid demise. Pound's poem about the Rhymers is situated within a history of the British avant-garde in *Hugh Selwyn Mauberley*, and it is a history of one tragic generation after another. "Yeux Glauques" tells of an age before the Rhymers when "Gladstone was still respected" and "Swinburne / And Rossetti still abused." And "Mr. Nixon" presents the Edwardian man of letters (modelled on Arnold Bennett) who advises *les jeunes* to "Accept opinion. The 'Nineties' tried your game / And died, there's nothing in it." For Pound, it is precisely Mr. Nixon's pandering to public taste that ennobles the Rhymers' fate. As Yeats had explained in "The Grey Rock," they kept the muses' higher laws. In *Hugh Selwyn Mauberley* the twentieth-century embodiment of their noble dream is found in "E. P." himself—and he too is trapped by his age, his companions killed for a "botched civilization," his efforts a "tragic" failure:

For three years, out of key with his time,
He strove to resuscitate the dead art
Of poetry; to maintain "the sublime"
In the old sense. Wrong from the start . . .

Hugh Selwyn Mauberley is steeped in Yeats's memories of his youth, and it reiterates a genealogy of modernism that is familiar to us from both Yeats's autobiography and Yeats's idiosyncratic edition of *The Oxford Book of Modern Verse:* from the Pre-Raphaelites, to Pater, Wilde, the poets of the Nineties, and on to the twentieth century. Yeats's version of the modern tradition was purely lyrical and private, eschewing the public mode of a Bennett, Kipling, or Shaw. It has become the most commonly invoked genealogy of modernism because Yeats passed it on to influential modernists; not only Pound but Eliot presented the genealogy in Yeats's terms. Before *The Trembling of the Veil* began to appear serially in 1922, Eliot invoked Pater only to dismiss him. But in 1923 Eliot would write that "Mr. Yeats' recent Memoirs which have been appearing in *The Dial* form a document of a very great interest for the generation of Oscar Wilde; and Mr. Yeats bears explicit testimony to the influence of Pater upon his generation." After reading Yeats's memoirs, Eliot's sense of the origins of modernism—and Pater's crucial place in the tradition—became identical with the genealogy Pound endorsed in *Hugh Selwyn Mauberley*. In "A Preface to Modern Literature" (1923) Eliot wrote that "Wells, Bennett, Chesterton, Shaw, Kipling are separated from us [moderns] by a chasm"; the moderns must find their tradition in Walter Pater, who "in an earlier epoch, was an heir of Arnold and Ruskin, and Wilde was the heir of Pater." Of the poets of the Nineties, Eliot says: "The greatest merit of this group of people is, to my mind, not to be found in their writings, but is rather a moral quality apparent in the group as a whole: it had a curiosity, an audacity, a *recklessness* which are in violent contrast with that part of the present which I denominate as the already dead." This is Yeats's vision of the tragic generation. Like Pound, Eliot was most taken with Yeats's sense of the nobility of their brief moment in the modern tradition. This *attitude* is the key-note of that tradition, and the one important characteristic that Yeats, Pound, and Eliot could be said to share. The Rhymers failed, but they alone opposed a suffocating literary climate. Pound and Eliot thought of themselves as the inheritors of that struggle.

It would take Eliot another decade to come to a full appreciation of Yeats's part in that struggle, but Pound saw Yeats's nobility from the beginning. And when Pound published *Hugh Selwyn Mauberley*, Yeats returned the compliment. He told Pound that the poem's "nobility" had moved him deeply: the first half of the sequence, ending in "Envoi," possessed "extraordinary distinction & an utterly new music"; the second part of the sequence, "Mauberley 1920," Yeats went on, contained

> lovely lines but I have not mastered the poems yet. But those first 14 pages, there I am certain, there certainly you have discovered yourself—a melancholy, full of wisdom, a self-knowledge that is full of beauty—style which is always neighbor to nobility when it is neighbor to beauty, a proud humility, that quality that makes one's hair stand up as though one saw a spirit. You have gripped all that now.

Here Yeats has turned Pound's praise of "The Grey Rock" back onto Pound's own *Mauberley*, acknowledging the higher sense of the literary occupation which the two poems share. The goals of the poets who met at Stone Cottage were not far from the goals of those who met above the Cheshire Cheese. By telling Pound that *Mauberley* had "that quality that makes one's hair stand up as though one saw a spirit," Yeats was including the younger poet among the noble company of the Rhymers: in "The Tragic Generation" Yeats wrote that he and the Rhymers "always discussed life at its most intense moment, that moment which gives a common sacredness to the Song of Songs, and to the Sermon on the Mount, and in which one discovers something supernatural, a stirring as it were of the roots of the hair."

Througout the rest of their lives, Pound and Yeats would continue to praise each other's verse for its nobility, for, as they learned from Matthew Arnold, there could be no higher praise. Arnold made the word "nobility" his own when he insisted (repeatedly) that the quality a translator of Homer most required was the quality Homer himself possessed above all others: "that he is eminently noble." Whether used by Arnold or Yeats or Pound, the word has a resonant ambiguity ("the last matter in the world for verbal definition to deal with adequately," said Arnold), a word suitable to praise the achievements of a brotherhood whose initiation rights are mysterious. In the first version of *A Vision* Yeats placed Pound in phase 12, in which one "spends his life in oscillation between the violent assertion of some commonplace pose, and a dogmatism which means nothing, apart from the circumstance that created it. If, however, he meets these accidents by the awakening of his *antithetical* being there is a noble extravagance, an overflowing fountain of personal life." In the later years of their friendship, Yeats did not often witness Pound's "noble extravagance," but when he did he found that it made Pound a poet he valued above all others. In his introduction to *The Oxford Book of Modern Verse* (1936) Yeats wrote that in certain moments in Pound's poetry he found "more deliberate nobility and the means to convey it than in any contemporary poet." But Yeats had to concede that this nobility was "constantly interrupted, broken, twisted into nothing by its direct opposite, nervous obsession, nightmare, stammering confusion; he is an economist, poet, politician, raging at malignants with inexplicable characters and motives, grotesque figures out of a child's book of beasts."

Pound did not get another chance to praise Yeats's verse for its nobility until after the older poet's death, and by that time Pound's nightmare and rage had caught up to him. In the *Pisan Cantos* he surveyed a ruined life and the wreckage of Europe; casting his mind back to a time before the world was given over to wars, he remembered Yeats's nobility most of all.

> Lordly men are to earth o'ergiven
> > these the companions:
> Fordie that wrote of giants
> > and William who dreamed of nobility.

The *Pisan Cantos* are Pound's autobiography, his own genealogy of the dream of nobility. The tissue of anecdotes which makes up the sequence is the final product of the "apostolic succession" that Pound valued so highly in his youth. Yeats is only one of a large cast of characters in the *Pisan Cantos*, yet Yeats's example as an earlier conservator of the better tradition permeates the entire sequence.

> La beauté, "Beauty is difficult, Yeats" said Aubrey Beardsley
> > when Yeats asked why he drew horrors
> > or at least not Burne-Jones
> > and Beardsley knew he was dying and had to
> > make his hit quickly

hence no more B-J in his product

So very difficult, Yeats, beauty so difficult

In these lines from Canto 80 Pound recalls an anecdote which Yeats told him and later included in his own autobiography: "I said to [Beardsley] once, 'You have never done anything to equal your Salome with the head of John the Baptist.' I think, that for the moment he was sincere when he replied, 'Yes, yes; but beauty is so difficult.'" In an earlier rendition of the anecdote published in "A Symbolic Artist and the Coming of Symbolic Art" (1898) Yeats makes the same comparison of Beardsley and Burne-Jones that Pound makes in Canto 80. Pound's memory of the anecdote probably stemmed from Yeats's conversation rather than his memoirs. He could have read this passage from Yeats's early essay in *The Dome*, but more likely he remembered that Yeats remembered.

> Men like Sir Edward Burne-Jones and Mr Ricketts have been too full of the emotion and the pathos of life to let its images fade out of their work, but they have so little interest in the common thoughts and emotions of life that their images of life have delicate and languid limbs that could lift no burdens, and souls vaguer than a sigh. . . .
> Once or twice an artist has been touched by a visionary energy amid his weariness and bitterness, but it has passed away. Mr Beardsley created a visionary beauty in *Salome with the Head of John the Baptist*, but because, as he told me, 'beauty is the most difficult of things', he chose in its stead the satirical grotesques of his later period.

The sense of the sheer difficulty of artistic creation, passed on from Beardsley to Yeats to Pound, is both a thematic and musical refrain throughout the *Pisan Cantos*. The entire sequence is a record of the struggle of creation under the most adverse conditions; "Down, Derry-down / Oh let an old man rest," ends Canto 83. In Canto 74 the phrase "beauty is difficult," or one derived from it ("lover of beauty"), is repeated seven times, each time, as Marjorie Perloff has pointed out, with a slightly different meaning.

"beauty is difficult" sd/ Mr Beardsley
and sd/ Mr Kettlewell looking up from a

> pseudo-Beardsley of his freshman composition
>   and speaking to W. Lawrence:
>   Pity you didn't finish the job
> while you were at it"
>   W. L. having run into the future non-sovereign Edvardus
> on a bicycle equally freshman
>   a.d. 1910 or about that.

In these lines beauty is difficult for John Kettlewell (a student Pound met when he read a paper on Cavalcanti to the St. John's College Essay Society at Oxford in 1913) as he attempts to imitate Beardsley's style. Beauty is difficult in quite another sense for William Lawrence, the brother of T. E. Lawrence and Vice-President of the Essay Society, who once ran into the future Edward VIII on a bicycle. For Pound, that story had a beauty worth preserving.

The threads of Pound's anecdotal memory unwind as Canto 74 continues, William Lawrence evoking T. E. Lawrence, Edward VIII evoking Lloyd George and Clemenceau ("frogbassador") at the Versailles peace conference, and John Kettlewell evoking Thomas Snow, lecturer on English language and literature at Oxford, whom Pound remembers quoting Sappho after his own lecture on Cavalcanti.

> beauty is difficult
>   in the days of the Berlin to Bagdad project
>   and of Tom L's photos of rock temples in Arabia Petra
> but he wd/ not talk of
>   LL.G. and the frogbassador, he wanted to
>   talk modern art (T. L. did)
>   but of second rate, not the first rate
>   beauty is difficult.
> He said I protested too much   he wanted to start a press
> and print the greek classics . . . periplum
>   and the very *very* aged Snow created considerable
> hilarity quoting the φαίνε-τ-τ-τ-τττ-αί μοι
> in reply to *l'aertremare*
>   beauty is difficult.

Beauty is difficult in art, in scholarship, in politics, and in the telling of a good story. These modes of beauty were inseparable for Pound, all three bound up in his memories of his early years in London, when Yeats first introduced him to the spirit of Aubrey Beardsley by telling him an anecdote.

As Canto 74 continues, we discover that Charles Granville and Ernest Rhys were "lovers of beauty," and we hear an anecdote about Rhys, a member of the Rhymers' Club, who was once an "engineer in a coal mine."

> a man passed him a high speed radiant in the mine gallery
> his face shining with ecstasy
> "A'hv joost . . . . Tommy Luff."
> and as Luff was twice the fellow's size, Rhys was puzzled.

That too was a story worth preserving. At the last repetition of the Yeats-Beardsley refrain, this long passage in Canto 74 culminates in a line Pound remembered from the first of his *Three Cantos* (1917):

> "ghosts move about me"   "patched with histories"
>   but as Mead said: if they were,
> *what have* they done in the interval,
>   eh, to arrive by metempsychosis at. . . . ?
> and there are also the conjectures of the Fortean Society
> Beauty is difficult.

Here Pound moves from his memory of the line (preserving the line break between "me" and "patched") that in a sense still begins *The Cantos* (Tiresias is the first of many ghosts patched with histories) to his memory of G.R.S. Mead, the leader of the Quest Society whom Pound met through Yeats. Remembering his own early interest in spirits and reincarnation, he also remembers Mead's more skeptical response. Pound told the whole anecdote in his *Guide to Kulchur:* "I know so many people who were Mary Queen of Scots," said Mead. "And when I consider what wonderful people they used to be in their earlier incarnations, I ask WHAT they can have been at in the interim to have arrived where they are." The beauty of ghosts patched with histories, of *The Cantos* themselves, is also difficult. But their beauty has a legacy that reaches back to Yeats and Beardsley and the Rhymers. Even when Yeats is not mentioned in the *Pisan Cantos* (and he does appear more often than any other ghost) the presence of his sensibility is always felt. A collector of anecdotes himself, Yeats passed on not only the stories but the belief that a noble tradition inheres in their preservation. Generations pass, poets fail, but we remember them, the tragic generations: Beardsley, Johnson, Dowson, Wilde, Pound. For Pound, their beauty is preserved by the simple fact that

> certain images be formed in the mind
> to remain there
> *formato locho*

III

7

Dialogues with the Dead

"The arrival of Zeppelins," Pound wrote to his father in the summer of 1915, "seems to have filled London with a quiet contentment." London's reaction to the first air raid, which occurred on the 31st of May, was not quite so calm as Pound would have had his worried family believe. Most Londoners were far from contented, but some found Pound's composure talismanic. Violet Hunt and her circle considered Pound's presence to be a charm against the German zeppelins—or if not Pound's presence, at least his Image. Hunt kept Gaudier-Brzeska's bust of Pound in her garden, maintaining that the sculpture warded off the airships.

Yeats felt none of the quiet contentment that Pound exuded, and he managed to convey the effect of one particularly spectacular raid in a letter to Lady Gregory. In the midst of a long discussion of new problems concerning Hugh Lane and the National Gallery, Yeats began a new paragraph ("Owing to threats—") but then suddenly broke it off and began again.

An exciting event has just happened which has put completely out of my head what I was going to say when I dictated the appropriate words 'Owing to threats'. There has been a Zeppelin raid. In the middle of that sentence there came a tremendous noise—series of them. We went down to the door (I am dictating in Miss Jacob's office opposite the British Museum)—it sounded as if the Museum was bombed. We saw a group of people running past and I shouted, 'Where is it?' And they said right overhead, so I thought it better that we should keep inside the house. However, as nothing happened we went across and stood under the Museum railings, where we found four or five other people. We then saw the Zeppelin at a comfortable distance—somewhere over the city I should think—shrapnel bursting round it with tremendous detonations. . . . It has the terrifying effect of thunder—I mean an emotional effect quite distinct from any consciousness of danger. . . . I have just said to Miss Jacobs, 'Twenty minutes is enough for the day of judgment so I will take up my letter.' I am so puzzled by those words, 'owing to threats' that I am half inclined to think that they were written automatically by Miss Jacobs.

Seen from a comfortable distance, the zeppelin raids were exciting, but even the excitement wore thin. When Robert Gregory told Yeats about another raid in London, Yeats passed the story on to his father in New York, commenting that "the mob cheered every bomb that fell and every shot from an anti-aircraft gun. High up a Zeppelin shone white under a cloud." Yeats felt no kinship with the "mob" who cheered such "bloody frivolity." But then he genuinely feared the raids and spent the winter of 1915–16 tucked away in Sussex with the talismanic Ezra.

During the summer of 1915 Pound could think of one constructive use for the German raids. "I believe one Zep was almost over the church at the corner," he wrote his father. "I offer five shillings to the first German who will bust that damn belfry or murder the vicar. Otherwise they seem unlikely to be of any real use to the community." The church was St. Mary Abbots, the vicar the Rev. Edward Pennyfeather, and the bells of St. Mary Abbots the death knells of Western civilization. Or so Pound wrote in the war number of *Blast*:

> Let it then stand written that in the year of grace, 1914, there was in the parish of Kensington a priest or vicar, portly, perhaps over fed, indifferent to the comfort of others, and well paid for official advertisement and maintenance of the cult of the Gallilean . . . that is to say of the contemporary form of that cult.
>
> And whereas the Gallilean was, according to record, a pleasant, well-spoken, intelligent vagabond, this person, as is common with most of this sect was in the most sorts the reverse . . . their hymns and music being in the last stages of decadence.

The said vicar either caused to be rung or at least permitted the ringing of great bells, untuneful, ill-managed, to the great disturbance of those living near to the church. He himself lived on the summit of the hill at some distance and was little disturbed by the clatter.

The poor who lived in the stone courtyard beneath the belfry suffered great annoyance, especially when their women lay sick. Protest was, however, of no avail. The ecclesiastic had the right to incommode them. The entire neighbourhood reeked with the intolerable jangle. The mediaeval annoyance of stench might well be compared to it. We record this detail of contemporary life, because obscure things of this sort are wont carelessly to be passed over by our writers of fiction, and because we endeavour in all ways to leave a true account of our time.

These bells, Pound continued, were an example of the kind of atavism that in his mind caused the war. "Once such bells were of use for alarm." Their ringing had purpose and meaning, but today they remain "without other effect than that of showing the ecclesiastical pleasure in aimless annoyance of others."

No bombs hit the belfry of St. Mary Abbots (though one did strike near Pound's father-in-law's office, leveling an old bicycle shed), but the war did continue to drain the energy from London's avant-garde; the special war issue of *Blast* marked the second and final appearance of the journal of the Great English Vortex. Pound had other schemes. During the summer of 1915 he wrote long manic letters to John Quinn, soliciting his support for a new magazine to be modeled on the *Mercure de France:* "My proposition received equal support from Mr Yeats, Mr Hueffer and from my own contemporaries." Quinn supported the proposition too, though instead of financing a new magazine, Quinn's money eventually went to the *Little Review,* where Yeats, Eliot, and Joyce would find wartime publication.

In the meantime Joyce required immediate attention. Throughout the summer of 1915 Pound and Yeats worked together to secure a pension for him from the Royal Literary Fund. The Italian declaration of war in May 1915 had forced Joyce to move from Trieste to Zurich. On July 15th he wrote to Pound that the "last raid of Italian airships, as I read, was directed against the Trieste shipyard, about five minutes from my house." He lived, as Pound wrote to the secretary of the Royal Literary Fund, in "obscurity and poverty, that he might perfect his writing and be uninfluenced by commercial demands and standards." At first, Pound did not approach the Fund himself, but asked Yeats to make the gesture. Yeats wrote to Edmund Gosse, "I have just heard that James Joyce, an Irish poet and novelist of whose fine talent I can easily satisfy you, is in probably great penury through the war. He was at Trieste teaching English and has now arrived at Zürich. He has children and a wife. If things are as I believe, would it be possible for him to be given a grant from the Royal Literary Fund?"

Gosse replied that he needed "to make perfectly sure of the *facts*." Yeats then told Pound to "get the facts," and Pound asked Joyce to "send on 'the facts.'" Pound then worked up a statement about Joyce's plight which concluded with a swipe at the publishers who had resisted the harsher realities of *Dubliners:* "Joyce says 'that as a matter of fact, they have not enough clothing as the summer in Switzerland is quite cold, in comparison with Trieste.' (He would rather this should not be known as he thinks it would place him at a disadvantage with publishers. As I dare say it would, the lice!)." Yeats forwarded this statement to Gosse, saying that the "typed passages I send are all from an intimate friend of Joyce." He did not mention Pound's name, but he was careful to disassociate himself from his young friend's excesses: "You must not attribute to me," he cautioned Gosse, "that remark about publishers."

With these "facts" in hand, Gosse petitioned the Literary Fund, and the pension was granted. Despite the efforts of his researchers, however, Gosse was left standing without the one fact he wanted most of all. At the end of the summer Yeats tried to make up for the oversight with a letter touched with a slightly facile enthusiasm: "My dear Gosse: I thank you very much for what you have done; but it never occurred to me that it was necessary to express sympathy 'frank' or otherwise with the 'cause of the Allies.' I should have thought myself wasting the time of the committee. I certainly wish them victory, and as I have never known Joyce to agree with his neighbors I [line missing] in Austria has probably made his sympathy as frank as you could wish." When Yeats wrote to Pound about the letter he had written in response to Gosse's request, he made the pun lurking in his description of Joyce's sympathies a bit clearer, emphasizing that he was sure that Joyce's residence among Austrians made his sympathy with the allies as "Frank" as Gosse could wish. A few days later Pound wrote to Joyce that Yeats "has had an amusing correspondence with Gosse in which Gosse complains that neither you nor W.B.Y. have given any definite statement of loyalty to the allies. . . . I think you'd calm G[osse]'s mind and comfort him if you sent him a note full of correct, laudable, slightly rhetorical (but not too much so) protestations of filial devotion to Queen Victoria and the heirs of her body."

Joyce's pension from the Royal Literary Fund was followed in 1917 by a Civil List Pension and in 1918 by Harriet Shaw Weaver's anonymous patronage; *Ulysses* progressed in the calm eye of a continent at war. Together, Pound and Yeats had initiated the first financial security and critical appreciation that Joyce received. And when the novelist wrote to thank them, each poet deferred to the other. "I am glad the committee has coughed up something," wrote Pound, but "I could have done nothing with 'em if it had not been for Yeats' backing." Yeats returned the compliment at length. "I am very glad indeed," he wrote to Joyce, "that 'The Royal Literary Fund' has been so wise and serviceable. You need not thank me, for it was really Ezra Pound who thought of your need. I acted at his suggestion, because it was easier for me to approach the Fund for purely personal reasons. We thought Gosse (who has great influence with the Fund people, but is rather prejudiced) would take it better from me. What trouble there was fell on Ezra."

Having secured the position of one of their novitiates, the Brothers Minor now had to think of themselves. Pound's gross income for the month of July had been £2/17, making a return to Stone Cottage and secretarial duties an economic necessity. "I am down here in the country," he told Joyce, "because I can't afford London, am behind in accounts, and hope to catch up." Yet Pound returned to Ashdown Forest for more sentimental reasons. On December 15, 1915 he told Harriet Monroe that "in the first rank [of poets] I put Masters, Frost, Yeats of course, Hueffer (tho out of it for a time), myself if permitted, and Eliot." Pound went on to explain why Yeats remained the greatest living poet—an admission he was not so willing to make to Joyce (who had told Yeats in 1902 that he was "too old" to be helped): "Yeats knows life, despite his chiaroscuro and his lack of a certain sort of observation. He learns by emotion, and is one of the few people who have ever had any, who know what violent emotion really is like; who see from the centre of it—instead of trying to look in from the rim." Pound was still tired of Hueffer's impressionism, and he acknowledged that Yeats's poetry provided him with an intensity of lived experience which the impressionist's emphasis on detached observation could not.

Four days after Pound sent this praise of Yeats to Harriet Monroe, Yeats himself told John Quinn of his own desire to return to Stone Cottage. At the conclusion of the previous winter Yeats had confessed that he never felt "at home in town after the country," and he looked forward to his third winter with Pound as a retreat from noisy London: "[Pound] has a beautiful young wife who does the housekeeping & both treat me with the respect due to my years and so make me feel that it is agreeable to grow old. I shall walk to the village post office every day and if I could have my will I would never see more of the great world than that but most of the year bad eyesight and the need of a woman friend tie me to this noisy London, which, by the by, looks its best now with the lights out for fear of Zeppelins." Pound and Yeats, accompanied once again by Dorothy Shakespear Pound, returned to their cottage at the edge of Ashdown Forest just before Christmas and remained there until the second week of March, when they returned to London to begin rehearsals for At the Hawk's Well. By the end of the winter Yeats had remade himself as a playwright; Pound was engrossed in his "poem including history."

During this final winter Pound and Yeats left London to escape not only the talk and clamor of the war but the real danger of air raids. Though Joyce was now safe in Switzerland, the two poets knew that others were not so fortunate. In September 1915 Yeats told Quinn, "I find I can keep the thought of the war away from me & go on with my work." At Coole the war seemed far away, but in London everyone spoke of its continuance: "many people that one knows have been killed and everyone that one knows has lost someone." A few weeks before they escaped to Sussex, Pound and Yeats attended a seance with Claire de Pratz, an Anglo-French novelist who had just arrived from Paris. Yeats recorded the event in his diary:

> Last Monday Madame Du Pratz said that she would die—"disappear" was her word—between Dec. 2 and Dec. 5 next. Pound and Sturge Moore were present.
>
> *November 23, 1915*
>
> Now Clare Du Pratz is in excellent health.

She remained in excellent health, but her feelings of impending doom were not unwarranted. Pound explained in a letter to his father that "Mlle de Pratz says that everyone in France who had heart trouble has died of the strain. James will never walk again they say. De Gourmont and Stuart Merrill are as much killed by the war as was Brzeska." Within the following year Pound would adopt Claire de Pratz's apocalyptic rhetoric when he discussed the war: "Flammarion [the French mystic and astronomer] or someone said that the sun was about to explode on, I think it was, February the fifth of this year. The end of the world is approaching. Perhaps."

The war made all of Europe acutely aware of the phenomenon of mass death in a new way. In Vienna Freud was writing in "Reflections upon War and Death" (1915) that "the war is bound to sweep away [the] conventional treatment of death. Death will no longer be denied; we are forced to believe in him. People really are dying, and now not one by one, but many at a time, often ten thousand in a single day." With this new awareness of death came a fascination with the life after death. Spiritualist experiments took on a new urgency as survivors of the war sought assurance that the souls of their loved ones had survived the Somme. In "Swedenborg, Mediums, and the Desolate Places," Yeats explained that "while the great battle in Northern France is still undecided, should I climb to the top of that old house in Soho where a medium is sitting among servant girls, some one would, it may be, ask for news of Gordon Highlander or Munster Fusilier, and the fat old woman would tell in Cockney language how the dead do not yet know they are dead, but stumble on amid visionary smoke and noise, and how angelic spirits seek to awaken them but still in vain." These spirits of the newly dead haunted the streets of London. Virginia Woolf wrote that "Nowadays I'm often overcome by London; even think of the dead who have walked in the city." D. H. Lawrence wrote poems about the ghosts of dead soldiers who could not rest in their French graves:

> There are so many dead,
> Many have died unconsenting,
> Their ghosts are angry, unappeased.
>
> So many ghosts among us,
> Invisible, yet strong,
> Between me and thee, so many ghosts of the slain.

> They come back, over the white sea, in the mist,
> Invisible, trooping home, the unassuaged ghosts
> Endlessly returning on the uneasy sea.

The ghosts of similar dead soldiers haunt *The Waste Land*, walking freely from the ships at Mylae to a postwar London bridge at dawn. But there were also more specific examples. On September 4, 1915, the son of Oliver Lodge (a physicist, university administrator, and former president of the Society for Psychical Research) was killed in France. The next year Lodge published *Raymond or Life after Death with Examples of the Evidence for Survival of Memory and Affection after Death*, an account of his communication with his son's spirit and a theoretical discussion of the afterlife. "I have endeavored," wrote Lodge, "to state the evidence fully and frankly for the persistent existence of one of the multitude of youths who have sacrificed their lives at the call of their Country when endangered by an aggressor of calculated ruthlessness."

Although Yeats refers to *Raymond* briefly in *A Vision*, Lodge's work is more interesting on its own terms for the way it makes explicit the link between war and spiritualism that is implicit in the work of Pound and Yeats. While Pound hoped that the zeppelins might destroy a church, he also knew that the war necessitated the construction of a new kind of spiritual reality. During the summer of 1915 he had begun drafting the poems he would eventually publish as *Three Cantos* (1917) and Cantos 4 and 5 (1919, 1921). In a draft for what would eventually become Canto 4, Pound asked "What is the poet's business?" and answered with these lines:

> Oh, take a heaven you know, and make the starry wood
> Sound like a grove well filled with nightingales,
> And call lights 'souls',
> And say: The lights ascending . . . like a covey of partridges.
> Thus much I saw above me, and beneath, looking into the water,
> Beheld the turret as a pillar of fire reflected,
> And thence to God,
> To the ineffable, *transhumanar non si potria per verba*.

> The soul starts with itself, builds out perfection,
> Confucius, Dante.
>   Or the best man killed in France,

Struck by a Prussian bullet at St Vaast
With just enough cut stone left here behind him.

We have seen that the presence of the war is felt only vaguely in
the final version of Canto 4, which opens with a vision of Troy in
ruins; but these cancelled lines reveal how Pound's presentation of
"ghosts [that] move about me / Patched with histories" in *Three
Cantos* was inextricably linked to his experience of the war. Like
Oliver Lodge, who invoked the spiritual presence of "one of the
multitude of youths who sacrificed their lives," Pound populated
his poem with the ghosts of myth and history, rebuilding a heritage
to replace what the war had obliterated. Like Odysseus calling up
the ghost of Tiresias, Pound would reconstruct a shattered universe.
He begins with Gaudier, "the best man killed in France," and builds
out to a celestial world, which, as Dante explained in the first canto
of the *Paradiso*, "per verba non si poria" [may not be told in words].

By the time Pound arrived at Stone Cottage in late December he
had stopped his work on these early drafts for the *Cantos*. He had
found his subject matter but he needed time to find the proper form.
And so he turned to the tradition, seeking models for his invoca-
tions of the dead. He and Yeats spent the winter reading through
Landor's *Imaginary Conversations*, which, as Pound would remark,
contained "a whole culture." Throughout the conversations, the
ghosts of various luminaries from history, myth, and literature meet
to discuss their lives and works. The impetus behind the traditional
form of these dialogues of the dead is expressed best by the passage
spoken by Socrates at the end of Plato's *Apology*:

> But if death is the journey to another place, and there, as men
> say, all the dead abide, what good, O my friends and judges, can
> be greater than this? If, indeed, when the pilgrim arrives in the
> world below, he is delivered from the professors of justice in this
> world, and finds the true judges who are said to give judgment
> there, Minos and Rhadamanthus and Aeacus and Triptolemus,
> and other sons of God who were righteous in their own life, that
> pilgrimage will be worth making. What would not a man give if
> he might converse with Orpheus and Musaeus and Hesiod and
> Homer?

So Landor's conversations commence, and we overhear Henry VIII
and Anne Boleyn, Filippo Lippi and Pope Eugenius, or Menelaus and
Helen exchanging remarks in some palpable elysium.

Landor remained with Pound until the end of his life. In Canto 95, a lament for the "historical blackout" Pound believed he had witnessed in his time, Pound drifted back to his final winter at Stone Cottage and with this fragmented line invoked his reading of Landor: " 'Are' as Uncle William said 'the daughters of Memory.' " The missing subject is of course "the muses"; Pound had supplied the entire line in the *Pisan Cantos:* "The Muses are daughters of memory." And in his notes for *'Noh' or Accomplishment* (1916) he had invoked this line once again to explain the apparition of an ancient spirit in *Kakitsubata:* "The Muses were 'the Daughters of Memory'." All these lines recall Landor's "Memory," which Yeats quoted in *Per Amica Silentia Lunae* (1918), his own meditation on ghosts patched with histories:

> A poet, when he is growing old, will ask himself if he cannot keep his mask and his vision without new bitterness, new disappointment. Could he if he would, knowing how frail his vigour from youth up, copy Landor who lived loving and hating, ridiculous and unconquered, into extreme old age, all lost but the favour of his Muses?

> The Mother of the Muses, we are taught,
> Is Memory; she has left me; they remain,
> And shake my shoulder, urging me to sing.

Yeats had cultivated such a vision of old age ever since as a young poet he wrote *The Wanderings of Oisin;* in later life he would play the wild old wicked man himself, and in phase 17 of *A Vision,* where we find Dante, Shelley, and Landor, we also find Yeats. In "To a Young Beauty" (1918), Yeats predicts what his own position in the afterlife might be, presenting an imaginary conversation with Landor and Donne.

> I know what wages beauty gives,
> How hard a life her servant lives,
> Yet praise the winters gone:
> There is not a fool can call me friend,
> And I may dine at journey's end
> With Landor and with Donne.

These lines may have been inspired by Landor's own remark in a dialogue between "Archdeacon Hare and Walter Landor": "I shall dine

late; but the dining-room will be well lighted, the guests few and select." Like Landor, Yeats preferred association with a few well-chosen
guests to commerce with "every Jack and Jill." Near the end of his
life, Pound chose similarly exclusive company for the final imaginary
conversation he foresaw in Canto 113.

> Yet to walk with Mozart, Agassiz and Linnaeus
>   'neath overhanging air under sun-beat
> Here take thy mind's space
> And to this garden, Marcella, ever seeking by petal, by leaf-vein
>   out of dark, and toward half-light.

For both Pound and Yeats, an art that forgets its past is not art at
all; memory was the mother of their muses. Yeats wrote in *Ideas of
Good and Evil,* one of Pound's sacred books, that "literature dwindles
to a mere chronicle of circumstance, or passionless fantasies, and passionless meditations, unless it is constantly flooded with the passions
and beliefs of ancient times." To a certain extent this flooding is inevitable. "When we delight in a spring day," mused Yeats, "there
mixes, perhaps, with our personal emotion an emotion Chaucer found
in Guillaume de Lorris, who had it from the poetry of Provence."
Even when the memory fades, the muses remain as her offspring, the
unconscious product of what Pound called "centuries of race consciousness" in *I Gather the Limbs of Osiris.*

Landor intrigued both Yeats and Pound because of his highly developed historical consciousness. In his 1917 essay on Landor, Pound
would proclaim that "no man has ever interpreted more different eras
with sureness and thoroughness"; while the "eighteenth and late seventeenth centuries put the classics into silk stockings," Landor was
the first great English writer to master the "power of looking out of
his own age, and of reaching the standpoint of another."

At Stone Cottage, Yeats was attempting to do just that in an imaginary conversation of his own. At the same time that he was reading
Landor, Yeats was writing his letters to "Leo Africanus." Leo, more
properly known as Alhassan ibn Mohammed Alwazzan, was a sixteenth-century Moorish traveller and scholar whose spirit first summoned Yeats in a seance on May 3, 1909. He spoke to Yeats several
times over the next few years, but Yeats remained skeptical. At first
he did not believe that Leo was the ghost of an actual historical per-
sonage, being more inclined to believe that either the medium or his

own mind was the source of Leo's presence. But Leo, being a true and persistent scholar, told Yeats, "You will find me in the Encyclopaedia." Yeats looked him up in *Chambers' Biographical Dictionary* to discover this:

> LEO AFRICANUS (properly Alhassan ibn Mohammed Alwazzan or Alwezaz) (1494–1552), a Cordovan Moor, who from *c.* 1512 travelled in northern Africa and Asia Minor. Falling into the hands of Venetian corsairs, he was sent to Leo X at Rome, where he lived twenty years, and accepted Christianity, but returned to Africa and (perhaps) his old faith, and died at Tunis. He wrote *Africae Descriptio* (1526) an account of his African travels in Italian (first printed 1550), long the chief source of information about the Sudan. Dr R. Brown re-edited John Pory's translation of 1600 (Hakluyt Society 1896).

Even with this confirmation of Leo's historical existence, Yeats was not convinced that Leo's voice was authentic (he thought it was more likely a "secondary personality" of the medium or the product of some living person's knowledge of Leo's life). Not until a seance on July 20, 1915 did Yeats begin to take the voices seriously. In an account of the seance written several weeks later Yeats explained that Leo insisted he was real:

> He was no secondary personality, with a symbolic biography as I thought possible but the person he claimed to be. He was drawn to me because in life he had been all undoubting impulse, all that his name and Africa might suggest symbolically for his biography was both symbolical and actual. I was doubting, conscientious and timid. . . . He asked me to write him a letter addressed to him as if to Africa giving all my doubts about spiritual things and then to write a reply as from him to me. He would control me in that reply so that it would be really from him.

These letters to and "from" Leo Africanus, written during the final Stone Cottage winter, were part of what Yeats would recall in his autobiography as his meditations on the "doctrine of 'the mask' which has convinced me that every passionate man . . . is, as it were, linked with another age, historical or imaginary, where alone he finds images that rouse his energy." When Yeats wrote this sentence he was actually thinking of the Nineties when he had first begun to construct the theory of the mask; encountering Leo added a new dimension to that theory. As Richard Ellmann has explained, Yeats began to believe that "his opposite, instead of being solely a mask, a conscious product of his own mind with slight independence of its creator, might be a spirit or daimon with a full personality of his own. [This] discovery . . . meant that the conflict which Yeats had visualized as internal and psychological might be an external battle between a living man and a dead one, between this world and the next."

Yeats wrote in his letter to Leo that "You were my opposite. By association with one another we should each become more complete; you had been unscrupulous & believing. I was over-cautious & conscientious." Yeats had already put this material into verse when he wrote his letters to Leo. On December 5th, two weeks before he began writing his imaginary conversation with Leo at Stone Cottage, Yeats had completed the final draft of "Ego Dominus Tuus."

> I call to the mysterious one who yet
> Shall walk the wet sands by the edge of the stream
> And look most like me, being indeed my double,
> And prove of all imaginable things
> The most unlike, being my anti-self,
> And, standing by these characters, disclose
> All that I seek; and whisper it as though
> He were afraid the birds, who cry aloud
> Their momentary cries before it is dawn,
> Would carry it away to blasphemous men.

When Yeats composed his letters to Leo after he had completed the poem, he seemed far less sure of this doctrine of the anti-self; the wildly poetic and sternly skeptical sides of his personality remained at odds. Once he had written the letters "from" Leo (hoping that Leo would "control" his thoughts) he concluded that he was "not convinced that in this letter there is one sentence that has come from beyond my own imagination." Nevertheless, Yeats was willing to entertain the possibility that Leo was an autonomous being and not merely a manifestation of his own psyche. Throughout the correspondence, Yeats took great care to emphasize the historical differences between Leo's time and his own; he tried to make the conversation take place not simply between two personalities but between two historical eras. As Yeats explained in one of the letters "from" Leo, using the terminology of both the twentieth and sixteenth centuries,

We [the spirits of the dead] are the unconscious as you say or as I prefer to say the animal spirits freed from the will, & moulded by the images of Spiritus Mundi. I know all & all but all you know, we have turned over the same books—I have shared in your joys & sorrows & yet it is only because I am your opposite, your antithesis because I am in all things furthest from your intellect & your will, that I alone am your Interlocutor. What was Christ himself but the interlocutor of the Pagan world, which had long murmured in his ear, at moments of self-abasement & defeat, & thereby summoned.

When Yeats composed the "Anima Hominis" portion of *Per Amica Silentia Lunae* in 1917, he would once again state this doctrine of the anti-self with greater clarity and assurance: "the Daimon comes not as like to like but seeking its own opposite, for man and Daimon feed the hunger in one another's hearts." The dialogue between self and anti-self enacts the confluence of past and present. Because the voice of Leo Africanus forced Yeats to consider the possibility that the anti-self might be the spirit of someone who had once walked the earth, a psychological theory was transformed into a theory of history. This would have everything to do with Yeats's desire to map historical events in *A Vision*, and, as we shall see, Pound's struggle to write a long poem in which ghosts assert the presence of a long dead past.

In writing his letters to and from Leo Africanus, Yeats was contemplating what Pound called the ancient dilemmas of the "immortality of the soul" and the "permanence or endurance of the individual personality" in his discussion of historical apparitions in the Noh plays. Yeats had been reading the seventeenth-century platonist Henry More; in the letters he wrote "from" Leo to himself he had Leo explain how More's idea of the "Spiritus Mundi" accounted for the permanence of the individual soul: "Henry More who has gathered up so much of the Platonism of the Renaissance insists in his essay upon the Immortality of the Soul—Chapter [   ]—that memory is not seated in the physical body as Saducees had begun to insist, but in a more delicate body. This body was he wrote what medical writers called the animal spirits a fine luminous & fluid substance defined by the channels of the nerves throughout the blood & the flesh. These animal spirits are but a coagulation, of what he called the 'Spiritus Mundi.' " Memory was the mother of the muses, Pound and Yeats agreed, but the memory of the individual was but a part of a larger memory that makes the entire past available to the present. Yeats had believed in something like a "great memory" for years, but he now saw that the idea of "a Great Memory passing on from generation to generation" was "not enough, for these images showed intention and choice." A sixteenth-century Moor had spoken to him and said: we need each other, we shall make each other more complete.

At Stone Cottage, Pound seemed to be saying the same thing to Yeats; the older poet saw his own sensibility challenged and completed by his younger companion. While Leo Africanus told Yeats, "I am your opposite, your antithesis because I am in all things furthest from your intellect," Pound wrote to Harriet Monroe that he and Yeats had returned to Sussex, the "antipodes of our two characters and beliefs being in more vigorous saliency." Yeats, associating Pound with his spiritual anti-self, was confronting his opposite in both heaven and earth. In his letter to Leo he used his daily fencing practice with Pound as a metaphor for his dialogue with the dead: "Sometimes when you are dreaming you will imagine you will dream that you witness or take part in a dispute, & afterwards when [you] examine the opinions discover that both disputants have made use of thoughts, that are a part of your daily mind, but should that make you believe you have not reasoned with yourself, whose was that other that opposed you, & when you lie in bed after fencing you see for certain minutes, a foil darting upon you from the darkness & whirling its point hither & thither? What hand holds the point upon you." In *Per Amica Silentia Lunae* Yeats used his fencing matches with Pound once again to describe his confrontations with the daimon: "I sometimes fence for half an hour at the day's end, and when I close my eyes upon the pillow I see a foil playing before me, the button to my face. We meet always in the deep of the mind, whatever our work, wherever our reverie carries us, that other Will."

Pound and Yeats probably found themselves "completed" by one another more in their attitudes than in their activities. They may have fenced in the evenings, but during the day, while Yeats wrote letters to Leo Africanus, Pound followed suit and fabricated his own dialogues of the dead. Landor's imaginary conversations had led him back to one of Landor's models, the dialogues of Bernard le Bovier de Fontenelle. By the end of February 1916 Pound had translated twelve dialogues from Fontenelle's *Nouveaux Dialogues des mortes* (1683). They were then published in twelve issues of the *Egoist* from May 1, 1916 to June 4, 1917, the same month in which the first of

Pound's *Three Cantos* appeared in *Poetry* magazine. Like *The Cantos*, the dialogues begin with a descent into hell.

Few of Landor's conversations are true dialogues of the dead. His characters exist in the natural world, and only rarely does he pair interlocutors who lived in different centuries. In the traditional form for the dialogue of the dead, beginning with Lucian in the second century A.D., the characters are usually shades of famous men and women who inhabit Hades and converse with such underworld luminaries as Pluto and Persephone as well as with the ghosts of famous men they did not know on earth. Fontenelle modeled his *Nouveaux Dialogues des morts* on Lucian's dialogues, but he burned some of the sulfur from the form. The infernal backdrop fades away, Pluto and Persephone do not appear, and the illustrious shades step forward to exchange their wits: Homer and Aesop, Socrates and Montaigne, Helen and Fulvia. Fontenelle divided his thirty-six dialogues into two sets each of six "Dialogues des morts anciens," "Dialogues des morts modernes," and "Dialogues des morts anciens avec les modernes." As the titles suggest, the dialogues make gentle play with the battle between the ancients and the moderns. But in the *Nouveaux Dialogues des morts* Fontenelle does not reveal himself to be the champion of the moderns that he seems in his *Digression sur les anciens et les modernes.* The dialogues give equal time to each side; each side stands revealed. As Molière says to Paracelsus in one of the dialogues Pound translated, "he who would paint for immortality must paint fools."

Pound distorted Fontenelle's balance: translating twelve of the thirty-six dialogues, he included six dialogues between the ancients and only three between the moderns and three between the ancients and moderns. Yet Pound probably agreed with Socrates, who speaks these words to Montaigne: "Be on your guard in one thing. Antiquity is very peculiar, it is the sole thing of its species: distance enlarges it. Had you known Aristides, Phocion, Pericles and me, since you wish to add me to the number, you would have found men of your time to resemble us. We are predisposed to antiquity because we dislike our own age, thus antiquity profits. Man elevates the men of old time in order to abase his contemporaries." Pound himself would say much the same thing a few years later, writing in the *New Age* that those who exaggerate the importance of the past "but accept the inheritance of the eighteenth century's inherited debate on the relative importance of classics and moderns. . . . The star turn of the ancientists is to play all antiquity, or the cream of antiquity, against the unselected product of a particular decade or century."

Pound continued to explore the relationship of the ancients and the moderns in "An Anachronism at Chinon" (1917), an original dialogue of the dead that he published in the *Little Review*. In this conversation between Rabelais and "an American student" (who bears an uncanny resemblance to the young E.P.), Rabelais tries to convince the student that the present age is superior to the one in which he lived: "they have not rung bells," he suggests, "expressly to keep you from reading." But, like Pound, the student has lived across the street from St. Mary Abbots: "Bells! later. There is a pasty-faced vicar in Kensington who had his dam'd bells rung over my head for four consecutive winters, L'Ile Sonnante transferred to the middle of London!" The dialogue ends in disagreement, Rabelais's and Pound's claims for the superiority of each other's centuries balanced in counterpoint.

This dialogue between what even Fontenelle might have been forced to name a modern and a postmodern does not take place in Hades; rather, the ghost of Rabelais appears to the student in present-day Chinon, Rabelais's birthplace. In this, as in all things Poundian, form follows content:

> *Student:* And yet I do not quite understand. Your outline is not always distinct. Your voice however is deep, clear and not squeaky.
> *Rabelais:* I was more interested in words than in my exterior aspect, I am therefore vocal rather than spatial.

The ghost of Rabelais is vocal rather than spatial, the embodiment of his art. He is one of Pound's many ghosts patched with history, and like the spirits who inhabit the Noh plays, *Three Cantos*, or Yeats's *The Dreaming of the Bones*, he appears as the spirit of the place, rising from the landscape like the djinn of Doughty's *Arabia Deserta*. If memory was the mother of the muses, then landscape was the mother of memory. Pound and Yeats learned this not only from Wordsworth but from an unreal city suddenly patched with the unappeasable ghosts of the recent war-dead.

Like Yeats, Pound had been obsessed with memory and history since the very beginning of his career, but beside the consciously modern realism of Joyce's prose, he found his own shadowy conversations inadequate. "Even my dialogues for the [Little] Review," he told Joyce, "are 'passéist' in the extreme." Pound's dissatisfaction with his dialogues of the dead was probably sharpened by Yeats's interest in the genre. While he wrote a dialogue about the ghost of Rabelais, Yeats wrote a dialogue about the ghost of Leo Africanus. And as one side of Pound still yearned for the artistic legitimacy conferred on him by association with Yeats, another side of him was faintly embarrassed by his own interest in the netherworlds of consciousness, especially when he corresponded with the novelist whom he and Yeats had given the financial security to write *Ulysses*—the book Pound considered to be the epitome of Flaubertian realism. When Pound returned to his ghosts in *Three Cantos* (a work as "passéist" as his dialogues), he wondered if he should "sulk and leave the word to novelists."

Yet he and Yeats shared other interests during the final winter at Stone Cottage. In 1914, after several years of neglect, Yeats returned to the unfinished manuscript of *The Player Queen* and, during the second winter in Sussex, told Lady Gregory that with Pound's help he had reduced the play to two manageable acts. Yeats continued to tinker with *The Player Queen* throughout 1915. After he returned to Sussex for the final winter, he wrote John Quinn that he had finished that play (though he would continue to rework it until 1919) and begun another. The new play was *At the Hawk's Well*, the first of Yeats's Noh-style plays for dancers. Pound naturally made this development in Yeats's dramatic practice possible with his translations of the Noh drama, but he also wrote plays of his own at Stone Cottage. These plays (which have only recently been published) are not "passéist" in the sense Pound used the word to describe his dialogues; they reveal Pound's attempts to forge a dramatic form that might please both Joyce and Yeats. When Pound and Yeats returned to London at the beginning of March 1916, they immediately began to prepare for the premiere of two one-act plays—one by Yeats and one by Pound. When it became clear that they would barely have enough time to prepare *At the Hawk's Well* for performance, Pound's play was cut from the program. But the unveiling of Yeats's new start as a dramatist was originally conceived as an event which would publicly acknowledge his three years of collaboration with Ezra Pound.

8

Theatre Business

The recognition of the greatness of a work of art, says Frank Kermode, is "the work of opinion, never to be observed without its shadow, ignorance." In making this statement, Kermode is thinking about the ninteenth-century rediscovery of Botticelli by Pater and Swinburne—critics who knew almost nothing about the painter, what little they did know being the product of their generation's vagaries of taste. Had they not been similarly ignorant, Pound and Yeats would never have rediscovered the Noh drama for themselves. They knew so little about the Japanese traditions that they were able to incorporate the Noh into existing traditions of Western drama.

Even before he had read any Noh plays Yeats upheld the ideal of Japanese symbolic drama in his 1911 lecture on "The Theatre of Beauty" (which he delivered again during his 1914 American lecture tour because Pound admired it): "Being a writer of poetic drama, and of tragic drama, desiring always pattern and convention, I would like to keep to suggestion, to symbolism, to pattern like the Japanese." Yeats also recognized that some of his early plays, especially *The King's Threshold* (1904), anticipated features he would discover in the Noh, just as his interest in Japanese theatre confirmed many of his established ideas about symbolic theatre rather than initiating a new phase in his dramatic writing. At the same time, however, Yeats's discovery of the Noh did rejuvenate his withered interest in theatre business. He had called it "the fascination of what's difficult" at just about the time he met Pound in 1909.

> My curse on plays
> That have to be set up in fifty ways,
> On the day's war with every knave and dolt,
> Theatre business, management of men.

As much as Pound's work on Fenollosa's transcriptions of the Noh interested Yeats, the texts alone were not enough to stimulate his fecund ignorance. Not until Michio Itow (whom Pound and Yeats erroneously assumed to be versed in Noh traditions) appeared in London did Yeats glimpse the possibility of circumventing the difficulties of theatre business by producing a Noh-style play of his own.

Itow was a dancer, but he had not seen a Noh production since the age of seven. His artistic aspirations originally leaned toward opera, and he came to Paris in 1911 to study singing. But as he remembered in his memoirs, Itow witnessed an event in Paris that changed his life: "I went to Paris in 1911 but was disappointed with Opera there as it didn't live up to my expectations. Only when Nijinsky, Blum and Hawkins came to Paris with the Ballet Russe did I see total art, combining dance, singing, and music, for the first time. Nijinsky was especially impressive, and I remember feeling completely drained after the performance and having spent the whole night walking the streets, my head afire with new ideas."

After watching Nijinsky perform, Itow began to study dance seriously. When Pound and Yeats met him in 1915, they thought they had discovered the living tradition of Noh dancing. But in their ignorance they had really discovered something better: a dancer trained in the same aesthetic tradition that produced Yeats's "The Symbolism of Poetry" and Pound's Imagist poems. In Paris Itow came to know Rodin and Debussy. He schooled himself in the aesthetics of Maeterlinck and the wardrobe of Oscar Wilde. "I wore my hair shoulder-length," Itow remembered, "dressed in velvet, and in short tried to look the European artist." When Pound first approached Itow about the Noh translations, Itow replied, "as far as I'm concerned there's nothing more boring than Noh." But as Itow became familiar with the plays, he came to see—as had Pound and Yeats— that "the ideas of European stage-artists of that time such as Gordon

Michio Itow photographed by Alvin Langdon Coburn in 1915.

Craig and Max Rheinhardt were really nothing but Noh." Rather than bringing an authentic understanding of the Noh to Pound and Yeats, Itow confirmed their own Western expectations, making Yeats's *At the Hawk's Well* possible. After Yeats's play convinced Itow of the value of the Japanese drama, Itow even planned to "try to do Oscar Wilde's *Salome* as a Noh." Two decades later Yeats would perform just that transformation in *A Full Moon in March.*

Before he arrived in London after the war broke out in 1914, Itow spent several years in Germany studying dance at the Dalcroze Institute near Dresden. Itow remembered that "in London, during the war, any attempts to speak German were met with hostile glares. Yet I could speak no English. Well, a little way into a street off Piccadilly Circus was a coffee-house. This was the Cafe Royale, that 'nest of artists' which Oscar Wilde used to haunt, dressed in velvet and sporting a sunflower in his lapel. Here it didn't matter if you spoke in German or French, so I was introduced and became a regular." At the Cafe Royale Itow met the heirs of Oscar Wilde—the artists Augustus John and Jacob Epstein, and the poet Ezra Pound. But Itow remained penniless and unknown until he was invited to a party given by Ottoline Morrell. There he was persuaded to dance and was then invited to a party given by Lady Cunard (in whose drawing room *At the Hawk's Well* would be given its premiere) where he repeated the performance. Itow recalled the evening in his memoirs:

> At supper, Lady Cunard, a refined, white-haired old gentleman and I all sat at a table together. The old man tried to carry on a conversation with me. However, it was English, so I didn't follow very well. He probably asked me about Japanese dancing and artistic matters, though I couldn't say for certain. I began to get frustrated, and interjected in halting English; "If you will allow me to speak in German I can answer a little more intelligently." Hearing this, the old man let out a hearty laugh: "I am an Englishman and can't speak Japanese. You are Japanese and can't speak English. If German mediates between us, then by all means let's speak in German." So saying he launched into really beautiful German.

The old gentleman turned out to be Asquith ("The person I had spoken to in German—the language of his enemy—had been the Prime Minister of England," Itow remembered), and their conversation became one of the many anecdotes Pound wove together to make the *Pisan Cantos:*

> So Miscio sat in the dark lacking the gasometer penny
> but then said: "Do you speak German?"

to Asquith, in 1914.

Yeats probably first saw Itow dance at one of the parties given by Lady Morrell and Lady Cunard. He wrote in the preface to *Certain Noble Plays of Japan* (1916) that his own *At the Hawk's Well* was "made possible by a Japanese dancer whom I have seen dance in a studio and in a drawing-room and on a very small stage lit by an excellent stage-light." In the drawing-room performance, "where no studied lighting, no stage-picture made an artificial world, [Itow] was able, as he rose from the floor, where he had been sitting cross-legged, or as he threw out an arm, to recede from us into some more powerful life. Because that separation was achieved by human means alone, he receded but to inhabit as it were the deeps of the mind. One realised anew, at every separating strangeness, that the measure of all arts' greatness can be but in their intimacy."

Itow's dancing was the product of Nijinsky's influence and not what Yeats supposed it to be, but in Itow's ability to create another world out of nothing, Yeats discovered how to produce drama without the bother of theatre business. Itow would create the strange abstracted world of *At the Hawk's Well* on April 2, 1916, after Pound and Yeats returned from their final winter together. But before they left for Sussex, Pound organized a kind of trial-run performance at the end of October 1915. He told Joyce that "Michio Itow is going to give some performances of Noh dancing, in proper costume, next week." Pound translated five "dance-poems" for the performance, emphasizing (like Yeats) the necessary exclusiveness of Itow's dancing when he printed them in an obscure journal in 1916. When Itow performed on a public stage, said Pound, "the finer movements . . . were lost and almost invisible"; but his "sword and spear dances" were seen properly when Itow "performed almost privately in a Kensington studio-theatre."

Like the poems of *Cathay*, the five dance-poems (which despite their excellence have never been reprinted) are a subtle commentary on the war that raged not so far from Kensington drawing rooms. The best of them is titled "In Enemies' Country just after War."

> Beneath the pale crust of the moon
> My sleeves are drenched with dew.
> Wind rushes against my face. I am cold.

> I start aside from the big snake on the pathway,
>> Startled I draw my sword,
>>> And slash at the old-pine-tree's shadow.

Pound knew that this poem's strength was its concision, and he noted that the last lines were necessarily obscure: "The translation might be clearer if one supplied the words, unnecessary in Japanese, 'start aside from what appears to be the snake, and slash at what is really the shadow,' but the essence of Japanese consists in leaving out just this sort of long explanation."

This kind of explanation was supplied by Itow's dancing, which accompanied the poems as they were read aloud. Pound saw the possibility of a viable theatre in Itow's performance: "Each dance was in itself a drama in miniature, having within the few lines of its text not only the crux of a play but almost the form and structure of full drama, Mr. Minami accompanying on a weird oriental flute and Mr. Utchiyama's voice booming ominous from behind the curtain. Itow himself, now rigid in some position of action impending, now in a jagged whirl of motions, slashing with the sword-blade, sweeping the air with the long samurai halberd." Pound's dance-poems are likewise each "a drama in miniature"; as his explanation of the last lines of "In Enemies' Country just after War" suggests, Pound cut the links of the narrative, leaving only the epiphanic moment of narrative closure. This, as he explained to William Carlos Williams in 1908, had always been the goal of his own poetry: "To me the short so-called dramatic lyric—at any rate the sort of thing I do—is the poetic part of a drama the rest of which (to me the prose part) is left to the reader's imagination or implied or set in a short note. I catch the character I happen to be interested in at the moment he interests me, usually a moment of song, self-analysis, or sudden understanding or revelation. And the rest of the play would bore me and presumably the reader." Most of Pound's Imagist poems are the distilled residue of a dramatic narrative. The famous story of how he came to write "In a Station of the Metro" (told in both "How I Began" and "Vorticism") details the process of transforming the motion of narrative into the stillness of epiphany; only the poem's title remains to help the reader construct the event which produced the vision. Given this aesthetic, Pound admired the Noh plays for the same reason he admired the dance-poems: the plays hold dramatic action within the resonant obscurity of the static Image, and the fact that their epiphanic intensity is sustained showed Pound that his poetry of concision could be extended without reintroducing the "prose" part of the drama.

So while Pound translated miniature dramas in the dance-poems, he continued to translate Noh plays, which gave him a model for dramatic poetry and Yeats a model for poetic drama. In 1915 he was still intent on embodying the link both he and Yeats sensed between the Noh and Irish folk literature in an idiom spiced with the Irish present participle: "It is a sad heart I have to see you looking up to Buddha, you who left me alone, as I was diving in the black rivers of hell." So read the Shite's speech in *Kayoi Komachi* as Pound published it in the May 1915 issue of *The Drama*. By this time Pound had discovered scholarly precedent for this home-grown anthropological insight; he read in Marie Stopes's *Plays of Old Japan: The Nō* that as "Synge and the Irish poets speak for the Irish people," so "do the Nō dramas represent the old spirit of Japan." But when Pound reprinted *Kayoi Komachi* in 'Noh' or Accomplishment (1916) he edited out much of the Irish lilt: "I've a sad heart to see you looking up to Buddha." Pound had already begun to feel (especially after he completed the more successful translations of the dance poems) that his versions of the Noh were inadequate. T. S. Eliot agreed. In his review of 'Noh' or Accomplishment, Eliot quoted the revised version of the Shite's speech from *Kayoi Komachi* (which retained some of its Irish flavor even in revision), calling the play "the least interesting" in the volume, "the one which is most remote from the idiom of Mr. Pound": "One feels that the original is not rendered because the translation is not English. . . . I should not read the Epistles of St. Paul in the language of Robert Burns, and I prefer the Noh in English. And Mr. Pound has no need of these accessories, for when he translates into English (and the Irish lapses are only occasional) he not only produces very fine poetry, but seems to bring us much nearer to the Japanese." Eliot went on to explain that the best passages occur when there is a "happy fusion of original and translator." Pound thought about translation in a slightly different way, however, believing that the texts of a given time and place required their own special language; the Noh drama could not be rendered in the same idiom as the poems of *Cathay* or *Lustra*.

Pound solicited help not from Eliot but from Yeats in forging his special idiom for the Noh plays. Before 'Noh' or Accomplishment was published, four of the plays (*Nishikigi*, *Hagoromo*, *Kumasaka*, and *Kagekiyo*) were printed in *Certain Noble Plays of Japan* along with Yeats's introduction. The plan for the book was worked out during the final winter at Stone Cottage, as Pound explained to John Quinn: "Yeats is booming in the next room, re-doing a lyric for his new playlet [*At the Hawk's Well*]. He is doing an introduction for my versions of a few of Fenollosa's japan plays, and I am highly honored." Yeats not only wrote the introduction but also read proof for the volume, making numerous suggestions and corrections in the language of Pound's translations.

In making these suggestions Yeats returned the lesson which he believed Pound had taught him. After their first winter together, Yeats had told an audience in Chicago that "a young man" had gone over all his work with him "to eliminate the abstract." Yeats went over the Noh translations with the same ideal in mind, questioning words such as "inexplicable," "ornate," "void," "tryst," and "largess." Forgetting that he had written of something called the "elaborate air" in "The Two Kings" (one of the poems Pound had helped to make "a new thing"), Yeats wrote, "I do not understand [the word] 'inexplicable'" beside this passage from *Hagoromo*: "Upon a thousand heights had gathered the inexplicable cloud, swept by the rain. The moon is just come to light the low house. A clear and pleasant time surely." His suggestion for several passages in *Nishikigi* were more specific. He singled out Pound's use of the words "ornate," "void," and "tryst," offering his own alternatives: "painted," "empty," and "marriage." In each case Yeats rejected the abstract and Latinate word, preferring the concrete word of everyday speech. "I cannot quite explain why," Yeats commented of the word "ornate," but it "does not seem to be good English in this sentence. It is probably a word that 'has not yet got its soul.'" " 'Void' is I think a poorer word than 'empty,'" he continued. " 'Void' is literary. It is not speech." This is just the kind of advice we have often imagined Pound giving Yeats. Yet the younger poet never confessed that he had Yeats go over his work to eliminate the abstract—and for good reason: Pound rejected every suggestion that I have cited. He accepted a few others, but wherever Yeats had replaced what he read as a "literary" word with one derived from "speech," Pound stuck with the "literary."

This is slim evidence from which to infer Pound's rationale for choosing the language of his Noh translations, but it does show once again that Pound considered the language of translation to be different from the language of poetry. That is the point Eliot missed in his review of 'Noh' or Accomplishment. Like the archaic language in Pound's translations of "The Seafarer" or the poems of Arnaut Daniel, the "literary" language of the Noh plays is designed to impart a particular sensibility—a sensibility that Pound considered aristocratic and self-consciously literary, the product of a culture that "listened to incense." Had Yeats's suggestions been made about poems Pound was collecting in *Lustra*, I suspect Pound would have listened; but then words like "ornate," "tryst," or "largess" do not appear in the poems of *Lustra*. The world of fifteenth-century Japan required an idiom different from that of twentieth-century London.

Even after revising the translations for publication in 'Noh' or Accomplishment, Pound ultimately was dissatisfied with them, "the scattered fragments left by a dead man, edited by a man ignorant of Japanese." But even as he wrote the translations at Stone Cottage he realized that they were the stepping-stones to better things. "Yeats is making a new start on the foundation of these Noh dramas," he wrote on March 9, 1916, just after the two poets had returned to London. Yeats had begun at Stone Cottage, as Pound explained in a letter he wrote to his father in February:

> He has done a new play of his own on the Noh model, and is preparing a new dramatic movement, plays which won't need a stage, and which won't need a thousand people for 150 nights to pay the expenses of production. His play and a brief skit of mine will be done in Lady Cunard's big room, in, I suppose, April. . . .
>
> Yeats seems to expect the new drama to do something, at least there will be no compromise, actors will wear masks, scenery will be mostly imagined, at most a cloth or a screen, and the dominion of Belasco . . . will no longer be coterminus with the known and inhabitable world.

David Belasco (1853–1931) was an American producer and playwright famous for his management of the Lyceum and Madison Square theatres and his productions of *Madame Butterfly* and *Lulu Belle*; in *The Great Gatsby* one of the party guests remarks, "This fella's a regular Belasco. It's a triumph. What thoroughness! What realism!" The epitome of what Yeats scorned as theatre business, Belasco stood for everything the new form of drama would reject: sensational realism, elaborate stage craft, and enormous crowds. Pound and Yeats would make no compromise with their audience, no concessions to the taste of the bourgeois "mob" who rioted at

The Playboy. Yeats wanted to create "an unpopular theatre and an audience like a secret society where admission is by favour and never to many." At the same time, Pound could not resist the temptation to satirize the aristocratic audience that would assemble in Lady Cunard's drawing room. He told John Quinn that Yeats "has a scheme for a Theatre-less stage—very noble & exclusive—his new play and a farce of mine are to be performed before an audience composed exclusively of crowned heads and divorcées." For Pound, "bourgeois" continued to be a state of mind; a prejudice against an ancient, abstract theatre could just as well be found in Lady Cunard's drawing room as in Madison Square.

Yeats realized that not only the audience but the actors would resist his new scheme for a drama of gesture and mask. Around the time that he and Pound were hammering out their new plays in 1916, Yeats wrote a dialogue called *The Poet and the Actress*. Although the Poet bears a clear resemblance to Leo Africanus, this dialogue (which has never been published) is not a dialogue of the dead like Pound's "An Anachronism at Chinon," but rather an exploration of the philosophical implications and practical difficulties of masking actors. The Poet offers the Actress a black box which he has brought back from Fez. He tells her that the box contains a mask, but the Actress protests that the natural beauty of her own face surpasses that of any mask. The Poet responds that for the phantasmagoric theatre he has in mind, the symbolic mask is the only way to express the "greater combat" between the dream and the reality: "Is not all comedy a battle—a sham fight often—but still a battle? Now the art I long for is also a battle but it takes place in the depths of the soul, and one of the antagonists does not wear a shape known to the world or speak a mortal tongue. It is the struggle of a dream with the world. It is only possible when we transcend circumstances and ourselves, and the greater the contest the greater the art." At the conclusion of the dialogue the Actress, still unwilling to don the mask, tells the poet to take his black box back to Fez. "There is no mask," replies the Poet, "I have never been to Fez." *The Poet and the Actress* pits Belasco's realistic theatre against Yeats's developing conception of a symbolic theatre of essences. As the final words spoken by the Poet emphasize, the symbolic theatre wins, because even the everyday events which realistic theatre purports to imitate are grounded in the interaction of the self and anti-self; only the mask is real, whether it has physical reality or not.

Pound was not so interested in these meditations on the theory of the mask, but, despite his reservations about the "crowned heads and divorcées" of Yeats's audience, he was deeply interested in the development of a private theatre, independent of the taste and financial support of the mob. He had been pleased with Itow's performance of his dance-poems because the audience was small and select enough to appreciate the delicate artistry. And, like Yeats, Pound had brooded about the inadequacy of the commercial theatre long before they began to organize the premiere of At the Hawk's Well. At the end of the summer of 1915 Joyce sent him the manuscript of Exiles, and Pound replied that "it won't do for the stage. . . . I don't believe an audience could follow it or take it in, even if some damd impracticable manager were to stage it. Not that I believe any manager would stage it in our chaste and castrated english speaking world." Pound even questioned Joyce's desire to write for the commercial theatre: "My whole habit of thinking of the stage is: that it is a gross, coarse form of art. That a play speaks to a thousand fools huddled together, whereas a novel or a poem can lie about in a book and find the stray persons worth finding, one by one seriatim."

Yeats's new dramatic program was designed to solve just this problem by wresting the theatre from the hands of the "mob" and placing it in the drawing rooms of the elite. Pound asked in "Mr. James Joyce and the Modern Stage" (written in September 1915 but published in The Drama in February 1916), "Must our most intelligent writers do this sort of [serious] work in the novel, *solely in the novel*, or is it going to be, in our time, possible for them to do it in drama?" In his introduction to Certain Noble Plays of Japan (published in the November 1916 issue of The Drama) Yeats answered Pound's question affirmatively:

> I have written a little play that can be played in a room for so little money that forty or fifty readers of poetry can pay the price. There will be no scenery, for three musicians, whose seeming sunburned faces will, I hope, suggest that they have wandered from village to village in some country of our dreams, can describe place and weather, and at moments action and accompany it all by drum and gong or flute and dulcimer. Instead of the players working themselves into a violence of passion indecorous in our sittingroom, the music, the beauty of form and voice all come to climax in pantomimic dance.

Yeats's development of this private form of theatre did not help
Pound find a place for Joyce's play, however; *Exiles* could not be
played in the drawing rooms of Kensington. Joyce continued to persuade Pound to try and place the play, but Pound continued to
object that he could find no audience large enough to make a production economically feasible: "I think you are a blind idealist
believing in ubiquitous intelligence among men. How many intelligent people do you think there are in England and America?" The
one intelligent reader Pound could think of was Yeats, and he persuaded him to consider Joyce's work for the Abbey.

Yeats began to read A *Portrait of the Artist as a Young Man* after
it was published in book form in 1917 and wrote to Pound, "I think
it a very great book—I am absorbed in it. If you have the play bring
it tomorrow night. If at all possible the Abbey should face a riot for
it." Yeats thought he might have found another Synge, but Pound
suspected that Yeats and the Abbey "damn well won't" take the
play, and they did not. The problem with Yeats's new dramatic program, Pound saw, was that it was suitable only for Yeats's new plays;
the trouble with theatre business had not been solved but circum-
vented. Joyce's *Exiles* was not produced but was finally published in
1918. And when Pound reviewed the play he reiterated the problem
with the commercial theatre that both he and Yeats had discussed
previously—but he did not mention Yeats's drawing room drama as
a possibility for "an interesting 'theatre' in our time": "A novel, to
be practicable, implies only 500 to 1,000 readers. It is just barely
possible to print for a public of that size. But a play, to be commer-
cially possible on the stage, implies at least twenty-one separate
audiences of 1,500 each, and demands that they assemble on twenty-
one consecutive nights. As there are not 30,000 people interested in
either serious literature or serious drama, it is hopeless sighing to
imagine there is going to be an interesting 'theatre' in our time."

Considering that Pound and Yeats had been conducting a public
dialogue in *The Drama* concerning the modern stage (Pound asking
in "Mr. James Joyce and the Modern Stage" for a way to produce intelligent plays for intelligent audiences and Yeats responding in "Certain Noble Plays of Japan" that he had made the breakthrough), it is
odd that Pound did not mention Yeats's Noh-style theatre in his later
essay on theatre business. His tacit dismissal of the aristocratic drama

may have been prompted by the fact that he himself was rejected from that exclusive company; the premiere of *At the Hawk's Well* was originally scheduled (as Pound told his parents and friends) as a double-bill. Even after the two performances of *At the Hawk's Well* in early April 1916, Pound still believed that one of his own plays was to be presented "somewhere or other *cum privilegio regis* for the delectation of duchesses (W.B.Y.'s select brand) but not for the vulgar herd." But like Joyce's *Exiles*, Pound's play was never performed. It was later rejected by the Abbey "on account of *indecency*."

Pound actually wrote several plays at the time Yeats was writing *At the Hawk's Well*, and, unlike *Exiles*, none of them was published in his lifetime. While it has not been possible to determine precisely which one of Pound's plays was to have been presented at Lady Cunard's, it seems likely that it was *The Consolations of Matrimony*. The manuscript of this one-act farce, signed with the pseudonym "Oge Terrence O'Cullough," contains a list of the Noh plays Pound was translating, and the play itself extends the experiments with Irish speech that Pound began in his translations. *The Consolations of Matrimony* recalls Synge's *The Playboy of the Western World* in both its language and its pointed mockery of the Irish story-teller.

During his three winters at Stone Cottage, Pound became increasingly interested in Synge. He began "John Synge and the Habits of Criticism," the review of Bourgeois's biography of Synge written during the first winter, with these sentences of praise: " 'She was so fine, and she was so healthy that you could have cracked a flea on either one of her breasts,' said the old sea captain bragging about the loves of his youth. It seems a shame that the only man who could have made any real use of that glorious phrase in literature, is dead. He has fallen prey to a dull and scholastic biographer who has gathered facts from the very parasites and detractors whom Synge has so causticly described as attending his funeral, 'small but select.' " Although Pound seems to imply that the sentence he quotes was written by Synge, it is not to be found in any of Synge's writings; Synge may have spoken the line to Yeats, or Pound may simply have made it up himself. Whatever its origin, the line remained important to Pound, and he remembered it thirty years later, quoting it in the *Pisan Cantos* immediately after Itow's anecdote about Asquith as an example of "precise definition":

> so that you cd/ crack a flea on eider wan
>   ov her breasts
> sd/ the old Dublin pilot.

Pound also used the line in his Syngean farce, *The Consolations of Matrimony*. (That he associates this play with Itow in the *Pisan Cantos* also suggests that it may have been the farce orginally scheduled for Lady Cunard's.) The play is composed entirely of a conversation between George Brannan and James Day. James laments the fact that he married at the age of twenty-two and has been "all the time with one woman." George, who has married more recently, brags that he has known many women, and James envies him for having a "mind full of things, to look back upon." Their conversation drifts idly from speculation about one woman after another, and the line Pound implied was Synge's is used to describe "the girl at the harbour":

> *James:* Do you mind now that girl at the mountain?
> *George:* (*after a reflective pause*) The one with a little round
>   belly, is it that one you mean? Nannie Keogh?
> *James:* It may be. You said she had a little round. . . .
> *George:* Ah go on with you.
> *James:* And the tinker's wife in the field?
> *George:* I do now.
> *James:* And the girl at the harbour, ah that was a fine girl.
> *George:* A fine girl, a strong girl.
> *James:* Ah.
> *George:* Ah you could have cracked a flea on either one of her
>   breasts.
> *James:* Ah.

Before the conversation turns to this catalogue of women, the play begins with George announcing that Tim Healan has returned from a trip to the United States. Tim had grown up in the same "small warty village" in Ireland as James and George, but his trip to America has given him new ideas about the state of matrimony. James, despite his dissatisfaction with monogamy, does not approve; nor does he approve of "the United States of America" where "they get a new divorce every week." George, on the other hand, senses the disparity between James's morals and desires, and suggests that if he followed Tim Healan's example, "you might at least get rid of your wife. . . .

And have a bold shine at an heiress, and give free vent to your powers of imagination."

James's powers of imagination are idle, so though he complains about his marital state with passion, none of that passion is directed towards the women of his dreams. He blames his fate on the village of Ballycurragh, "where there wasn't a horse begat, or a man shaved, or hen went off with the cock of another man's hen yard, or a boar gelded, or a priest drunk, since Adam was three months old. Ah, it's a slow place, and a dull place, and no part of the world." But James's inability to see that his village is as much a part of the world as the United States of America is just what Pound mocks in *The Consolations of Matrimony*. The play concludes as a boy rushes onto the stage with a message from Tim Healan: "Dear Mr. Day: You need not worry. I shall look after your wife, and you needn't bother to hunt for you won't find us." James flees the stage in pointless pursuit, and George concludes the action with a line that underscores the irony of both the play's all too well-made plot and James's impotent powers of imagination: "This *is* a bloody slow place."

Although *The Consolations of Matrimony* focuses its irony on Ireland, the play really had its origins in Pound's own experience as an American thrust into the intricacies of Edwardian society. When Dorothy Shakespear's parents finally approved Pound's proposal of marriage in 1914, Pound received a letter from his future father-in-law: "As you are not a British Subject it is important to ascertain definitely whether a marriage carried out with the formalities required by the Laws of England is all that is necessary." The Shakespears knew that Pound (unlike James Day) was capable of acting on his powers of imagination. In his reply to Henry Hope Shakespear, Pound himself took delight in exposing the decorously concealed point of their correspondence: "Of course divorce is a much more difficult job in America than you seem to think, and as for Pennsylvania, originally a quaker colony, the original inhabitants were so on guard against illegitimacy that it [was] practically impossible even to cohabit without being legally married." Masquerading as a satire of Irish morality, *The Consolations of Matrimony* was also an expression of Pound's complicated feelings about the monogamous life.

The manuscript of *The Consolations of Matrimony* is not a fair copy; Pound seems to have abandoned the play without polishing it. Even in its unfinished form, the drama is well paced, and yet it is difficult to imagine it as a prelude to the delicate intricacies of *At the*

Hawk's Well. But Yeats's play is also about a young man destined to remain impotent, and like Pound's play, it conceals a strong autobiographical undercurrent: like the young Cuchulain, the childless, middle-aged, and unmarried Yeats was searching for rejuvenation. Yet it seems unlikely that either Pound or Yeats would want to emphasize the personal aspect of their plays; in originally planning to place Pound's farce side by side with Yeats's adaptation of the Noh, the two poets were thinking of the traditional relationship of the Noh and the Kyogen. Brinkley's work explained to them that the Noh "was solemn and stately" but needed to be balanced by "some lighter scenes, and to satisfy that requirement farces were compiled for independent acting between the Nō. These farces (*Kyōgen*) were essentially of a histrionic character, the dance being omitted altogether, or entirely subordinated to the action of the piece and the dialogue." Pound did not translate any of the Kyogen, but the Fenollosa papers contain numerous Kyogen outlines. And although he was familiar with the form, Pound's own farce failed to adhere to one important convention. Brinkley explains that both the Noh and the Kyogen "were essentially a pastime of the upper classes, and to that reason, perhaps, is to be chiefly attributed their authors' obedience to the rules of pudicity." Pound's indecorous farce did not obey them, and it was finally judged an unsuitable companion for *At the Hawk's Well*, whether performed in Lady Cunard's drawing room or the Abbey Theatre.

Whatever the content of Pound's farce, he and Yeats quickly discovered that they did not have time to prepare even one short play for performance. Yeats had begun writing *At the Hawk's Well* at Stone Cottage by February 4, 1916, and by February 16th he and Pound were already planning the first performance for the first week in April. Yeats wrote to Allan Wade, who would play the Old Man in the premiere, that he wanted to talk over his as well as Pound's and Edmund Dulac's ideas about the project. Pound would prompt the production and Dulac would design the masks and costumes. Yeats himself wrote the play with unusual swiftness, finding his scenario (as Richard Taylor has discovered) in *Yoro* (The Sustenence of Age), a play which Fenollosa translated but which Pound did not finish for inclusion in '*Noh*' or *Accomplishment*. *Yoro* begins with an exchange between an imperial messenger and a father and son who have discovered the waterfall of immortality. Yeats transformed the waterfall into Connla's Well of Celtic legend; the pine trees that overhang the waterfall in the Noh drama became the hazel trees of *At the Hawk's Well*. But Yeats based his own play on *Yoro* only to invert the myth. In the Japanese play the god who controls the waterfall allows men to drink its water; in *At the Hawk's Well* the hazel trees are stripped of their leaves; the well is dry. An old man has waited fifty years and fallen asleep each time the waters filled the well; a young man (Cuchulain) journeys to the well only to be seduced by the well-guardian's dance as the waters rise and recede once more.

By the middle of February 1916 Yeats had written both a prose and verse version of his divagation from *Yoro*. The choral description which begins the rejected prose version initiates Yeats's transformation of the fecund Japanese landscape into an ancient Irish wasteland: "The night is coming on; the mountain side is darkening. The leaves of the hazel have fallen, driven by the autumn [winds], and half choked up the dry bed of the well. And too weary with her work clearing the well, the guardian of the fountain sits alone upon the stone margin. Nearby, stirred by the falling wind, the dry leaves rustle the green, and the great heap stirs and flutters."

It was Yeats's usual practice to write his poetry out as prose and then recast it into verse. Although he transformed much of his prose version of *At the Hawk's Well* into blank verse, this opening prose passage was recast into verses with anywhere from two to five stresses.

> Night falls;
> The mountain-side grows dark;
> The withered leaves of the hazel
> Half choke the dry bed of the well;
> The guardian of the well is sitting
> Upon the old grey stone at its side,
> Worn out from raking its dry bed,
> Worn out from gathering up the leaves.
> Her heavy eyes
> Know nothing, or but look upon stone.
> The wind that blows out of the sea
> Turns over the heaped-up leaves at her side;
> They rustle and diminish.

During the first Stone Cottage winter Yeats told Pound that *"vers libre* is prose," but in these lines Yeats was experimenting with a kind of free verse. The lines are carefully cadenced and bound together with repetitions—much as Pound's "The Return" (the free verse poem that Yeats admired most) is "free" only in the sense that its controlled pattern of accent and stress are not regularized. The rustling of the withered hazel leaves serves as what Pound would have called an "equation" for the well-guardian's fatigue in the same way that the "wet leaf that clings to the threshold" embodies the hesitant woman in Pound's "Liu Ch'e."

Yeats probably chose to cast his play's opening in this form because he associated free verse with dejection and sterility. In his introduction to *The Oxford Book of Modern Verse* (1936) he wrote that Eliot rejected traditional rhythms and metaphors to describe his "modern" world: "in describing this life that has lost heart his own art seems grey, cold, dry." Like many early readers of *The Waste Land*, Yeats assumed that Eliot's poem was (in I. A. Richards' phrase) "radically naturalistic," a mirror of the "modern" world rather than one source for the metaphors a generation would use to characterize that world. But it is no surprise that Eliot's metaphors were borrowed from earlier elegiac poets for earlier "modern" worlds: Arnold, Morris, and Yeats himself. Just before he came to Stone Cottage for his final winter with Pound (and just before he drafted *At the Hawk's Well*), Yeats wrote "Lines Written in Dejection," whose free verse rhythms are a mirror of his own "grey, cold, dry" mind.

> All the wild witches, those most noble ladies,
> For all their broom-sticks and their tears,
> Their angry tears, are gone.
> The holy centaurs of the hills are vanished;
> I have nothing but the embittered sun;
> Banished heroic mother moon and vanished,
> And now that I have come to fifty years
> I must endure the timid sun.

"Lines Written in Dejection," Yeats's most radical experiment in free verse, shares a wasteland sensibility with the opening lines of *At the Hawk's Well*; for Yeats, free verse is necessarily a sign of a desiccated sensibility, not the technical exercise it is for Pound. Eliot stands between them. When he attended the premiere of *At the Hawk's Well* he found the wasteland sensibility and the quest for water he would soon transform into his own. Many years later he re-

called that he saw Yeats "very differently" after he attended the play:
"I remember well the impression of the first performance of *The
Hawk's Well*, in a London drawing room, with a celebrated Japanese dancer in the role of the hawk, to which Pound took me. And
thereafter one saw Yeats rather as a more eminent contemporary than
as an elder from whom one could learn." But Eliot did continue to
learn from him. When he described the important innovation in the
use of myth in *At the Hawk's Well*, he also described the way he
himself would mythologize his personal experience in *The Waste
Land:* "with the Cuchulain of *The Hawk's Well*, the Cuchulain,
Emer and Eithne of *The Only Jealousy of Emer* . . . the myth is
not presented for its own sake, but as a vehicle for a situation of universal meaning."

Once Yeats had written out his play in prose and then recast it in
verse at Stone Cottage, all of its essential parts were in place. The
only important point that remained unclear was the dance with
which the play would climax. Yeats could not imagine how this
scene would take shape and simply wrote in his prose draft, "Chorus
describes first part of dance." Not yet knowing how effective Itow's
dance would be, he first planned to have the chorus narrate its significance; by the third week of February 1916 Yeats had begun to write
the lyrics that would open and close the play as well as a long lyric
interlude which the musicians were to sing during Itow's dance. In rehearsals, once Yeats perceived that the dance was more than adequate
to induce a sense of supernatural revelation, he cut all but eight of
the twenty-eight lines that make up the lyric interlude. Yet the deleted lines are instructive, for they reveal explicitly the emotions
which Yeats felt the dance itself could embody. This quatrain, sung
by the musicians three times during the deleted interlude, describes
the hawk's actual movement, along with Cuchulain's infatuation with
her otherwordly, deathless eyes.

> The horror of unmoistened eyes
> Slips by me with side-long head
> From stone to stone, or half flies
> The unappeasable gray wings spread.

Yeats wrote to Lady Gregory from Stone Cottage on February 23rd
that his play was growing into richer poetry now that he was writing
the lyrics, but the dramatic structure of the play demanded that this

lyric be cut; Yeats later inserted the reference to the hawk's "unmoistened eyes" (essential for its contrast to the life-giving water of immortality which those eyes force Cuchulain to forget) into the Old
Man's description of the Woman of the Sidhe: "There falls a curse /
On all who have gazed in her unmoistened eyes."

After the first and second recitation of the deleted "unmoistened
eyes" lyric in the Stone Cottage drafts of the play, Cuchulain inter-
jects a prayer to God to save him from the hawk's deathless body.
These lines, along with others in which Cuchulain threatens to tame
the hawk, were saved in the final version of At the Hawk's Well. But
after the third repetition of the "unmoistened eyes" lyric in the Stone
Cottage drafts, Yeats also cut a quatrain in which the musicians, in
contrast to Cuchulain, express their terror at the dance.

> Keep me from dancing feet and terrible eyes,
> Two feet seeming like two quivering blades,
> Eyes long withered and yet seeming young
> Keep from me—How should I bear those eyes.

In the final published version of At the Hawk's Well no descriptive
references to the dance are present. With his training in modern
dance—not the tradition of the Noh—Itow was able to make his
dance threatening (alleviating the need for the comparison to "quiv-
ering blades"); and even with the headdress designed by Dulac, Itow
was able to express Yeats's sense of the hawk's terrible and unappeasable eyes. Both poet and actor had succeeded in rendering that
battle "in the depths of the soul" that Yeats described in The Poet
and the Actress.

Most of the revisions Yeats made in At the Hawk's Well after he
left Stone Cottage were deletions. He had little time for anything
more intricate. After he and Pound returned to London in the first
week of March rehearsals began immediately for a performance that
would take place only three weeks later. To save more time, At the
Hawk's Well was designed as a chamber production, requiring a
minimum of scenery, lighting, and no stage at all. This rejection of
all manner of theatre business was dictated not only by Yeats's aesthetic but by a wartime economy. In Switzerland, Stravinsky was
writing Les Noces and L'Histoire du Soldat, major works for ensem-
bles of only eight or ten musicians; never again would he score a work
for the Romantic orchestra Le Sacre du printempts requires. Both

Stravinsky and Yeats reacted against the musical and theatrical ideal fostered by Wagner's massive music-dramas, but both artists were also encouraged to reduce the size of their productions by forces Yeats suggested in a letter to Ernest Boyd: "The anxiety of the war and the many deaths reduced our audience both in Dublin (where we could play only the more popular pieces and those at a loss) and in England till we were losing heavily. If however we can hold on at music halls we will restore our fortunes and be able to open soon again. In any case however we will start again after the war." Pound had one solution to this problem in addition to Yeats's plan for a drawing-room theatre. In January 1915 Yeats wrote to Lady Gregory from Stone Cottage that the Abbey "may have to close down and, Ezra Pound suggests, put in a cinematograph."

Not simply a play conceived to alleviate the need for "theatre business," *At the Hawk's Well* was designed to make theatre possible during wartime. And as Yeats and Pound soon discovered, even the small-scale production of a one-act play in a stylish drawing room entailed new sorts of fascination for the merely difficult. Rehearsals did not run smoothly. The musicians demanded a guitar, which Dulac transformed into an instrument of the Irish heroic age with a cardboard disguise. "One cannot discuss anything," Yeats wrote, "with a feud between Dulac and a stupid musician at every rehearsal." Though the dance sequence choreographed by Itow was successful in transporting the audience to another place and time, Yeats was dismayed at Henry Ainley (playing Cuchulain) who "waves his arms like a drowning kitten." Pound prompted the actors during both the rehearsals and the performance, telling Quinn that he had "some undefined marginal function which consists partly in watching W.B. rushing about a studio shouting 'Now . . . . . NOW . . . . Now . . . . . Now you really must . . . . etc . . etc. I am a TIGER when I get to rehearsing." At one rehearsal, when Ainley failed to appear, Pound took his place as Cuchulain. Yeats remembered the effect of his performance: "A man who loves verse and the visible arts has, in a work such as I imagined, the advantage of the professional player. The professional player becomes the amateur, the other has been preparing all his life, and certainly I shall not soon forget the rehearsal of *At the Hawk's Well*, when Mr. Ezra Pound, who had never acted on any stage, in the absence of our chief player rehearsed for half an hour."

Yeats wanted his lines declaimed as verse, nobly, and with a minimum of expression. Untrained in what Yeats called the "subjective" tradition of acting (except for a brief stint as a member of the chorus in a 1903 production of *Iphigenia among the Taurians*), Pound was better equipped by his experience as a poet to speak the lines in Yeats's play. This stylized method of acting impressed Eliot, who after attending the premiere of *At the Hawk's Well* wrote in a review of a production of *The Duchess of Malfi* that no "modern actor, with his interpretive gifts, would allow the poetry to reach the audience. . . . For poetry is something which the actor cannot improve or 'interpret'; . . . in consequence, the ideal actor for a poetic drama is the actor *with no personal vanity*." Building on Yeats's example, Eliot would write plays suited for just such an actor. He originally planned his first play, *Sweeney Agonistes*, as a verse drama featuring (like *At the Hawk's Well*) "certain things in it accentuated by drumbeats." He would later tell a director interested in producing the fragmentary play that she should read Pound's *'Noh' or Accomplishment* and Yeats's essay on the first performance of *At the Hawk's Well*; the action of *Sweeney Agonistes*, Eliot said, "should be stylized as in the Noh."

Eliot was invited to the premiere of *At the Hawk's Well* on April 2nd because he was one of the few, as Yeats explained in his essay on the first performance of the play, who really "cared for poetry": " 'At the Hawk's Well' was performed for the first time in April, 1916, in a friend's drawing-room, and only those who cared for poetry were invited. It was played upon the floor, and the players came in by the same door as the audience, and the audience and the players and I myself were pleased. A few days later it was revived in Lady Islington's big drawing-room at Chesterfield Gardens for the benefit of a war charity. . . . And round the platform upon three sides were three hundred fashionable people including Queen Alexandria, and once more my muses were but half welcome." Yeats stressed that his new kind of drama would succeed only among the most exclusive aristocracy of the arts, not among the larger audience for the second performance, which Pound ridiculed as "selected royalty (mostly aged and female)." But while Yeats preferred the premiere at Lady Cunard's, Pound thought the second show at Lady Islington's was the superior performance; he told Quinn that the play was "a success. Not right as yet, but [it] went much better than could have been expected from the shape it was in on Sunday."

Despite his feeling that only a small percentage of the charity au-

dience appreciated his delicate drama, Yeats took pleasure in inform-
ing a photographer that he did not desire or require publicity:

> we found a newspaper photographer planting his camera in a
> dressing-room and explained to him that as fifty people could pay
> our expenses, we did not invite the press and that flashlight photo-
> graphs were not desirable for their own sake. He was incredulous
> and persistent—a whole page somewhere or other was at our dis-
> posal—and it was nearly ten minutes before we could persuade him
> to go away. What a relief after directing a theatre for so many
> years—for I am one of the two directors of the Abbey Theatre in
> Dublin—to think no more of pictures unless Mr. Dulac or some
> other distinguished man has made them, nor of all those paragraphs
> written by young men, perhaps themselves intelligent, who must
> applaud the common taste or starve!

It is fitting that the three winters of collaboration between Pound
and Yeats should have ended with these performances of Yeats's play.
The intricacies of At the Hawk's Well were designed for the Brothers
Minor and their novitiates; the mob was railed at Synge and balked
at Joyce were not invited, denied even the consolation of the common newspaper story about the private entertainment of the privileged few. Photographs were prohibited, not so much because the
images were to be kept secret, but because the makers of the images
were mired in common taste. The premiere of At the Hawk's Well
was photographed by Alvin Langdon Coburn, for whom Yeats had
sat in 1908 and Pound in 1913. Coburn was no newspaper photographer; a close friend of Shaw's, he had provided the photographs for
the New York edition of Henry James's novels, and in 1917 (with
Pound's help) he would create what many consider to be the first
purely abstract photographs. "No press, no photographs in the papers,
no crowd," Yeats told Quinn of the premiere of his play. "I shall be
happier than Sophocles. I shall be as lucky as a Japanese dramatic
poet at the Court of the Shogun."

Yeats wrote three more plays for dancers after At the Hawk's Well,
and even his plays not modeled directly on Pound's translations of
the Noh were influenced by their anti-realistic aesthetic. He remarked
in "Certain Noble Plays of Japan" that each play focused "upon a
single metaphor, as deliberate as the echoing rhythm of line in Chinese and Japanese painting." Yeats used this "rhythm of metaphor"
to organize his later plays; Pound used it to organize the early cantos.

Michio Itow photographed by Alvin Langdon Coburn in costume for his role in *At the Hawk's Well*.

In a note appended to his essay "Vorticism" he wrote, "I am often asked whether there can be a long imagiste or vorticist poem. The Japanese, who evolved the hokku, evolved also the Noh plays. In the best 'Noh' the whole play may consist of one image. I mean it is gathered about one image. Its unity consists in one image, enforced by movement and music. I see nothing against a long vorticist poem." The Noh showed Pound how to extend the aesthetic of his dance-poems in a longer form. With Pound's help, Eliot also saw this "rhythm of metaphor" in the Noh plays. He explained in his essay on "The Noh and the Image" that at their best, the plays are organized by a "unity of the image" which is "also the unity of certain cantos of Dante." Had he written the essay a few years later, Eliot might have ended that sentence with the words "certain cantos of Pound."

Pound once told Harriet Monroe that the theme of his own *Three Cantos* (1917) was "roughly the theme of 'Takasago,'" a Noh play he did not include among his translations. This Japanese version of the myth of Baucis and Philemon does appear throughout the early cantos, but the Noh influenced Pound's tentative beginning for a long poem more profoundly than these allusions suggest. Each of the early cantos has its own "rhythm of metaphor," and like many of the Noh plays each canto is organized around a place made sacred by myth and history—a place like the Abbey of Corcomroe in Yeats's *The Dreaming of the Bones*—where "ghosts move about me / Patched with histories." If Yeats's Stone Cottage studies in the Noh and the occult converged in *The Dreaming of the Bones* and *Per Amica Silentia Lunae*, Pound's studies in the same subjects were annealed in *Three Cantos*.

9

Ghosts Patched with Histories

On the afternoon of Saturday, August 10, 1901, Anne Moberly and Eleanor Jourdain, the principal and vice-principal of St. Hugh's College, Oxford, were strolling through the gardens of Versailles and found themselves transported back into the eighteenth century. At the time, neither one of them comprehended what had happened. In a narrative written a few months later, Anne Moberly described the experience this way:

> We walked briskly forward, talking as before, but from the moment we left the lane an extraordinary depression had come over me. . . . In front of us was a wood, within which, and overshadowed by trees, was a light garden kiosk, circular, and like a small bandstand, by which a man was sitting. There was no greensward, but the ground was covered with rough grass and dead leaves as in a wood. The place was so shut in that we could not see beyond it. Everything suddenly looked unnatural, therefore unpleasant; even the trees behind the building seemed to have become flat and lifeless, *like a wood worked in a tapestry.*

Nothing these two women reported they saw that day—the woods, the kiosk, a woman sitting on a terrace—existed in 1901. After ten years of research in the French national archives, they confirmed to their satisfaction that all these things had existed in the year 1789.

The woman whom Anne Moberly saw on the terrace was determined to be none other than Marie Antoinette.

In 1911 Anne Moberly and Eleanor Jourdain (using the pseudonyms Elizabeth Morison and Frances Lamont) published *An Adventure*, a book which presented their accounts of this vision of the past as well as their subsequent documentation of its historical veracity. The records of their research, now deposited in the Bodleian Library, were scrupulously dated to prove that they had not undertaken it before their adventure at Versailles. At the time of its publication, *An Adventure* created an enormous stir—not only because of its subject matter but because the publisher, Macmillan, guaranteed the respectability of its authors—and it was subsequently expanded and reissued in four editions. Even today the book remains a widely debated example of what psychologists refer to as "retrocognition."

At Stone Cottage, *An Adventure* (and other books like it) became central to the development of both Yeats's *Per Amica Silentia Lunae* (1918) and Pound's *Three Cantos* (1917). In fact, when the compositional histories of these apparently vastly different works are laid side by side, we can see that they are both responses to the material Pound and Yeats studied together in Ashdown Forest. Yeats's middle-period essays and Pound's early cantos are both meditations on the nature of the artist's relationship to the spirits of his ancestors. And Yeats's essays shed an illuminating light on Pound's attempts to find a poetic form for the visionary sense of the past he had been struggling to express ever since he published "Histrion" in 1908.

> 'Tis as in midmost us there glows a sphere
> Translucent, molten gold, that is the "I"
> And into this some form projects itself:
> Christus, or John, or eke the Florentine;
> And as the clear space is not if a form's
> Imposed thereon,
> So cease we from all being for the time,
> And these, the Masters of the Soul, live on.

In his explanatory notes for Lady Gregory's *Visions and Beliefs in the West of Ireland*, Yeats refers to more than two dozen books of folklore, demonology, philosophy, poetry, and occult phenomena. With the exception of Sinistrari's *De Daemonialitate* (given to him by Pound during their first winter together), he spends more time discussing *An Adventure* than any other book. Commenting on Lady

Gregory's story about a woman who claimed to have seen an ancient castle and drawbridge appear at Coole lake, Yeats wrote that in *An Adventure* "an elaborate vision of this kind is recorded in detail and, accepting the record as accurate, the verification is complete. Two ladies found themselves in the garden of the Petit Trianon in the midst of what seemed to be the court of Marie Antoinette, in just the same sudden way in which some countryman finds himself among ladies and gentlemen dressed in what seem the clothes of a long passed time."

Yeats goes on to speculate on possible explanations for historical vision that have more to do with his dialogue with Leo Africanus and *Per Amica* than with *An Adventure* itself. First he invokes Madame Blavatsky's idea of the "mind of God" in which "all things past and to come were present" as an explanation of the adventure. Not content to let this theory rest on so questionable an authority as Madame Blavatsky, Yeats points out that the theory is "ancient," invoking Cornelius Agrippa, Henry More, Éliphas Lévi, and Swedenborg to prove it. In the final paragraphs of his discussion of *An Adventure* he invokes authorities even closer to his own concerns as a poet:

> I was once talking with Professor [William] James of experiences like to those in *The Adventure* and said that I found it easiest to understand them by believing in a memory of nature distinguished from individual memory, though including and enclosing it. He would, however, have none of my explanation and preferred to think the past, present and future were only modes of our perception and that all three were in the divine mind, present at once. It was Madame Blavatsky's thought, and Shelley's in the *Sensitive Plant*:
>
>> "That garden sweet, that lady fair,
>> And all sweet shapes and odours there,
>> In truth have never passed away;
>> 'Tis we, 'tis ours, are changed, not they.
>>
>> "For love, and beauty, and delight,
>> There is no death nor change; their light
>> Exceeds our organs, which endure
>> No light, being themselves obscure."

The same concoction of poetry, philosophy, and the occult would emerge as Yeats's theory of the "Anima Mundi" in *Per Amica Silentia Lunae*, in which the muses are indeed shown to be the daughters of memory. This extended meditation on *An Adventure*, composed at Stone Cottage, reveals Yeats in the process of hammering his thoughts into unity. In "Swedenborg, Mediums, and the Desolate Places," the essay Yeats also drafted in Sussex, he began to incorporate the insights derived from Shelley, James, More, Agrippa, Swedenborg, and *An Adventure* into his own theory: "I was comparing one form of belief with another," he wrote of his occult investigations, "and, like Paracelsus who claimed to have collected his knowledge from midwife and hangman, I was discovering a philosophy." That philosophy was what he had called the "Great Memory" in *Ideas of Good and Evil* and what he would soon call, bolstered by his studies in Renaissance Neoplatonism, the "Anima Mundi." Yeats wrote in "Swedenborg, Mediums, and the Desolate Places" that while reading Swedenborg, he came across "a discovery one had thought peculiar to the last generation, that the 'most minute particulars which enter the memory remain there and are never obliterated', and there as here we do not always know all that is in our memory, but at need angelic spirits who act upon us there as here, widening and deepening the consciousness at will, can draw forth all the past."

Following his completion of "Swedenborg, Mediums, and the Desolate Places" in 1914, Yeats became more deeply involved in his dialogue with Leo Africanus, discovering that there was indeed an "angelic spirit "who deepened his consciousness at will. In 1917 he recalled his Stone Cottage investigations of Noh drama and the occult and presented his theory with a bit more polish in *Per Amica Silentia Lunae*:

> Spiritism, whether of folk-lore or of the séance-room, the visions of Swedenborg, and the speculation of the Platonists and Japanese plays, will have it that we may see at certain roads and in certain houses old murders acted over again, and in certain fields dead huntsmen riding with horse and hound, or ancient armies fighting above bones or ashes. We carry to *Anima Mundi* our memory, and that memory is for a time our external world; and all passionate moments recur again and again.

Yeats is describing what his reading in the literature of psychical research might have led him to call an "adventure," a psychic experience that transports us to another place and time. These "adventures" make the past available as an eternally present moment, called up from the vast store house of the "Anima Mundi."

Yeats does not mention *An Adventure* in either "Swedenborg, Mediums, and the Desolate Places" or *Per Amica*, but the book remained in the background of his visionary system. Discussing the process of the "dreaming back" in the final version of A *Vision* (1937), Yeats writes that one "thinks of those apparitions haunting the places where they have lived that fill the literature of all countries and are the theme of the Japanese Nō drama." He then recalls *An Adventure*, characterizing it as a book which "describes with minute detail a vision of Marie Antoinette and her Court, and of the gardens of the Petit Trianon as they were before the Revolution, and the research that proved the vision's accuracy." Not only the mechanism but the substance of the vision appealed to Yeats: *An Adventure* revealed a glimpse of the courtly world that existed before the rise of the modern middle class, who, as Yeats wrote in "The People," fill the "unmannerly town / Where who has served the most is most defamed." *An Adventure* showed both Yeats and Pound an example of how two people had actually walked in "the green shadow of Ferrara wall" and "climbed among the images of the past."

The importance of the ideas of the "dreaming back" and the "Anima Mundi" that Yeats found embodied in *An Adventure* are obvious in his own work; not so clear is the centrality of these same ideas to Pound's efforts to write a "poem including history." Soon after the final winter at Stone Cottage, Pound wrote a preface for a reading of Alfred de Musset's brief play, "A Supper at the House of Mademoiselle Rachel." He explained to his audience that the play contained "very little drama" and should be understood as a "reconstruction" of the past.

> You tell me you do not want Japanese things, that these new plays must be European. Still it is a Japanese play [*Nishikigi*] that gives me the closest parallel to my thought. . . . No, I am not going to be oriental. I think you all have your heroes and heroines. You all have your periods. You all think you were Mary Queen of Scots, or Joan of Arc, or Charlotte Corday, or someone. I have taken an unpopular period. I have taken a period out of fashion. I have taken Rachel and de Musset. All wrong? The eighteen-thirties? Still if you went to the Tuileries and really saw Marie Antoinette? If suddenly by the Tiber you saw re-acted, re-arranged, re-presented the events and heard the exact speeches on the morning after the Duke of Gandia was murdered?
>
> Ah no, you would not complain about my giving you Japanese

emotion, you would call it European emotion. And then the rational continent always says you English are mad about ghosts.

Not only *Nishikigi* but also *An Adventure* (in which the two women went to Versailles and really saw Marie Antoinette) provided Pound with a drama of "reconstruction," a drama in which ghosts assert the presence of the past. Pound was already thinking about the ghosts he would present in *The Cantos* as he wrote these sentences; in Canto 5 he would reconstruct the murder of Giovanni Borgia, Duke of Gandia.

Pound emphasized in his introduction to de Musset's play that these historical adventures should be presented as "an illusion that should be not quite an illusion," and he quoted these lines from *Nishikigi* to illustrate the point.

> Let it be a dream, or a vision,
> Or what you will, I care not.
> Only show me the old times over-past and snowed under;
> Now, soon, while the night lasts.

The ghostly presences in the Noh plays appealed to Pound because they are utterly precise and concrete; like Yeats, he saw this quality in the "adventures" that occur throughout many of the plays. In his notes for *Suma Genji* (in which a priest has a vision of an ancestral hero) Pound remarks that the reader must "put himself in sympathy with the priest eager to see 'even in a vision' the beauty lost in the years, 'the shadow of the past in bright form.'" In "Fenollosa on the Noh," an essay Pound transcribed to accompany his translations, Fenollosa concludes that because of their use of "great types of human character, derived from Japanese history," the Noh plays became "a storehouse of history." Yeats might have called them the manifestation of the Anima Mundi.

Another of the plays, *Kakitsubata*, reaches its climax when the spirit of Kakitsubata appears in ancient clothing: "A hat and a robe of remembrance! / I am come clothed in a memory." This memory, as both Pound and Yeats realized, was more than personal memory. In his commentary on these lines, Pound refers to Landor's "Memory"—as Yeats would do in *Per Amica Silentia Lunae:* "The Muses were 'the Daughters of Memory.'" It is by memory that this spirit appears, she is able or 'bound' because of the passing thought of these iris [growing in the marsh where she appears]. That is to say, . . . she demonstrates the 'immortality of the soul' or the 'permanence or endurance of the individual personality' by her apparition—first, as a simple girl of the locality; secondly, in the ancient splendours." In speaking about memory, Pound knew that he was beginning the ancient questions of the "immortality of the soul" and the "permanence of the individual personality," but he had little desire to dogmatize about these esoteric topics in 'Noh' or Accomplishment; he knew that Yeats was laying out the theory of the universal memory in his essays.

Yet Pound did conduct some research of his own. In "An Anachronism at Chinon," his imaginary conversation between an American student and the ghost of Rabelais, Pound included a brief quotation from Cicero in one of Rabelais's speeches: "All that I believed or believe you will find in De Senectute: '. . . that being so active, so swift in thought; that treasures up in memory such multitudes and varieties of things past, and comes likewise upon new things . . . can be of no mortal nature.'" The full passage from which these phrases are excerpted in the De Senectute reveals that Pound had found even more ancient precedent for the "immortality of the soul" than Yeats found in Agrippa or Swedenborg:

> I used to be told that Pythagoras and his disciples . . . never doubted that our souls were emanations of the Universal Divine Mind. Moreover, I had clearly set before me the arguments touching the immortality of the soul, delivered on the last day of his life by Socrates, whom the oracle of Apollo had pronounced the wisest of men. Why multiply words? That is my conviction, that is what I believe—since such is the lightning-like rapidity of the soul, such its wonderful memory of things that are past, such its ability to forecast the future, such its mastery of many arts, sciences, and inventions, that its nature, which encompasses all these things, cannot be mortal. . . . And a strong argument that men's knowledge of numerous things antedates their birth is the fact that mere children, in studying difficult subjects, so quickly lay hold upon innumerable things that they seem not to be then learning them for the first time, but to be recalling and remembering them. This, in substance, is Plato's teaching.

Pound also knew that this eternal memory was the substance of Plato's teaching, for in The Spirit of Romance he quoted the significant passage from the Phaedrus as a commentary on the first canto of ‚the Paradiso: "And this is the recollection of those things which our souls saw when in company with God—when looking down from above on that which we now call being, and upward toward the true being." Mortal man's knowledge, Pound and Yeats agreed, came ultimately from his participation in eternal memory. In "The Approach to Paris," his primer in French poetry, Pound invoked Richard of St. Victor to explain how the Platonic theory of recollection could be employed in poetry: "Richard of St. Victor who was half a neoplatonist, tells us that by naming over all the beautiful things we can think of, we may draw back upon our minds some vestige of the unrememberable beauties of paradise. If we are not given to mystical devotions we may suspect that the function of poetry is, in part, to draw back upon our mind a paradise, if you like, or, equally, one's less detestable hours and the outrageous hopes of one's youth."

Pound's poetic goal was the cultivation of "adventures," the soul's visionary memories of the paradise or the past it once knew. He even adopted the term "adventure" from his study of the occult with Yeats. In an essay on Arnold Dolmetsch, published during his second winter at Stone Cottage, Pound reported that in the presence of Dolmetsch he "had two sets of *adventures*. First, I perceived a sound which is undoubtedly derived from the Gods, and then I found myself in a reconstructed century—in a century of music, back before Mozart or Purcell, listening to clear music, to tones clear as brown amber." Pound began the essay by recounting the first of these adventures.

> I have seen the God Pan and it was in this manner: I heard a bewildering and pervasive music moving from precision to precision within itself. Then I heard a different music, hollow and laughing. Then I looked up and saw two eyes like the eyes of a wood-creature peering at me over a brown tube of wood. Then someone said: Yes, once I was playing a fiddle in the forest and I walked into a wasps' nest.
>
> Comparing these things with what I can read of the earliest and best authenticated appearances of Pan, I can but conclude that they relate to similar occurrences. . . .
>
> Our only measure of truth is, however, our own perception of truth. The undeniable tradition of metamorphoses teaches us that things do not remain always the same. They become other things by swift and unanalysable process.

Pound offers an explanation for the reality of his "adventure" that even the authors of *An Adventure* did not put forward. First, because perception is the only measure of truth, his vision of Dolmetsch as Pan must stand as fact. Pound compares himself to a primitive visionary who has no means of distinguishing his imaginative visions from the "real" world around him; "These things are for them *real*," Pound wrote of this kind of visionary experience in "Psychology and Troubadours." Second, these visionary experiences, subjective and unverifiable as they might be, stand in a long tradition of similar experiences recorded in the literature of folklore, mythology, and the occult. Pound sought to situate his own work in this tradition. In his article on Dolmetsch, he generalized from his own "adventure" to construct his own theory of an artist's relationship to the memories stored in the "Anima Mundi": "When any man is able, by a pattern of notes or by an arrangement of planes or colours, to throw us back into the age of truth, everyone . . . gives honour to the spell which has worked, to the witch-work or the art-work, or to whatever you like to call it." An "arrangement of planes or colours," a "witch-work" that "throws us back into the age of truth"—that is what Pound sought to fabricate in the early cantos. Like Dolmetsch or the authors of *An Adventure* Pound professed to hear the music of lost dynasties, but his problem was to discover a way of transcribing those melodies into a long poem. *Three Cantos* is a record of that struggle.

Pound may have begun working on the poems which became *Three Cantos* as early as 1910, but it was not until the summer of 1915 that he began to work intensively. On September 25th he told his father that he was "at work on a very long poem." The previous winter at Stone Cottage had given him new material; Yeats told Quinn that he had made Pound read Icelandic sagas and Doughty's *Travels in Arabia Deserta* but then "allowed him to raise his spirits with Sordello." Pound had read Browning's *Sordello* before, but reading the poem aloud to Yeats gave him a new start on his own work. On December 18, 1915, just before he left for the third winter in Sussex, Pound conveyed his new enthusiasm for Browning in a letter to his father:

> If you like "Perigord" you would probably like Browning's "Sordello". . . . It is a great work and worth the trouble of hacking it out.
> I began to get it on about the 6th reading—though individual passages come up all right on the first reading.
> It is probably the greatest poem in English. Certainly the best long poem in English since Chaucer.
> You'll have to read it sometime as my big long endless poem

that I am now struggling with starts out with a barrel full of allusions to "Sordello."

Pound's *Three Cantos* do begin with an extended meditation on *Sordello*, which was eventually reduced to the four lines which open the final version of Canto 2. During the summer of 1915 the meditation on *Sordello* did begin a "big long endless poem," for Pound's manuscript drafts show that at that time *Three Cantos* consisted of one giant, disorganized poem only tentatively divided into cantos. This leviathan contained not only material that Pound would include in *Three Cantos* but also drafts of lines that would appear in Cantos 4 and 5. Pound explained in his letter of December 18th that he was already planning the fifth canto: "I must have the lot typed out and send it to you as a much belated Xmas [present]. Though I dare say the present version needs a lot done to it. It will be two months at least before I can send it, I suppose, as I don't want to muddle my mind now in the Vth Canto by typing the first three cantos, and I don't want to leave the only copy with a typist while I'm out of town [at Stone Cottage]."

Pound continued shaping this material through 1916. Early versions of the first *Three Cantos* appeared in *Poetry* during the summer of 1917, just as Yeats was completing *Per Amica Silentia Lunae*. The poem's opening address to Browning is misleading; in *Three Cantos* Pound does not continue the technique of *Sordello* and *The Ring and the Book* (as he does in "Near Perigord") so much as create a method for historical vision suggested by works such as *An Adventure*. Instead of presenting figures dug up from the past by borrowing Browning's conceit of the stage and diorama box, Pound presents his characters in "adventures," visions of a world normally unavailable to human sense. After the opening address to Browning in *Three Cantos* I, Pound utters the crucial line of the poem ("Ghosts move about me / Patched with histories"), then offers a vision of the spirits floating over the waters of Lake Garda. As in his Imagist poems, he stresses the Pre-Raphaelite clarity of the visionary experience.

> And the place is full of spirits.
> Not *lemures*, not dark and shadowy ghosts,
> But the ancient living, wood-white,
> Smooth as the inner bark, and firm of aspect,
> And all agleam with colors—no, not agleam,
> But colored like the lake and like the olive leaves.

. . . .
'Tis the first light—not half light—Panisks
And oak-girls and the Maenads
Have all the wood. Our olive Sirmio
Lies in its burnished mirror, and the Mounts Balde and Riva
Are alive with song, and all the leaves are full of voices.

These "adventures" in *Three Cantos* are organized around specific geographical locations to emphasize their origin in the meeting of a particular consciousness and a particular place. Pound had already exploited this technique in "Provincia Deserta," and we have seen that Yeats explained the theory behind it in *Per Amica Silentia Lunae*: "Spiritism . . . will have it that we may see at certain roads and in certain houses old murders acted over again, and in certain fields dead huntsmen riding with horse and hound, or ancient armies fighting above bones or ashes." The spirits of *Three Cantos* appear as the spirits of the dead appear in the Noh plays *Kakitsubata* or *Nishikigi*, eternally associated with the place in the landscape where they lived or died. In a 1918 essay on Chinese poetry Pound remembered why Yeats found *Nishikigi* in particular so intriguing: "Chinese poetry is full of fairies and fairy lore. Their lore is 'quite Celtic.' I found one tale in a Japanese play; two ghosts come to a priest to be married, or rather he makes a pilgrimage to their tomb and they meet him there. The tale was new to me, but I found that Mr. Yeats had come upon a similar story among the people of Aran." Yeats not only discovered this correlation between Eastern and Western traditions, but used it as the basis for *The Dreaming of the Bones* (1919), the second of his plays for dancers. In this play Yeats marries *Nishikigi* with the Irish legend of Diarmuid and Dervorgilla and filters both through the 1916 Easter Rebellion. The ghosts of Diarmuid and Dervorgilla appear as the spirit of Kakitsubata appears in the Noh play, in ancient dress— "clothed in a memory." They also appear as the spirits appear in *Three Cantos*, evoked from the landscape charged with the "Anima Mundi." In the twelfth century, Diarmuid and Dervorgilla began the English domination of Ireland by conspiring with Henry II; in the fourteenth century Donough O'Brien similarly enlisted Scottish aid for his rebellion. After the 1916 rebellion the ghosts of Diarmuid and Dervorgilla appear to a fugitive revolutionary at the ruined Abbey of Corcomroe, near which O'Brien met his death after his aborted insurrection:

> Why does my heart beat so?
> Did not a shadow pass?
> It passed but a moment ago.
> Who can have trod in the grass?
> What rogue is night-wandering?
> Have not old writers said
> That dizzy dreams can spring
> From the dry bones of the dead?

To distort Pound's famous phrase, *The Dreaming of the Bones* is a play including history, and it uses the same conceit ("ghosts patched with histories") as *Three Cantos* to bring the past alive in the present. In Yeats's play, the sacred place is the Abbey of Corcomroe; in the first of *Three Cantos* the place is Sirmio, and in the second it is the Dordogne valley in France. Here Pound comes upon the ghosts of "the ancient people":

> So the murk opens.
> > Dordoigne! When I was there,
> There came a centaur, spying the land,
> And there were nymphs behind him.
> Or going on the road by Salisbury
> Procession on procession—
> For that road was full of peoples,
> Ancient in various days, long years between them.
> Ply over ply of life still wraps the earth here.
> Catch at Dordoigne.

Pound's use of these "adventures" as a method for including history in *Three Cantos* is as much a metaphor for historical reconstruction as Browning's use of the showman's booth. Yet Pound's method had some grounding in the occult literature that bolstered Yeats's conception of the Anima Mundi; *Per Amica Silentia Lunae* helps to explicate *Three Cantos* as much as it does *The Dreaming of the Bones*.

At the same time that all these works were drafted, Pound wrote his own version of *The Dreaming of the Bones* in a brief play titled *Tristan*. While Yeats had crossed *Nishikigi* with the story of Diarmuid and Dervorgilla, Pound married it with the tale of Tristan and Iseult. In Pound's version of the play, the part of Yeats's fugitive revolutionary is taken by a young French sculptor who embarks on a walking tour in Cornwall and stops at a ruined castle to watch a quince tree blossom; instead of flowers, he sees the ghosts of Tristan and Iseult appear. The sculptor has no idea that he has come to Tintagel, the ancient castle of King Mark, or that the quince tree has grown from Tristan's grave; he believes that its magical blossoming is caused by the gulf stream. Yet the ruined castle is as enchanted a place as the Abbey of Corcomroe in *The Dreaming of the Bones* or the iris marsh in *Kakitsubata*, and like the ghosts of those plays, Tristan and Iseult appear in the medieval costume of their time. Like Yeats's Diarmuid and Dervorgilla, Pound's ghosts are "neither alone, nor together"; they are "torn between two lives / Knowing neither." Only after they have receded back into the landscape does the sculptor discover that the name of the castle is Tintagel, and the conclusion of the play recalls *At the Hawk's Well* as the sculptor realizes he has missed what he came for (the blossoming of the tree) only to have seen something far more mysterious: "The green leaves have surrounded the flowers. / I have not known how it happened."

Three Cantos progresses as if it were a sequence of the spiritual encounters presented in *Tristan;* but in these early cantos (as in the Imagist poems) Pound omits most of the dramatic situation and presents the "adventures" more suddenly. In the drafts of *Three Cantos* written during the summer of 1915, however, his use of "adventures" to structure the poem is especially apparent because he still surrounds each of the visions of the past with a dramatic frame. A portion of the manuscript headed "Fragment Modern World" begins with an account of a dream-vision of Bartolomeo D'Alviano (1455–1515), a condottiere who like Sigismundo Malatesta was equally at home as a commander of troops and patron of poets:

> Now I will fall asleep, will hear in swevyn,
> Move in the past, take note, glue ear to key holes,
> I was the valet to Ser D'Alviano
> In 1520 in the (Dolomites), came a bleared evening,
> Snow from the alps, north of Bergamo,
> A wheeze of light, short days, and cringing shadow,
>   al poco giorno ed al gran cerchio d'ombra,
> I brought the early candles   set them down
> On the bare table, took an arquebus
> to oil and clean, but the further door,
> piled up the fire.

As this passage continues, Pound presents a conversation between D'Alviano and Girolamo Fracastoro (a poet D'Alviano patronized), Giovanni Cotta (with whom D'Alviano founded the academy at Pordenone), and Andrea Navagero (who delivered D'Alviano's funeral oration). This portion of the manuscript would eventually coalesce (without the visionary introduction) in Canto 5 when all these men reappear to discuss the murder of Giovanni Borgia, Duke of Gandia. In Canto 5 Pound repeats the same line from Dante's sestina that he used in the draft ("al poco giorno ed al gran cerchio d'ombra"— "at the short day and at the great circle of shadow"):

> For the gossip of Naples' trouble drifts to North,
> Fracastor (lightning was midwife) Cotta, and Ser D'Alviano,
> Al poco giorno ed al gran cerchio d'ombra,
> Talk the talks out with Navighero,
> Burner of yearly Martials,
> > (The slavelet is mourned in vain)
> And the next comer says "Were nine wounds,
> "Four men, white horse. Held on the saddle before him . . ."
> Hooves clink and slick on the cobbles.
> Schiavoni . . . cloak . . . "Sink the damn thing!"
> Splash wakes that chap on the wood-barge.
> Tiber catching the nap, the moonlit velvet,
> A wet cat gleaming in patches.

Pound's source for these lines describing the murderers throwing Giovanni Borgia's corpse into the Tiber was a diary entry in William Roscoe's *The Life and Pontificate of Leo the Tenth*, which he read at Stone Cottage during the winter of 1915–16. The murder took place during the reign of Leo X—the same pope who brought Alhassan ibn Mohammed Alwazzan to Rome and named him Leo Africanus. So as Pound read the life of Leo X, mining it for luminous particulars for the poem, Yeats discovered more of the real history of his daimon. Both poets were getting the facts straight about the ghosts that inhabited their work.

After this glimpse of the Italian renaissance in the 1915 drafts, Pound turns to a tale he remembered from the *Mahābhārata*, which he had read during the first winter at Stone Cottage.

> Turn to Vyasa's wood,
> > "there's war about you!

The Huns are at the gates! The middle ages
Had some such squaling pig loose once a fortnight,
Get to your work, say of Vyasa's wood,
That Ubanuban, or whatever his name was,
Walked beneath snakelike trees, a tangle, a jungle,
That doubled octopus, your indian art, these squirms,
contortions, what can you hold of it.
This Ubanasan, plunged down in a cave,
                    full of black dusk,
Above him clung the spirits, shriveled and querulous
     Dark souls, souls of his fathers,
                                        crying for generation,
Hung by their heels, squeaking with little noises,
Crying for blood libations.

This passage begins with a reference to the mythology behind Yeats's "The Valley of the Black Pig"; in the notes to *The Wind Among the Reeds* Yeats wrote that "all over Ireland there are prophecies of the coming rout of the enemies of Ireland, in a certain Valley of the Black Pig"; he suggested that this battle would be "the battle between the manifest world and the ancestral darkness at the end of all things." What Pound mistakenly remembered as the story of "Ubanuban" or "Ubanasan" involves the same confrontation. In *The Book of the Beginning* (the first of the eighteen books of the *Mahābhārata*), Ugraśravas tells the story of Jaratkāru, who discovers his own ancestors "hanging in a cave with their faces down, hanging on to a single remaining strand of grass; and he saw a rat that lived in the cave gnawing slowly through this string. They were bereft of food and emaciated and wretched in their cave; and they suffered and yearned for deliverance." His ancestors, who have been condemned to this hell because their lineage is barren, enjoin Jaratkāru to return from the cave and marry. This tale must have seemed to Pound to be a distant parallel to Odysseus's descent into the underworld, which would first appear at the end of *Three Cantos* III before it became the program piece for the entire poem in Canto 1; Pound's comparativist mind had connected the story with an Irish legend, and he probably planned to sift it together with Homer later on. Although none of this Indian legend was preserved even in *Three Cantos*, Pound saw in the *Mahābhārata* another possible source of ghosts patched with histories.

In the final version of Canto 1 Pound no longer explicitly presents himself as a visionary, one who "falls asleep" and "moves in the past"; he emphasizes the textuality rather than the ghostliness of his historical figures. The final version of Canto 5 begins with a vision of the ancient city of Ecbatana, which then fades as Pound questions his "adventure" as a convincing mode for including history in the poem. But in the 1915 drafts for the passage, he flaunts his visionary prowess:

> "All is within us", purgatory and hell,
> Seeds full of will, the white of the inner bark
> the rich smooth colours,
>   the foreknowledges of trees,
> sense of the blade in seed, to each its pattern.
> Germinal, active, latent, full of will,
> Later to leap and soar,
>   willess, serene,
> Oh one could change it easy enough in talk.
> And no one vision will suit all of us.
>
> Say I have sat then, the low point of a cone,
> hollow and reaching out beyond the stars,
> reaches and depth, the massive parapets,
> Walls whereon chariots went by four abreast.
> Viae strade, 20 yards down, massive and wide,
> Armed toga'd people rushing along between,
> populous business that was none of mind.
>
> Egypt lies northward, the celestial nile,
> deep-blue, and wide, cuts through the low brown land,
> old men and camels working at water wheels.
>
> Night-blue beyond us, infinite seas and stars.
>
> But starting, always, pointed, the bottom vertex,
> always a vertex.

More than anything Pound wrote, these lines reveal that for his private purposes, Vorticism was a theory of intellectual vision. Yeats had concluded in his notes in *Visions and Beliefs* (along with Madame Blavatsky and William James) that the experience recounted in *An Adventure* was possible because all events, past and future, are present at once in the mind of God. For Pound, all events—from the Italian Renaissance to ancient Egypt or India—are present in the mind of the individual; the point of the vortex is the single consciousness, but it widens to include the entire universe: " 'All is within us', purgatory and hell."

Pound had first explained this theory of the "phantastikon" and the "germinal consciousness" in "Psychology and Troubadours," the lecture he presented to the Quest Society in 1912: "Their thoughts are in them as the thought of the tree is in the seed, or in the grass, or the grain, or the blossom." In 1913 he discussed the theory with Yeats. "I dare say we've the whole divina commedia going on inside of us," he told Dorothy Shakespear. "Yeats rather objects to cells being intelligent, but, I think the 'Paradiso' is a fair stab at presenting a developed 'phantastikon.' " As Pound groped to find a form for his long poem, he tried to do the same thing. His early drafts are more openly visionary even than the published *Three Cantos*, but that poem is similarly structured as a sequence of "adventures" in which Pound begins with a particular mind in a particular place and then (to borrow his own metaphor) extends the cone of the vortex to include a vision of a world that is normally beyond human comprehension, the Anima Hominus completed in the Anima Mundi.

The 1915 drafts do not include one essential task which Yeats undertook in *Per Amica* and which Pound began in "An Anachronism at Chinon": an investigation of the sources of the idea of the Anima Mundi in Neo-Platonism. But Pound did complete that task in the final version of *Three Cantos* III. While Yeats focused on Henry More, Pound chose John Heydon, a seventeenth-century Neo-Platonic occult philosopher whom he and Yeats read at Stone Cottage:

> Another's a half-cracked fellow—John Heydon,
> Worker of miracles, dealer in levitation,
> In thoughts upon pure form, in alchemy,
> Seer of pretty visions ("servant of God and secretary of nature").

Pound was particularly interested in Heydon's thoughts on "pure form." He invoked Heydon in his book on Gaudier-Brzeska (along with the clavichord he had purchased from Dolmetsch with Yeats's wedding gift) to explain the appeal of abstract forms in modern art: "A clavichord or a statue or a poem, wrought out of ages of knowledge, out of fine perception and skill, that some other man, that a hundred other men, in moments of weariness can wake beautiful sound with little effort, that they can be carried out of the realm of annoyance into the calm realm of truth, into the world unchanging, the world of fine animal life, the world of pure form. And John Heydon, long before our present day theorists, had written of the joys of pure form . . . inorganic, geometrical form, in his 'Holy Guide.' " Throughout *Gaudier-Brzeska*, Pound uses the word "form" in a Platonic rather than a material sense. Building on the visionary poetics of the Image, he asserts that the abstract forms of modern art are designed to invoke imperceptible realities. Not only Kandinsky's *On the Spiritual in Modern Art* (1911) but also John Heydon's *Holy Guide* (1662) supported Pound's doctrine. When he wrote in *Gaudier-Brzeska* that Heydon extolled the joys of "pure form" long before such modern authorities as Kandinsky, he was thinking of passages such as this one from *The Holy Guide*: in contrast to the beauty "that is acknowledged by the whole generations of men, to be in Trees, Flowers, and Fruits," Heydon suggests that his readers contemplate the "*Cone, Sphere*, or *Cylinder*," and then asks "whether the sight of these do not gratifie the minds of men more, and pretend to more elegancy of shape, than those rude cuttings or chippings of Freestone that fall from the Masons hands. . . . And it is observable, that if Nature shape any thing near this *Geometrical* accuracy, that we take notice of it with much content and pleasure, as if it be but exactly round, as there be abundance of such stones upon *Masque*, a hill in *Arabia*. . . . These stones, I say, gratifie our sight, as having a nearer cognation with the soul of man that is rational and intellectual."

The abstract forms designed by Epstein and Gaudier-Brzeska, Pound maintains, are similarly designed to invoke a reality beyond the senses. As Pound wrote in "Vorticism," the Image causes "form to come into being." And as Yeats explained in "Swedenborg, Mediums, and the Desolate Places," forms "are related by 'correspondence' or 'signature' to celestial incomprehensible realities." Pound made his Platonic conception of geometric form even clearer in his 1921 essay on Brancusi when he compared the contemplation of Brancusi's sculpture with gazing into a crystal ball. The two experiences, Pound explained, are both alike and dissimilar:

> Admitting the possibility of self-hypnosis by means of highly polished brass surfaces, the polish, from the sculptural point of view,

results merely from a desire for greater precision of the form, it is also a transient glory. But the contemplation of form or of formal-beauty leading into the infinite must be dissociated from the dazzle of crystal; there is a sort of relation, but there is the more important divergence; with the crystal it is a hypnosis, or a contemplative fixation of thought, or an excitement of the 'subconscious' or unconscious (whatever the devil they may be), and with the ideal form in marble it is an approach to the infinite *by form*, by precisely the highest possible degree of consciousness of formal perfection; as free of accident as any of the philosophical demands of a 'Paradiso' can make it.

By the use of perfect forms, as Heydon had suggested in the seventeenth century, the artist may capture the divine essence in his work. As Pound saw in Cicero, Richard of St. Victor, and Plato, contemplation can lead the individual soul to remember the world of perfection it knew when it was still part of what Cicero called "the Universal Divine Mind." It is just this kind of great memory that Pound had in mind when he offered one of the most famous images for his own work in the *Pisan Cantos*.

> This liquid is certainly a
>   property of the mind
> nec accidens est   but an element
>   in the mind's make-up
> est agens and functions   dust to a fountain pan otherwise
>   Hast 'ou seen the rose in the steel dust
>   (or swansdown ever?)
>   so light is the urging, so ordered the dark petals of iron
>   we who have passed over Lethe.

The rose in the steel dust, the design created when iron filings are passed over a magnet, is the manifestation of the perfect world ("Dove sta memoria") on earth. When Pound used the image in his 1915 essay on Vorticism, he compared the rose in the steel dust to the "automatic painting" performed by artists who claim that "the painting is done without volition on their part, that their hands are guided by 'spirits' or by some mysterious agency over which they have little or no control." Three decades later, when he returned to the rose in the steel dust in *Guide to Kulchur*, Pound compared the conception of eternal form which it embodied to Yeats—who had spent the last three decades immersed in his wife's automatic writing:

"I made it out of a mouthful of air"

wrote Bill Yeats in his heyday. The *forma*, the immortal *concetto*, the concept, the dynamic form which is like the rose pattern driven into the dead iron-filings by the magnet, not by material contact with the magnet itself, but separate from the magnet. Cut off by the layer of glass, the dust and filings rise and spring into order. Thus the *forma*, the concept rises from death.

Pound remembered Yeats's "He Thinks of Those who have Spoken Evil of his Beloved" from *The Wind Among the Reeds*, in which Yeats contrasts other men's passing fancies with the eternal statement of his own art: "But weigh this song with the great and their pride; / I made it out of a mouthful of air." Yeats would later theorize that the mouthful of air, the inexplicable inspiration, was not something he controlled but a voice from the Anima Mundi that came to him. He sensed little connection between his occult doctrines and Pound's *Cantos*, which he thought of as "a portable substitute for the British Museum." But that vast museum stands, as Richard Sieburth has suggested, as the incarnation of the Anima Mundi, the patterned abstract rose that corresponds to the eternal storehouse of all history: "The vast mnemonic system of the *Cantos* is nothing less than an attempt to create, within the space of a single poem, a simulacrum of that Great Memory which Pound (like Yeats) believed was as essential to the survival of culture as instincts are to the survival of the body."

Later in his life Pound returned to Heydon and his ideas of eternal memory and pure form in the *Rock-Drill Cantos*; as he composed them, he even wrote to George Yeats from St. Elizabeths, asking her to send the copy of Heydon's *Holy Guide* that he and Yeats had read at Stone Cottage. In the first *Three Cantos* that grew directly out of his Stone Cottage reading, however, Pound was not so interested in Heydon's conception of pure form as in his "adventures"—his accounts of visionary experience. Quoting the phrase Heydon uses to describe himself on the title page of the *Holy Guide* ("A Servant of God, and a Secretary of Nature"), Pound then recounts one of Heydon's visions in *Three Cantos* III.

> Thus Heydon, in a trance, at Bulverton,
> Had such a sight:
> Decked all in green, with sleeves of yellow silk

Slit to the elbow, slashed with various purples.
Her eyes were green as glass, her foot was leaf-like.
She was adorned with choicest emeralds,
And promised him the way of holy wisdom.
"Pretty green bank," began the half-lost poem.

Pound discovered this vision at the end of *The Rosie Cross Uncovered*, the sixth and final book of the *Holy Guide*, though he probably did not know that like almost everything else in the *Holy Guide*, the vision and the "half-lost poem" with which it concludes was plagiarized (in this case from Thomas Vaughan's *Lumen de Lumine*). Heydon presents this dream-vision at the end of the guide in order to "shew who taught these Secrets, and shewed me these things."

Walking upon the plain of *Bulverton Hill* to study Numbers and the nature of things, one evening, I could see between me and the light, a most exquisite Divine beauty; her frame neither long nor short, but a man decent stature; attir'd she was in thin loose Silks, but so green that I never saw the like, for the color was not earthly, in some places it was fancied, with gold & silver Ribbands, which looked like the Sun and Lyllies in the field of grass; her head was overcast with a thing floating Tiffany; which she held up, with one of her hands, and looked as it were from under it; her eyes were quick, fresh, and Celestial, but had something of a Start, as if she had been puzzled with a suddain occurence.

Pound thought that Heydon's vision was "lacking the vigor of gods"; in contrast, Pound's own visions in *Three Cantos* are "living, wood-white, / Smooth as the inner bark, and firm of aspect." Nevertheless Pound invokes Heydon as a precedent for his own "adventures" throughout *Three Cantos*. After recounting Heydon's vision Pound offers his own vision of Heydon. While *Three Cantos* I and II are peopled with Pound's visions of historical and mythical figures, only now in *Three Cantos* III does Pound establish himself as the inheritor of "the old way"—the tradition of the medieval dream-vision poem.

Take the old way, say I met John Heydon,
Sought out the place,
Lay on the bank, was "plungèd deep in swevyn;"
And saw the company—Layamon, Chaucer—

Pass each in his appropriate robes;
Conversed with each, observed the varying fashion.
And then comes Heydon.
                    "I have seen John Heydon."
Let us hear John Heydon!
                    "Omniformis
Omnis intellectus est"—thus he begins, by spouting half
    of Psellus.
(Then comes a note, my assiduous commentator:
Not Psellus De Daemonibus, but Porphyry's Chances,
In the thirteenth chapter, that "every intellect is omniform.")

Omniformis omnis intellectus est: every intellect is omniform, capable of assuming every shape. Three Cantos are based upon this
principle—Pound's ability, as inheritor of "the old way," to visualize
a "phantastikon" of ghosts and goddesses. Pound took the Latin
phrase from Porphyry's De Occasionibus, but Heydon also had a
great deal to say about the protean capabilities of the mind. Yeats's
notes for Lady Gregory's Visions and Beliefs reveal that Yeats was as
impressed as Pound with this aspect of the Holy Guide. Yeats borrows the same phrase ("servant of God and secretary of nature")
that Pound quotes in Three Cantos III to introduce Heydon: "John
Heydon, 'a servant of God and secretary of nature,' writing in 1662
in The Rosie Cross Uncovered which is the last book of his Holy
Guide says that a man may become one of the heroes: 'A hero,' he
writes, 'is a daemon, or good genius, and a genius a partaker of divine
things and a companion of the holy company of unbodied souls and
immortal angels who live according to their vehicles a versatile life,
turning themselves proteus-like into any shape." Yeats quotes this
passage from the same section of the Holy Guide from which Pound
adapted his dream-vision. And Yeats's point is the same as Pound's:
every intellect is capable of assuming every shape. Yeats had been
worrying this principle for some time. In his dialogue with Leo Africanus he had asked, "Does in fact the human mind possess a power
like that of the amoeba of multiplication by division?" and by the
time he wrote Per Amica Silentia Lunae he could state without question that "The soul has a plastic power, and can after death, or during
life, should the vehicle leave the body for a while, mould it to any
shape it will by an act of imagination." Probably without any consciousness that he was doing so, Yeats provided the theoretical foun-

dation of Pound's *Three Cantos* in his mid-life meditation on his own work.

While Pound found precedent for the poet's imaginative powers in the dream-visions of Chaucer and Heydon, Yeats pointed out that there were more recent precursors. After quoting Heydon in his notes for *Visions and Beliefs*, Yeats set out "to prove that the shape-changer is a part of general literature." Because he wrote at Stone Cottage, he had "but Wordsworth and Milton" at hand, and he took his examples from the first book of *Paradise Lost* and from Wordsworth's "The White Doe of Rylstone."

> When the white doe of Rylstone shows itself at the church door according to its Sunday custom, one has one tale to tell, another another, but an Oxford student will have it that it is the faery that loved a certain "shepherd-lord."
>
> " 'Twas said that she all shapes could wear."

And Milton writes like any Platonist of his time:

> "For Spirits, when they please,
> Can either sex assume, or both; so soft
> And uncompounded is their essence pure,
> Not ty'd or manacled with joint or limb,
> Nor founded on the brittle strength of bones,
> Like cumbrous flesh; but, in what shape they choose,
> Dilated or condensed, bright or obscure,
> Can execute their aery purposes,
> And works of love or enmity fulfill."

Unlike Yeats, Pound was not interested in exploring these Romantic precedents for the mechanisms of *Three Cantos*; he preferred to locate his ancestry in Heydon. Yet as much as Keats's "Sleep and Poetry," *Three Cantos* is a paean to the poetic imagination and its ability to envision distant realities. As Yeats remarks in *Per Amica* (quoting an entry from his diary), *Three Cantos* reveals the attempt to "imagine ourselves as different from what we are." Pound is the poet Yeats describes turning "from our own age" and trying "to feel Chaucer nearer than the daily paper."

Although *Per Amica* may be seen to provide a kind of commentary on *Three Cantos*, Pound's poem holds a place in his poetic development that is closer to that which "Sleep and Poetry" holds in Keats's: both works are tentative and somewhat immature, a testing ground for structures and concerns both poets would treat with greater power. In contrast, *Per Amica Silentia Lunae* is a work of mid-life re-evaluation rather than youthful initiation. Pound recognized the in-adequacy of his work, and except for the translation from Divus's Homer which concludes the third canto, almost all of *Three Cantos* would be scuttled when Pound reorganized the opening of the poem for *A Draft of XVI Cantos* (1925).

It has become a critical commonplace that Pound's reading of *Ulysses* gave the impetus for the reworking of the early cantos and led Pound to make the Odyssean passage from *Three Cantos* III the program piece for the entire poem. I think we can also see that long before Pound read Joyce's masterpiece, his investigation of the oc-cult with Yeats led him to include the passage in the poem in the first place. After their first winter at Stone Cottage, Pound wrote Yeats a letter offering him a suggestion for his essay on "Swedenborg, Mediums, and the Desolate Places." "I don't want to be stuffy about Swedenborg's originality," wrote Pound, "but I have just come on a line in the 11th book of the Odyssy [sic] . . . 'The departing soul hovers about as a dream'—it might not make a bad chapter heading or motto."

Yeats did not use this line but he did conclude his essay by quoting some other equally appropriate lines from the eleventh book of the *Odyssey* (in Lang and Butcher's 1879 translation):

> Certainly in most writings before our time the body of an apparition was held for a brief, artificial, dreamy, half-living thing. . . . [A passage comes to mind] in the *Odyssey* where Odysseus speaks not with 'the mighty Heracles', but with his phan-tom, for he himself 'hath joy at the banquet among the deathless gods and had to wife Hebe of the fair ankles, child of Zeus and Hera of the golden sandals', while all about the phantom 'there was a clamour of the dead, as it were fowls flying everywhere in fear, and he, like black night with bow uncased, and shaft upon the string, fiercely glancing around like one in the act to shoot'.

Like the Pound of Canto 1, Yeats was interested in speaking with Homeric phantoms. And although Pound did not translate any of the lines Yeats quotes in this passage, Yeats does refer to the pouring of blood for ghosts in both of the essays he wrote for *Visions and Be-*

liefs in the West of Ireland. In "Witches and Wizards and Irish Folk-lore," he ends the tale of a man who draws blood from a ghost by recalling "the measure of blood Odysseus poured out for the shades." In "Swedenborg, Mediums, and the Desolate Places," after giving many examples of the invocation of spirits, Yeats concludes that "All these shadows have drunk from the pool of blood and become delirious." Even before their first winter at Stone Cottage Yeats wrote in his "Preliminary Examination" of the automatic writing of Elizabeth Radcliffe that in hearing the voices of the dead, "One remembers also the shades before they drank the blood-offering of Odysseus. They are not of us and it is but natural that they come to us with difficulty." Finally, in *Per Amica Silentia Lunae*, written while *Three Cantos* was going to press in 1917, Yeats wrote that a spirit may become visible "by building into its substance certain particles drawn from the body of a medium. . . . The witch, going beyond the medium, offered to the slowly animating phantom certain drops of her blood." So begins *The Cantos*.

In their joint investigations of occult legends and doctrines, Yeats and Pound must have shared their thoughts on the eleventh book of the *Odyssey*. When this passage from the *Odyssey* is read in the context of Yeats's essays, we can see more clearly that *The Cantos* begin with a seance, an invocation of the dead. The line which Pound suggested to Yeats as a motto for "Swedenborg, Mediums, and the Desolate Places" ("the departing soul hovers about as a dream") comes from the passage in the eleventh book of the *Odyssey* which describes the appearance of Anticlea, Odysseus's mother, in the pool of blood. In the version of Canto 1 which now stands at the opening of *The Cantos* this particular passage does not appear; however, Pound did include it in the version of his Homeric translation which concludes *Three Cantos*:

> Came then Anticlea, to whom I answered:
> 'Fate drives me on through these deeps: I sought Tiresias.'
> I told her news of Troy, and thrice her shadow
>   Faded in my embrace.
> Then had I news of many faded women—
> Tyro, Alcmena, Chloris—
> Heard out their tales by that dark fosse, and sailed
> By sirens and thence outward and away,
> And unto Circe buried Elpenor's corpse.

Pound did not include the precise line he suggested to Yeats in this condensed translation of Anticlea's appearance, yet the shadowy nature of the departing soul is made clear by Pound's inclusion of Odysseus's attempt to embrace his mother's shade. Pound probably cut this passage from the final version of Canto 1 for the same reason that he thought the passage was appropriate to Yeats's discussion of departing souls: the lines had occult connotations. When Pound yanked his translation of Divus's Homer from *Three Cantos*, deleting his meditation on Heydon's visions, he no longer wished to emphasize the spiritualist overtones of the *nekuia*. The Stone Cottage years had come to an end.

≽≼

Read side by side, *Three Cantos* and *Per Amica Silentia Lunae* emerge as the culmination and synthesis of three winters of collaborative research. Their range of reference is remarkably similar: Noh drama and Renaissance Neoplatonism figure largely in both, and each work contains passing references to most of the authors in the Stone Cottage curriculum—Doughty, Landor, Wordsworth, Browning, and Homer filtered through John Heydon or Henry More. In addition to these allusions, *Three Cantos* and *Per Amica* share some of the same attitudes toward poetic experience. As Ronald Bush has pointed out to me, both works reveal a poet groping for a new life. Each work is a kind of protracted crisis-ode, an assertion of visionary powers haunted by the suspicion that these powers are fading fast. At the end of the "Anima Hominis" portion of *Per Amica*, Yeats imagines himself as the aged, desiccated Wordsworth, and at the end of *Three Cantos* I, Pound surveys his "adventures" and calls them "sweet lie[s]": "And now it's all but truth and memory, / Dimmed only by the attritions of long time."

Pound was thirty-one years old when he published *Three Cantos* in 1917; Yeats was fifty-one when he completed *Per Amica* in the same year. And so these similar works of imaginative crisis occupy different positions in the two poets' careers. In *Three Cantos* Pound asks the question that Yeats had asked after he completed *The Wind Among the Reeds* as a much younger man: having perfected one mode of poetry (in Pound's case the Imagist lyrics collected in *Lustra*), how do I continue to be a poet without either repeating myself or risking an unmastered style? In *Per Amica Silentia Lunae* Yeats asks the question Pound would not be forced to ask until he wrote the *Pisan Cantos* as a much older man: having spent all my youth as a poet, having sacrificed my personal life to my ambition and having little to show for it, how do I turn to something outside myself for nurture and solace? A sentence Lawrence Lipking has written to describe *Per Amica* describes the *Pisan Cantos* equally as well: "The book seems half a prayer or desperate plea for some outward sign of regeneration."

In both the *Pisan Cantos* and *Per Amica Silentia Lunae* the poets look for that outward sign of regeneration in memory, both personal and Platonic, the Anima Hominis drenched in the Anima Mundi. At the climax of his prose poem Yeats recounts his experience of a feeling of blessedness that he would return to in the fourth segment of "Vacillation":

> At certain moments, always unforeseen, I become happy, most commonly when at hazard I have opened some book of verse. Sometimes it is my own verse when, instead of discovering new technical flaws, I read with all the excitement of the first writing. Perhaps I am sitting in some crowded restaurant, the open book beside me, or closed, my excitement having overbrimmed the page. I look at the strangers near as if I had known them all my life, and it seems strange that I cannot speak to them: everything fills me with affection, I have no longer any fears or any needs; I do not even remember that this happy mood must come to an end. It seems as if the vehicle had suddenly grown pure and far extended and so luminous that the images from *Anima Mundi*, embodied there and drunk with that sweetness, would, like a country drunkard who has thrown a wisp into his own thatch, burn up time.

Fearing that his psychological isolation might envelop him totally (as it had enveloped Wordsworth), Yeats becomes possessed by the universal soul of the world. Pound, writing in physical conditions that mirrored his prison of consciousness with frightening precision, recounts a similar experience at the climax of the *Pisan Cantos*. The eyes of his composite daimon appear to him in his isolation to tell him that "What thou lovest well remains." And for a moment, like Yeats, he feels that he could burn up time.

> there came new subtlety of eyes into my tent,
>   whether of spirit or hypostasis,

but what the blindfold hides
or at carneval
                 nor any pair showed anger
Saw but the eyes and stance between the eyes,
colour, diastasis,
     careless or unaware it had not the
     whole tent's room
nor was place for the full $\Sigma\iota\delta\grave{\omega}s$
interpass, penetrate
     casting but shade beyond the other lights
         sky's clear
         night's sea
         green of the mountain pool
         shown from the unmasked eyes in half-mask's space.

Part of the lost world restored to Pound at Pisa—as we have seen over and over again—was the time he spent with Yeats at Stone Cottage. In the years that passed between, Pound often expressed antipathy for Yeats's work. Although *Three Cantos* and *Per Amica* are the parallel endpoints to three years of collaboration, the two works did not seem to Pound to be related—except by their inadequacy. "I don't think Yeats' *Silentia Lunae* hangs together," Pound wrote in 1918. "And I find *Noh* unsatisfactory. . . . it's all too damn soft." It is important to see that Pound's criticism of Yeats is linked to his rejection of his own work on the Noh plays and the early cantos. His impatience with Yeats's spooks is a reflection of his discomfort with his own interest in the occult. Pound considered Yeats "on psychism" to be " 'reasonable' to a point," and that point was the one Pound himself was unwilling to cross. Yet in 1918 Pound quite remarkably realized that he had his own blind fanaticism: Yeats "will be quite sensible," he told John Quinn, "till some question of ghosts or occultism comes up, [and] then he is subject to a curious excitement, twists everything to his theory, usual quality of mind goes." The same thing happened to Pound in regard to his own esoteric religion of social credit and usury. He admitted to Quinn that he himself had a "touch" of Yeats's fanaticism when it came to Christianity, but he tried to defend his fervour, maintaining that "most of the tyrannies of modern life" are "based on Xtn taboos, and can't really be got rid of radically until Xtianity is taken lightly and sceptically, until, that is, it drifts back into the realm of fairy-lore and picturesque superstition." Ironically, the ancient realm of fairies and superstitions was the world the fanatic Yeats opened more fully to Pound at Stone Cottage, and *Three Cantos* is peopled with the ghosts, nymphs, centaurs, oak-girls, and panisks of Ashdown Forest.

Although Pound hid these occult origins of *The Cantos*, another interest he shared with Yeats left a permanent stamp on the poem. In "The Constant Preaching to the Mob" a brief tirade published in *Poetry* magazine in 1916, Pound repeated once again the attitude toward his audience that he had worked out with Yeats: poems are "made for no man's entertainment," he said before quoting a few world-weary lines from the Anglo-Saxon "Wanderer." "Such poems are not made for after-dinner speakers," he continued, "nor was the eleventh book of the Odyssey." For Pound, Odysseus became the archetype of the exiled artist, the poet armed with magical powers against a bourgeoisie that, as he and Yeats had pointed out to George Moore, is not so much a social class as a state of mind. Pound also wrote in "The Constant Preaching to the Mob" that the lines he quoted from the "Wanderer" ("For the doom-eager bindeth fast his blood-bedraggled heart in his breast") were "an apology for speaking at all, and speech only pardoned because his captain and all the seafaring men and companions are dead." When Pound wrote this essay, the reality of his artistic community, the Brothers Minor, had ended. Yeats would not appear in *The Cantos* again until after the Second World War when all of Pound's own companions were dead. But the quality in Yeats which Pound admired most, his refusal to compromise with his audience, hangs, for better and for worse, over the entire poem.

The Secret Society
of Modernism

Pound began his first "Status Rerum" (1913) by proclaiming that "Mr. Yeats [is] the only poet worthy of serious study." In "Status Rerum—the Second," published in April 1916 after three years at Stone Cottage, his opinion had not changed: "Looking at the names of English writers in my first *Status Rerum*, I find that not one of them has bettered his position one iota. Only Mr. Yeats and Mr. Hueffer have done work worthy of notice. The rest have either stagnated or relapsed completely into silence." When Yeats's new edition of *Responsibilities and Other Poems* appeared later that year, Pound made his praise more specific.

> [Yeats] is the only poet of his decade who has not gradually faded into mediocrity, who has not resigned himself to gradually weaker echoes of an earlier outburst. . . .
> There is a new robustness; there is the tooth of satire which is, in Mr. Yeats' case, too good a tooth to keep hidden. *The Coat*, the wild wolf-dog that will not praise his fleas, *The Scholars*, are all the sort of poem that we would gladly read more of. There are a lot of fools to be killed and Mr. Yeats is an excellent slaughtermaster, when he will but turn from ladies with excessive chevelure appearing in pearl-pale nuances.

With these sentences, as so many times before, Pound was tracing both Yeats's and his own development from a *fin de siècle* "dolce stil nuove" to a poetry that grappled more tough-mindedly with modern-day realities; as Yeats's "Upon a Dying Lady" and Pound's "Portrait d'une Femme" reveal, both poets felt that the songs and Ladies of the troubadours were no more. When Yeats told Olivia Shakespear that Elkin Mathews was complaining about the frankness of some of Pound's poems in *Lustra* ("not only men come into this shop, *but ladies*," said Mathews), she replied, "Well, I suppose we are ladies of *some* sort. Or if we aren't, who IS? ! ! !"

Yeats had revealed his satiric tooth as early as 1910 with the epigrammatic lines of *The Green Helmet* addressed "To a Poet, who would have me praise certain bad poets, imitators of his and mine." This poem, concluding with the wolf-dog that will not praise its fleas, was one of Pound's touchstones for the "new" Yeats, and he invoked it in both his 1914 and 1916 reviews of *Responsibilities*. As we have seen, not only did Yeats strike this satiric note in his poetry long before Pound, but it was due to Yeats's more vigorous effort to transform his style that Pound (the imitator) came to write the epigrammatic poems collected in *Lustra* (1916) instead of his own pearl-pale nuances.

> Nine adulteries, 12 liaisons, 64 fornications
>   and something approaching a rape
> Rest nightly upon the soul of our delicate friend Florialis,
> And yet the man is so quiet and reserved in demeanour
> That he passes for both bloodless and sexless.
> Bastidides, on the contrary, who both talks and
>   writes of nothing save copulation,
> Has become the father of twins,
> But he accomplished this feat at some cost;
> He had to be four times cuckold.

Yeats felt that with these lines Pound had grasped "the true quality, the real, the hellenic epigram," but Pound made the satiric tooth his own in a way that Yeats did not, and the older poet confessed that *Lustra* as a whole offered "no asylum for his affections." That did not prevent Yeats from helping Pound to get the book published after they left Stone Cottage for good in 1916. He joked with Pound, suggesting that Coburn's charismatic photograph of Pound (originally planned as the frontispiece of *Lustra*) "ought to placate the public and console them for the verses that follow." But Yeats also persuaded Pound's publisher, Elkin Mathews, to reconsider when the suppression of Lawrence's *The Rainbow* had made him disinclined to bring out the more indecorous poems of *Lustra*. Pound sent Mathews several long, raging letters and composed a statement saying that the "deletions in this book are none of mine and I do not give them my approval. . . . If the writers of the past had been dependent upon the present regulations or habits of book-printing the following authors and books could not have come down to us as they stand, they would have been either suppressed or interfered with in some way." Pound then offered a list of authors which included Sappho, Catullus, Horace, Villon, Rabelais, Dante, Shakespeare, Pope, Fielding, Flaubert, and Tolstoi. "I write for a few hundred people," he continued, "who are already aware of the classics, and who will be for the most part greatly surprised that any such difficulty in printing exists in this twentieth century."

A copy of the proofs of *Lustra*, with poems marked for deletion, was sent to Yeats who then (as Pound told Harriet Monroe) went to see Mathews and "quoted Donne, and said a man ought to be allowed to be as indecent as he liked." On May 29, 1916, Yeats then told Mathews that he agreed with everything Pound had said about classic authors. He added that since Pound was willing to leave some poems out of the collection, they should be able to come to an agreement. The next day Pound explained to Mathews that his poems were "clean cut satire, written in the speech of the best English classics and with the vocabulary of all the classics that ever were." Finally, two versions of *Lustra* were published. A trade edition excluded nine poems, but a private edition, available only by request, contained the full range of Pound's ire.

By 1916 Pound had made Yeats's own "tooth of satire" seem rather dull in comparison to his own; Yeats, Pound recognized, had already moved on to a different mode. In his introduction to Pound's *Certain Noble Plays of Japan* Yeats had written that "Realism is created for . . . all those whose minds, educated alone by schoolmasters and newspapers, are without the memory of beauty and emotional subtlety." In contrast, Pound was deeply invigorated by what he thought of as Joyce's "realism," and so in his review of *Responsibilities and Other Poems* conceded, after mentioning Yeats's satires, that despite his "occasional bits of realism, the tone of the new book is romantic. Mr. Yeats is a romanticist, symbolist, occultist, for better or worse, now and for always. That does not matter. What does matter is that he is the only one left who has sufficient intensity of temperament to turn these modes into art." Yeats's intensity, his commitment to the seriousness of poetry, was (for Pound) the crucial aspect of his work. Pound knew that Yeats was at heart "a romanticist, symbolist, occultist" because he had already seen the poems of *The Wild Swans at Coole* which were not printed in the new edition of *Responsibilities*.

When the June 1917 issue of the *Little Review* appeared under Pound's auspices, it contained seven poems Yeats would collect in *The Wild Swans at Coole*: "The Wild Swans at Coole," "Presences," "Men Improve with the Years," "A Deep-Sworn Vow," "The Collar-Bone of a Hare," "Broken Dreams," and "In Memory." A year later Pound looked back over these poems and declared that he had "published some of Mr. Yeats's best poems, poems obviously destined for posterity as are those in his 'Wind Among the Reeds.' " The omission of the satiric poems of *Responsibilities* from this appraisal of Yeats's finest work is telling. Pound read Yeats's career not as Eliot's New Critical progeny would do, sensing a constant progress from the poetry of the Nineties through *Responsibilities* to *The Wild Swans at Coole* and beyond; although he valued the work of Yeats's middle period, Pound saw that between 1900 and 1916 Yeats was unsure of himself, and he read Yeats's career in the same way that Harold Bloom has: "*The Wind Among the Reeds* is a better volume of poetry than Yeats was to write until *The Wild Swans at Coole*." For contemporary readers of Yeats, the irony of Pound's judgment of the older poet's poetic development is that Pound has so often been credited with producing the Yeats of *Responsibilities*. A more careful reading of their relationship shows that Yeats was far more influential in producing the Pound of *Lustra*. Pound's poetic development during these years was a steady climb; being the apprentice he had nowhere else to go.

Pound was particularly attracted to poems such as "The Wild Swans at Coole" because in them Yeats once and for all rejected the nostalgia which had clouded the poems written about Maud Gonne during the second Stone Cottage winter.

> I have looked upon those brilliant creatures,
> And now my heart is sore.
> All's changed since I, hearing at twilight,
> The first time on this shore,

> The bell-beat of their wings above my head,
> Trod with a lighter tread.

These lines, with their personal gloss on the "All changed, changed utterly" of "Easter 1916," brought Yeats firmly into the present. His memoirs of the Nineties were written, he no longer yearned for forgotten beauty. Pound saw a confidence in this verse, emotionally and stylistically, which he had not seen since *The Wind Among the Reeds*—the achievement against which Pound measured all of Yeats's later work.

"Easter 1916" itself was another poem which showed Pound that Yeats had finally transformed himself into a new poet equal in power to the early "romanticist, symbolist, occultist." On the day after Easter, just a few weeks after Pound and Yeats finished the rehearsals for the premiere of *At the Hawk's Well*, the Dublin post-office was blown up. Yeats had remarked in his introduction to *Certain Noble Plays of Japan* that he had written the play "for my own country." Now the country required something different, and on May 11th, the day before the leaders of the uprising were executed, Yeats told Lady Gregory that he was "trying to write a poem." The line that would not leave his head was "terrible beauty has been born again."

> We know their dream; enough
> To know they dreamed and are dead;
> And what if excess of love
> Bewildered them till they died?
> I write it out in a verse—
> MacDonagh and MacBride
> And Connolly and Pearse
> Now and in time to be,
> Wherever green is worn,
> Are changed, changed utterly:
> A terrible beauty is born.

Reading these lines in 1916 (the general public would not receive them until 1920), Pound saw the synthesis of Yeats's effort to remake himself as a poet, and he saw that the excursion into satire had been one stage along the way. Like the poems of *Lustra*, "Easter 1916" addresses contemporary events ("I had no idea that any public event could so deeply move me," said Yeats), but Pound saw that Yeats remained "a romanticist, symbolist, occultist" as he transfigured those events by the very power of poetic incantation. The surging lines of "Easter 1916" are as distinct as they could possibly be from the wind whispering in the reeds, but as Pound recognized, they were born "of a no less powerful magic."

At first, Pound was not so moved by the Easter rebellion as Yeats was; on May 1st he told John Quinn that he was "going out to chaff Yeats about the Dublin republic. He don't like republics, he likes queens preferably dead ones." After discussing the event with Yeats, his tone darkened considerably:

> There seems to be no doubt [he wrote Quinn] that Ireland has been bungled, but damn it all, all the brains in the country are turned into something else. etc. etc. etc. etc.
>
> You are dead right when you say the struggle is for something bigger than the rights of small nations, and that the self-preservation is more than the sentimental appeal.
>
> . . . Damn it all, the government, i.e. the executive must *know*, I mean they must understand *why* things happen if they are to act intelligently. In the case of the Irish outbreaks they didn't know. Nobody seems to have known. Yeats certainly didn't know.

Pound went on to explain some of Yeats's thoughts about the uprising, thoughts that cast a cold eye on Yeats's own comment about the "dream" of the revolutionaries in "Easter 1916": Yeats, Pound told Quinn, "has said for years that Pearse was half-cracked and that he wouldn't be happy until he was hanged. He seemed to think Pearse had Emmet mania, same as some other lunatics think they are Napoleon or God." That was one way to interpret the Easter uprising; another is suggested by the note Yeats appended to "September 1913" for the new edition of *Responsibilities and Other Poems:* "'Romantic Ireland's dead and gone' sounds old-fashioned now. It seemed true in 1913, but I did not foresee 1916. The late Dublin Rebellion, whatever one can say of its wisdom, will long be remembered for its heroism. 'They weighed so lightly what they gave,' and gave too in some cases without hope of success." Nobility, as Pound saw early on, was still Yeats's highest value. And when Pound constructed his postwar hell in Canto 14, he included, sunk beneath the "sows eating their litters,"

> reversed, foot-palm to foot-palm
>   hand-palm to hand-palm, the agents provocateurs
> The murderers of Pearse and MacDonagh.

The Easter rebellion quickly pushed Stone Cottage and *At the Hawk's Well* into the past, and Yeats put the uprising behind him just as quickly, spending July and August in France (where he proposed to the newly widowed Maud Gonne MacBride) instead of returning to Dublin to manage the Abbey Theatre. He had suggested Pound as his replacement. "I recognize that the 'Abbey" will be a circus," Pound told Quinn. "Still there is a salary, AND I should only be there for four months, AND it might be entertaining, AND W.B.Y. probably would have had to give up his trip to France if I hadn't said I would take the job *in case he couldn't get anyone else.*" The Brothers Minor were still looking out for one another's welfare, but Lady Gregory rejected the plan, and St. John Greer Ervine was engaged as manager instead of Pound. After three winters of collaboration, Pound and Yeats began to go their very separate ways. Yeats returned to Stone Cottage in 1917, not with Pound but as Pound had done during the summer of 1914: with his new wife. Yeats and Georgie Hyde-Lees were married on October 20th. A few years earlier, on a holiday with Dorothy Shakespear, Georgie Hyde-Lees had seen a vision of Pound sitting at the top of one of the trees of Ashdown Forest. When she and Yeats spent their honeymoon in Forest Row, on the other side of the forest from Stone Cottage, she began the automatic writing that would crystallize in *A Vision.* A new order of the secret society of modernism was founded.

When Pound first came to Stone Cottage in 1913 he still dreamed of a Brothers Minor; he wrote with an unjaded excitement that his "gang" was finally coming together. His time with Yeats provided solace (both economic and emotional) from the war's destruction of his dream of a larger artistic community. Yet if Pound came to Ashdown Forest hoping to found the Brothers Minor, he left with the members of the entire secret society of modernism firmly in place. Yeats had introduced him to Joyce's work, and *A Portrait of the Artist as Young Man* appeared in the *Egoist.* The *Catholic Anthology*, including both Yeats and Eliot, was planned at Stone Cottage as a riposte to the "democratic beer-garden" that the once exclusive Imagist movement had become. Blunt had been properly honored, Synge, Gaudier-Brzeska, and the Rhymers properly eulogized, and George Moore and Amy Lowell denied titles in the ranks of the nobility. By 1916, when Pound left Stone Cottage for good, both the members and the attitudes of his secret society were set for many years to come. And throughout the Stone Cottage years, to borrow Richard Ellmann's phrase, Yeats held eminent domain: if rarely an exemplar of modernist sensibility, he was a constant model for the noble mission of an artistic elite and a direct connection to its aristocratic heritage.

The metaphors of the occult—the brothers, the secret societies— serve to characterize the Stone Cottage winters well because Pound and Yeats used the metaphors themselves. No matter what their interests or activities, one keynote echoes through their work: the opposition of the artist's aristocratic "state of mind" to the unpurged sensibility of the "mob." The sentence A. E. Waite (Yeats's colleague in the Order of the Golden Dawn) used to describe occult circles in *The Real History of the Rosicrucians* (1887) applies equally as well to the modernists' conception of their own function in society: "Beneath the broad tide of human history there flow the stealthy undercurrents of the secret societies, which frequently determine in the depths the changes that take place upon the surface."

Yeats wrote in "The Autumn of the Body" (1898) that the "arts are . . . about to take upon their shoulders the burdens that have fallen from the shoulders of priests." While Pound was an instructor at Wabash College in 1907 he wrote to Viola Baxter that she should read "all of Wm. Butler Yeats that you can lay hold of" and then went on to explain his own aesthetic: "Religion I have defined as 'Another of those numerous failures resulting from an attempt to popularize art.'" At Stone Cottage, artists adopted the rhetoric if not the burden of priests. When Joyce's *Portrait* appeared in the *Egoist,* it was printed side by side with Olivia Shakespear's translation of *Le Comte de Gabalis:* the juxtaposition is revealing. As Stephen Dedalus renounces the Jesuits for a higher order, the priesthood of the imagination, Olivia Shakespear's "Memoirs of a Charming Person" reveals how the literature of the occult was transformed into the sacred texts of the secret society of modernism. In another translation published in 1914 by an actual occult society called "The Brothers," *Le Comte de Gabalis* ended with this paragraph:

> Thus ends the Discourse of the Comte de Gabalis. He returned the next day and brought the speech that he had delivered to the Subterranean Peoples. It was marvelous! I would publish it with the series of Discourses which a certain Vicomtesse and I have had with this Illustrious Man, were I certain that all my readers would have the proper spirit, and not take it amiss that I amuse myself

at the expense of fools. If I see that people are willing to let my
book accomplish the good that it is capable of doing, and are not
unjustly suspecting me of seeking to give credit to the Occult Sciences under the pretence of ridiculing them, I shall continue to
delight in Monsieur le Comte, and shall soon be able to publish
another volume.

Throughout *Le Comte de Gabalis* the narrator's attitude towards the
teachings of the Comte is always ambiguous and often ironic. That
ambiguity is swept away by "The Brothers," who offer annotations
that double the length of the romance as well as a translation that
tips towards the certainty of belief. Olivia Shakespear, whose title
for her translation suggests drawing-room comedy rather than cabala,
translated the final paragraph quite differently:

> Thus he ended our conversation. I had many others with him,
> and would give their substance were I sure that my readers would
> recognize the fact that I am no believer in the Secret Sciences,
> whilst pretending to laugh at them. If I were certain of not being
> misunderstood on this point, I would go on amusing myself with
> the Count, and would soon give another volume to the world.

Unlike "The Brothers," Olivia Shakespear is not worried about the
"proper spirit" of her readers or concerned that her translation "accomplish the good it is capable of doing." Furthermore, her prose
is constructed to make sure she is misunderstood on this point: "I
am no believer in the Secret Sciences, whilst pretending to laugh at
them." The awkward syntax and peculiar logic of this phrase obscure
the issue of belief altogether. Even the endings of the more famous
sacred books of modernism—"Shantih shantih shantih" or "yes I
said yes I will yes"—are, by comparison, less ambiguous because of
the resonance of their incantatory power. After Pound and Yeats
read *Le Comte de Gabalis* in the privacy of Stone Cottage, Olivia
Shakespear transformed it into "Memoirs of a Charming Person" in
order to introduce the secret society of ⹁readers to the doctrines of
" 'symbolism' in its profounder sense" while requiring them to believe only in the sanctity of modernism.

From 1911 to 1916 Pound often felt that he and Yeats were
joined "in one movement" to preserve that sanctity, but the two
poets never again worked together so closely after Stone Cottage,
and, although they sustained their friendship, their sympathy for
each other's work diminished. In a sense, the final winter at Stone

Cottage was the beginning of the end of their secret society. That winter ended dramatically, as Pound remembered in Canto 83.

> did we ever get to the end of Doughty:
>> The Dawn in Britain?
>>>>> perhaps not
>> Summons withdrawn, sir.)
> (bein' aliens in prohibited area).

In the first days of February 1916 a policeman walked down the hidden lane from Coleman's Hatch to Stone Cottage and told Pound that he and his wife were aliens in a prohibited area; wartime regulations required that they report to the local police station, and they had not done so. Yeats, who was amused, explained the problem to John Quinn: "I think people here are cheerful about the war. All except Ezra Pound who having spent the last six weeks with me here in Sussex without discovering that we are in a 'prohibited area,' has to appear before the magistrate on the charge of not registering himself and to prove himself no spy. After his third visit from a policeman he left the house this afternoon with such energy that he tore the coat hook from the wall." Quinn, who was also amused, replied that "Pound's experience with regard to the prohibited area was a little bit like my smoking in the outer room of the income tax office, when you went there on your income tax when the little cockney Englishman, greater in circumference than in height, came out and said: 'See ere, don't yu know ware you arr? Yu arr in er Majesty's tax orrfice. Yu mite as well smauke in Sommerset aause.' "

Pound himself was not amused, and he battled the authorities with his characteristic excess of energy. He wrote to Lucy Masterman, asking her to persuade her husband (who was a member of Asquith's cabinet) to intercede: "I am so unused to be summoned before courts of law . . . and the local police do not inspire confidence as they seem most vague as to their duties. There is no copy of regulations in the post-office where one would naturally expect to find such notices and I signed all the blanks they brought round when they got sufficiently animated to do so and I wasted my substance driving cross country to Grinstead when requested to go there." Pound added that his case was surely doomed since "any proper rural magistrate" would "probably see red at the first sight of an artist of any sort."

Pound must have continued to play the part of an "artist" even in 1916, perhaps with the same turquoise earring and velvet jacket he had sported in London. Perhaps it was the "respectable elderish female" whom Pound saw spying in the windows of Stone Cottage who tipped off the police about the questionable characters renting the Welfare farmhouse. However conspicuous as an alien or artist, Pound was impatient for results and persuaded Yeats to write to G. H. Mair before hearing from C.F.G. Masterman. While conveying the seriousness of the situation, Yeats simultaneously offered a hint of his own amusement at Pound's urgency:

> When I arrived home tonight I found my household disturbed. A policeman had been round and Ezra Pound and his wife had to go off to the Police Station at East Grinstead, seven miles. It seems that we are in a prohibited area, and we never knew it, and what makes it worse we have been in it for the last six weeks. The trouble is that Ezra Pound is an American and that his wife though she has never been out of Europe in her life has become an American by marrying him. I have cross questioned the two aliens carefully and they seem to be generally observing the laws, but can not give me a coherent account of what the police want. The police are referring the matter, it seems, to some higher policeman who may descend upon us any day.

Yeats went on to explain that they were originally told that the prohibited area was a fifteen-mile belt bordering the sea (Stone Cottage is about twenty miles from the coast), but were then informed that it included the whole country. "Ezra is my secretary at present," Yeats continued, "and I am very busy and it would greatly upset my plans if we have to move out of this."

The day after Yeats dictated this letter to Pound, Pound reconsidered his tactics and decided to make the trip into London to obtain a passport at the American embassy. Yeats wrote a second letter to Mair, explaining the new plan of attack, and after the affair was settled, Pound explained the outcome to his father: "The Home Office has kindly saved me from the depredations of the Sussex authorities, as we have been here some time without finding out that we ought to have registered. Finally managed to get identified. Yeats took a few shots at it, got a letter from the poet laureate which would have hanged all three of us in any country in Europe, a perfect ecstasy of timidity on old [Robert] Bridges part, derived from reading Conan Doyle." The laureate's letter is a comic masterpiece.

My dear Yeats,

    I have received your letter asking me to write something to identify Ezra Pound.

    I do not know how much you are yourself suspected. If you have been able to identify yourself to the Chief Constable, there should be no further difficulty—but he may be open to the suspicion that you yourself are not what you pretend to be. As your letter was typewritten, though your signature was all right enough, I thought I would telegraph to your housekeeper in town asking where you were; but I have had no answer and must write this before post time.

    Assuming that you are W. B. Yeats, then the man with you is unquestionably the Ezra Pound, who is your secretary, and whom I know, and with whom I have had correspondence. He has written several volumes of verse, the titles of two of them being "Canzoni & Ripostes" and "Personae & Exultations." I have not a *Who's Who* later than 1912, and his name is not in that. His address in London that I have is 5 Holland Place Chambers, but that may have been before his recent marriage. Of course I have no *proof* of his being American, but I have always understood that he was, and *have not the slightest doubt of it*. My naming his poems will probably identify him with the description in [the current] *Who's Who*.

    You omitted in your letter to show me any *proof* that E. P. was really with you, but it happened that he corrected two sentences in the typewritten letter with a pen, *and I recognised his handwriting* before I had read the letter. I think it was at first glance, anyhow I have no doubt about its being his writing.

    If the Chief Constable thinks that you may be two people personating W. B. Yeats and Ezra Pound, then there may be some difficulty; but if he is satisfied about you, I feel fully able to reassure him about your companion.

    And how is he going to identify *me?* The simplest way seems to be to return the envelope of the letter which you wrote to me and that seems satisfactory enough for the occasion.

    I will keep this open till the last moment in case I get [an] answer to my telegram.

    Given his own sense of the gravity of the situation, Pound did not find this mockery of wartime regulations amusing; that he did not write Bridges to thank him for his help suggests that he and Yeats kept the letter to themselves. Pound did write to thank C.F.G. Masterman, explaining that the "cop appeared this morning . . . &

informed me that the summons was withdrawn. For which the exquisite smoke of our frankincense arises before you." This last remark was not insincere; public authorities had attempted to infiltrate
the aristocracy of the arts (which owed no allegiance to any nation)
and the aristocracy of the arts had prevailed. Pound and Yeats, who
admired the Japanese custom of "listening to incense," were free to
devote themselves to the delicate intricacies of Noh drama and
Doughty's prose.

Throughout the *Pisan Cantos* Pound's ability to recall the details
of speech and place of wartime London is remarkable. His aside in
his 1916 letter to Masterman ("The summons was withdrawn")
suggests that the phrase in Canto 83 ("Summons withdrawn, Sir")
was the actual phrase the Sussex policeman uttered at the door of
Stone Cottage. The memory of this event, a symbolic end to the
noble dream of the Brothers Minor, must have been especially
charged for Pound as he wrote the Pisan sequence in the Detention
Training Center. Authorities had come for him for the second time
in his life, and there was no one left to write to. The memory of the
Sussex authorities stung, for Pound was still an alien in a prohibited
area; after recalling the policeman at Stone Cottage in Canto 83, the
eyes of Canto 81 (now internalized) reappear to accuse and console:

> A fat moon rises lop-sided over the mountain
> The eyes, this time my world,
>   But pass and look *from* mine
>   between my lids
>   sea, sky, and pool
>   alternate
>   pool, sky, sea.

Pound's juxtaposition of his two confrontations with the authorities is instructive, for it helps to separate what was truly valuable
about the dream of a secret society of the arts from its lamentable
political consequences. Faced with Yeats's proposal of eugenics in
On the Boiler (1939) or Pound's radio broadcasts, one must wonder
if such excesses are the inevitable conclusion of the anti-democratic
attitudes fostered in such secluded places as Stone Cottage. So it
sometimes seems:

> I don't believe in the "public." Liberty, equality, fraternity,
> democracy, all very well. I think there ought to be as much of 'em

as possible. BUT art exists in spite of them—Any art that matters. Literature is the same as painting or sculpture. "Aristocracy" (a pink candle-shade stretched over cash) or cash erects a barrier around art and defends it long enough for it [to] come into maturity.

This aristocracy, composed of a few artists, a few people who know, a small amount of money, has to subjugate a certain milieu. . . . This subjugation is a purely unscrupulous process made possible by both the aspirations and the asininity of the subjected. The rest are a herd of sheep.

However I shall never be thrown into prison without trial as Voltaire was. I shall never be burnt at the stake for heresy as several nice people were in Spain so recently as 1758, so I have no heavy complaint against things in general.

In this letter to John Quinn, written just a few months after the poets left Stone Cottage for good, Pound was able to predict his ultimate fate—yet he saw it as something that could never happen; the real political consequences of his art were unimaginable. In 1923 Pound admitted proudly that he had learned from Yeats to "make NO compromise with the public," and if we take him to be addressing an artistic audience as an artist, the remark is (at least to some tastes) acceptable. We can hear a long line of poets behind him saying the same thing. ("I have not the slightest feel of humility towards the Public— . . . a thing I cannot help looking upon as an Enemy," said Keats. And Swinburne: "art and poetry are in no wise given for the sustenance or the salvation of men in general, but reserved mainly for the sublime profit and intense pleasure of an elect body or church.") Yet in *Jefferson and/or Mussolini* (1935) when Pound extrapolates his refusal to compromise from the artistic to the political arena, it becomes intolerable: "The fascist revolution was FOR the preservation of certain liberties and FOR the maintenance of a certain level of culture, certain standards of living, it was NOT a refusal to come down to a level of riches or poverty, but a refusal to surrender certain immaterial prerogatives, a refusal to surrender a great slice of the cultural heritage."

Beyond the walls of Stone Cottage, the secret society of modernism is troubled by this tension between the dream of an artistic elite that eschews public responsibilities and the extension of the dream's values into the hard reality of politics. When T. S. Eliot writes in "Tradition and the Individual Talent" (1919) that the poetry of the present is necessarily bound up in the poetry of the past, he is (even to some postmodern tastes) acceptable: "the most individual parts of [a writer's] work may be those in which the dead poets, his ancestors, assert their immortality most vigorously." Yet when Eliot self-consciously rewrites his early manifesto in the introduction to *After Strange Gods* (1934) we feel the manacles descending: "The problem [of tradition], naturally, does not seem to me so simple as it seemed then, nor could I treat it now as a purely literary one." Tradition "is not solely, or even primarily, the maintenance of certain dogmatic beliefs; these beliefs have come to take their living form in the course of the formation of a tradition. What I mean by tradition involves all those habitual actions, habits and customs, from the most significant religious rite to our conventional way of greeting a stranger, which represent the blood kinship of 'the same people living in the same place.'" In these sentences Eliot has transformed a theory of literary influence into a theory of racial purity, and the step is a small one. Digging more deeply into his earliest writings, one senses that it might have been no step at all. When Eliot declared that *"vers libre* does not exist" in "Reflections on *vers libre*" (1917), he seemed to address a purely aesthetic question; yet he continued: "Only in a closely-knit and homogeneous society, where many men are at work on the same problems, such a society as those which produced the Greek chorus, the Elizabethan lyric, and the Troubadour canzone, will the development of such forms ever be carried to perfection." Eliot was more honest in the 1928 preface to *The Sacred Wood* when he looked back on his early formalism and confessed that it was an "artificial simplification": "we cannot say at what point 'technique' begins or where it ends," and as soon as we begin talking about poetry, "we appear already to be leaving the domain of criticism of 'poetry.'"

In one of his obituary notices for Remy de Gourmont (1915) Pound wrote that "Nietzsche has done no harm in France because France has understood that thought can exist apart from action." In the case of the moderns one might wish that thought could be divorced from action, but the line is too fine to draw; in *Jefferson and/ or Mussolini* Pound wrote that no *"real* intelligence exists until it comes into action." After Pound's incarceration at Pisa, a selection of his radio broadcasts were published as *If This Be Treason*: the volume was concerned almost exclusively with literary criticism. The selection was certainly prejudiced in Pound's favour, but as Jeffrey

Perl has pointed out, it is crucial to realize "the extent to which Pound risked prosecution for a capital crime in order to broadcast literary propaganda." As in Eliot's work, however, it is not easy to mark the point where aesthetics spill into politics, where the secret society of the arts at Stone Cottage becomes the "Ezuversity" meeting at Rapallo. And given Pound's myopic single-mindedness, it is a pleasure to step outside his secret society to read the Marianne Moore who said that "Truth is no Apollo Belvedere, no formal thing," or the Wallace Stevens who asked "Where was it one first heard of the truth?" and answered "The the."

But before I turn Stone Cottage into a cautionary tale, I think different sorts of distinctions can be made. In the nineteen-twenties and thirties, when the interests of Pound and Yeats could not have diverged more dramatically, both poets supported Mussolini. In 1922, during the Irish civil war, Yeats wrote that the "Ireland that reacts from the present disorder is turning its eyes towards individualist Italy." Like some intellectuals *entre deux guerres*, Yeats saw a possible cure for modern anarchy in a fascist ideology which had not yet become inextricably associated with the Holocaust. But as Elizabeth Cullingford has exhaustively shown, Yeats did not fully understand what his endorsement of Mussolini entailed, and, after Mussolini's invasion of Abyssinia, Yeats rejected him as he had rejected the Germany that invaded Belgium and the England that prevailed over Ireland: "All through the Abyssinian war my sympathy was with the Abyssinians, but those feelings were chilled by my knowledge that the English government was using those feelings to help an Imperial policy I distrusted."

Pound, in contrast, supported Il Duce to the bitterest of ends. He had built *The Cantos* and a self-enclosed world of poetic and political ideology around the conflation of Jefferson's and Adams's America with Mussolini's Italy, and to reject Mussolini would have meant the toppling of his life's work; one faulty presupposition led inevitably to another. Pound began to lose touch with any sense of political reality, continuing to invoke Mussolini's draining of the swamps long after such socially constructive acts were rendered irrelevant by events the rest of the world could not ignore.

Pound was able to idealize the Italian state not because he extrapolated the values of a secret society of artists into a political world, but because he ultimately did the opposite. Pound journeyed to England in search of an artistic community. He glimpsed the possibility of a London Vortex, watched the war destroy it, and settled into Stone Cottage with the greatest living poet for three years of the most crucial artistic friendship of his life. When these years were over, London soon became as deadening to Pound as Crawfordsville, Indiana; and after London, Paris proved another disappointment, despite the presence of Ford, Hemingway, Joyce, Cocteau, and Picasso. In 1920, just before he left London, Pound told Williams that "there is no longer any intellectual *life* in England save what centres in this eight by ten pentagonal room; now that Remy and Henry are gone and Yeats faded." Pound's inability to sympathize with Yeats's later work was his own misfortune, for his own work could not withstand the self-imposed isolation. If in 1920 Pound thought that his own mind was the only source of light in London, by 1930 he believed that it was the only beacon in the Western world.

When Pound stationed himself in Rapallo, he became the member of a secret society of one. The dream of community and collaboration, embodied in Stone Cottage, was rejected—not brought to its inevitable fruition—in Pound's later career. Yeats, who sometimes remained in touch with the world, could sense the futility of his own excesses. Working in complete isolation, Pound constructed a private version of the world. Like Yeats, he ended his work by concluding that "my glory was I had such friends"—but only after it was too late. When, just a few years after Yeats's death, Pound wrote in the *Pisan Cantos* (recalling the line from "The Seafarer") that "Lordly men are to earth o'ergiven," the companions had really been gone for almost twenty years.

Pound returned to Sussex only spiritually in the *Pisan Cantos*, but Yeats in the last decade of his life found another aristocracy of the arts at Penns in the Rocks, Dorothy Wellesley's estate, about four miles east of Stone Cottage. Behind the house rises a massive outcropping of rock that gives the estate its name. And at the top of the hill Dorothy Wellesley erected a small temple. On its floor these words are carved:

> To the poets who loved Penns
> W. B. Yeats
> Walter de la Mare
> W. J. Turner
> Ruth Pitter
> V. Sackville West

Dorothy Wellesley
They learn in suffering
What they teach in song

This list of poets recalls some of the illusions of Yeats's old age; his
edition of *The Oxford Book of Modern Verse* contains many more
pages of poetry by either Dorothy Wellesley or W. J. Turner than
by Pound or Eliot or Auden. But Yeats remained (for whatever reasons) part of a community. He listened. The words of Thomas Nashe
that Dorothy Wellesley had cut into the wall of the poets' temple
do not seem an inappropriate testament to the secret society it com-
memorates: "Happie, thrice happie are they whom God hath doubled his spirit upon & given a double soule unto to be poets." These
words, with the lines about suffering from Shelley's "Julian and
Maddalo" cut below the poets' names, recall the ideal of tragic joy
embodied in Yeats's last poems. "All men live in suffering," says
"The Wild Old Wicked Man," but the meditative voice of "Lapis
Lazuli" cautions that those who are worthy of

their prominent part in the play,
Do not break up their lines to weep.
They know that Hamlet and Lear are gay;
Gaiety transfiguring all that dread.

In "Lapis Lazuli" Yeats resists the temptation to answer the historical imperative of "Aeroplane and Zeppelin" with drastic action; instead, he presents the artist who neither ignores his world nor engages
it directly. As they climb the mountainside, Yeats's Chinamen pause
in a "half-way house," a place where they cannot remain forever. The
servant plays a mournful melody; the three men contemplate the
world they've left below. The imagined scene is Yeats's ideal community: "Their eyes mid many wrinkles, their eyes, / Their ancient
glittering eyes, are gay."

Not suffering mixed with joy but suffering mixed with penance are
the mark of Pound's last words. Whether in the *Pisan Cantos* or
the final *Drafts and Fragments* Pound is in utter solitude, the true
seafarer at last. Memories of a community sustained him. And what
is universally acknowledged as the most beautiful passage in the
Pisan Cantos, the prayer that concludes Canto 81, grew from his
memories of Stone Cottage. On January 18, 1914, we have seen,

Yeats and Pound hired a motorcar to drive from the cottage to Newbuildings Place for a noble feast of peacock amid Burne-Jones tapestries and a secret society of poets. Pound remembers standing beside Yeats as the door opened to reveal Wilfrid Scawen Blunt, the last of the great Victorians. Yet the curious thing about Pound's memory of this scene is that he offers it as recompense for political errors; the line between the political and the aesthetic continues to blur. If Pound's dream had remained within the closed world of the arts, if his Yeatsian desire to preserve a noble "state of mind" had not become a political strategy, these lines might have been all anyone would need to pardon the vanity of another tragic generation.

> But to have done instead of not doing
>   this is not vanity
> To have, with decency, knocked
> That a Blunt should open
>   To have gathered from the air a live tradition
> or from a fine old eye the unconquered flame
> This is not vanity.
>   Here error is all in the not done,
> all in the diffidence that faltered . . .

Notes

Previously Unpublished Material

Yeats's letters to Mabel Beardsley are held in either the Princeton University Library or the Harry Ransom Humanities Research Center at the University of Texas at Austin. Those to Lady Gregory and G. H. Mair are part of the Henry W. and Albert A. Berg Collection at the New York Public Library, Astor, Lenox and Tilden Foundations, while those to John Quinn are part of the John Quinn Collection, Rare Books and Manuscripts Division of the New York Public Library, Astor, Lenox and Tilden Foundations. Yeats's letter to Lennox Robinson is in the Morris Library at the Southern Illinois University at Carbondale. His letters to Pound (along with Robert Bridges's letter to Yeats) are part of the Pound Archive in the Collection of American Literature, Beinecke Rare Book and Manuscript Library, Yale University.

Pound's letters to Harriet Monroe are part of the *Poetry* Magazine Papers, Department of Special Collections, University of Chicago Library. His letters to John Quinn are held in the Rare Books and Manuscripts Division of the New York Public Library. Excerpts from Pound's letters to his mother and father are cited from D. D. Paige's transcriptions of the correspondence in the Pound Archive, Beinecke Library, Yale University; the originals are not available for inspection. These letters are identified both by date and by the letter number assigned to them by D. D. Paige.

Two of Pound's unpublished poems ("War Verse" and "1915: February") and part of a third ("Morning on the Farm: An Impression à la Vachel Lindsay") are transcribed from typescripts in the *Poetry* Magazine Papers at the University of Chicago Library. The typescript of Pound's *This Generation* as well as the drafts of the so-called Ur-Cantos are part of the Pound Archive, Beinecke Library, Yale University.

In quotation of these manuscripts, I have sometimes made minor alterations of spelling and punctuation to clarify the sense.

Abbreviations

Au   *The Autobiography of William Butler Yeats* (New York: Macmillan, 1965).

AV-A *A Critical Edition of Yeats's A Vision* (1925), ed. George Mills Harper and Walter Kelly Hood (London: Macmillan, 1978).

AV-B W. B. Yeats, *A Vision* (New York: Macmillan, 1956).

CEP   *The Collected Early Poems of Ezra Pound*, ed. Michael John King (New York: New Directions, 1976).

E&I   W. B. Yeats, *Essays and Introductions* (New York: Macmillan, 1961).

EPWL *Pound/Lewis: The Letters of Ezra Pound and Wyndham Lewis*, ed. Timothy Materer (New York: New Directions, 1985).

Ex   W. B. Yeats, *Explorations*, sel. Mrs. W. B. Yeats (New York: Macmillan, 1963).

GB   Ezra Pound, *Gaudier-Brzeska: A Memoir* (New York: New Directions, 1970).

GK   Ezra Pound, *Guide to Kulchur* (New York: New Directions, 1968).

J/M   Ezra Pound, *Jefferson and/or Mussolini* (London: Stanley Nott, 1935).

LE   *Literary Essays of Ezra Pound*, ed. T. S. Eliot (New York: New Directions, 1968).

Mem   W. B. Yeats, *Memoirs*, ed. Denis Donoghue (New York: Macmillan, 1973).

Myth W. B. Yeats, *Mythologies* (New York: Macmillan, 1959).

P   *Personae: The Collected Shorter Poems of Ezra Pound* (New York: New Directions, 1971).

PD   Ezra Pound, *Pavannes and Divagations* (New York: New Directions, 1958).

PJ   *Pound/Joyce: The Letters of Ezra Pound to James Joyce*, ed. Forrest Read (New York: New Directions, 1967).

PL   *The Selected Letters of Ezra Pound*, ed. D. D. Paige (New York: New Directions, 1971). Since the British edition of the letters is printed with different pagination, the American edition will be cited by both page number and letter number.

PMN   Ezra Pound, *Plays Modelled on the Noh* (1916), ed. Donald

Gallup (Toledo: Friends of the University of Toledo Libraries, 1987).

PSL   *Ezra Pound and Dorothy Shakespear: Their Letters 1909–1914*, ed. Omar Pound and A. Walton Litz (New York: New Directions, 1984).

SP   Ezra Pound, *Selected Prose 1909–1965*, ed. William Cookson (New York: New Directions, 1973).

SR   Ezra Pound, *The Spirit of Romance* (New York: New Directions, 1952).

T   Ezra Pound, *Translations*, ed. Hugh Kenner (New York: New Directions, 1963).

UPII   *Uncollected Prose by W. B. Yeats*, Vol. 2, ed. John P. Frayne and Colton Johnson (New York: Columbia University Press, 1976).

V&B   *Visions and Beliefs in the West of Ireland*, collected and arranged by Lady Gregory with two essays and notes by W. B. Yeats (1920; rpt. New York: Oxford University Press, 1970).

VP   *The Variorum Edition of the Poems of W. B. Yeats*, ed. Peter Allt and Russell K. Alspach (New York: Macmillan, 1957).

VPl   *The Variorum Edition of the Plays of W. B. Yeats*, ed. Russell K. Alspach (New York: Macmillan, 1966).

YL   *The Letters of W. B. Yeats*, ed. Allan Wade (New York: Macmillan, 1955).

References to *The Cantos of Ezra Pound* (New York: New Directions, 1975) are given as 81/521 to designate Canto 81, page 521.

Preface

p. ix   *"the dream of"*   Au 196.
         "God knows what"   80/516.
         "Lordly men are"   74/432–33.

Prologue

p. 3   *In the eighth century:*   Information concerning the history of Ashdown Forest is derived from Garth Christian, *Ashdown Forest* (Forest Row, Sussex: The Society of Friends of Ashdown Forest, 1976).

p. 4   *"I am on"*   Yeats to Mabel Beardsley, 15 January 1915.

p. 5   "*Georgie had an*"   PSL 269.
            "*You & W.B.Y.*"   PSL 258.
            "*not yet got*"   PSL 274.
p. 6   "*When my father*"   This history of the Welfare family, written
            by William Welfare Jr., was given to me by Mr. and Mrs.
            Roy Welfare.
p. 7   "*I can see*"   This and the following anecdotes about Pound and
            Yeats at Stone Cottage were told by Alice Welfare to
            Patricia Hutchins and are quoted from Hutchins's unpub-
            lished essay, "W. B. Yeats and Ezra Pound in Sussex."
            "*It is a pretty*"   PSL 249–50.
p. 8   "*the advice to*"   83/534.
p. 10   "*don't seem much*"   Pound to his mother, January 1905 (25).
            "*The problem for*"   *The English Auden*, ed. Edward Mendelson
            (New York: Random House, 1977), p. 367.
            "*I am homesick*"   CEP 86.
            "*the greatest living*"   PL 7–8 (4).
            "*to have a month*"   Pound to his mother, June 1908 (88).
            "*1902 to 1908*"   Pound, ed., *Profile* (Milan: Giovanni Scheiwil-
            ler, 1932), p. 13.
p. 11   "*Mr Yeats in*"   CEP 8.
            "*Naught but the wind*"   CEP 9.
            "*he is introducing*"   Pound to his father, 11 February 1909 (99).
            "*resuming the nights*"   Ernest Rhys, *Everyman Remembers*
            (New York: Cosmopolitan, 1931), p. 243.
            "*who does stained*"   Pound to his father, 21 February 1909, in
            Hugh Witemeyer, " 'Of King's Treasuries': Pound's Allusion
            to Ruskin in *Hugh Selwyn Mauberley*," *Paideuma* 15 (1986):
            27.
            "*to make the milieu*"   Pound to Harriet Monroe, 11 October
            1912.
            "*the most charming*"   PSL 5.
            "*sitting on the*"   PSL 4.
p. 12   "*At first he was*"   PSL 3.
            "*I shall never*"   Douglas Goldring, *South Lodge: Reminiscences
            of Violet Hunt, Ford Madox Ford, and the English Review
            Circle* (London: Constable, 1943), p. 49. For more infor-
            mation about the interaction of the various poetic societies
            in prewar London, see Ronald Schuchard, " 'As Regarding
            Rhythm': Yeats and the Imagists," *Yeats: An Annual of
            Critical and Textual Studies* 2 (1984): 209–26.
            "*No special furor*"   Pound to his father, 1909 (108).
p. 13   "*the only living*"   Pound to his mother, 1 January 1910, in
            Thomas Parkinson, "Yeats and Pound: The Illusion of In-

fluence," *Comparative Literature* 6 (1954): 258.

"*things of Yeats*"   Pound to his father, 1909 (119).

"*the old brown*"   VP 206–207

"*There are also*"   SR 159.

"*new commonness*"   VP 198.

p. 14   "*Mr. Yeats has perfect*"   Pound, "Hark to Sturge Moore," *Poetry* 6 (June 1915): 141.

Symons was writing: Yeats to John Quinn, 12 January 1909.

"*if he dies*"   Mem 154.

"*I often wonder*"   Mem 171–72.

p. 15   "*All the great*"   Mem 214.

"*King of the Cats*"   Yeats to his sister, April 1909, in Joseph Hone, *W. B. Yeats 1865–1939* (New York: Macmillan, 1943), p. 245.

"*renounce the deliberate*"   Au 335.

"*I shall read*"   Mem 224–25.

p. 16   "*In the generation*"   Joseph Ronsley, ed., "Yeats's Lecture Notes for 'Friends of my Youth' " in *Yeats and the Theatre*, ed. Robert O'Driscoll and Lorna Reynolds (Niagara Falls: Maclean-Hunter Press, 1975), p. 78.

"*is rumored that*"   Pound to his mother, 2 March 1910 (157).

"*a solitary volcano*"   Pound to his father, 1910 (170).

"*I sat alone*"   William Carlos Williams, *Autobiography* (New York: Random House, 1951), p. 115.

"*the darkness gathered*"   Robert O'Driscoll, ed., "Yeats on Personality: Three Unpublished Lectures" in *Yeats and the Theatre*, p. 34. This essay reprints a stenographer's transcription of what Yeats actually said in his lectures.

"*beauty like a tightened*"   VP 256.

p. 17   "*That is the spirit*"   Letter of 27 November 1910 in a private collection, in A. Walton Litz, "Pound and Yeats: The Road to Stone Cottage," in *Ezra Pound Among the Poets*, ed. George Bornstein (Chicago: University of Chicago Press, 1985), p. 132.

"*bring a less*"   VP 814.

"*Yeats did not*"   T. S. Eliot, "Ezra Pound," *Poetry* 68 (1946): 326.

"*about but kings*"   VP 257.

p. 18   "*Some may have*"   CEP 207.

"*there's no use*"   CEP 174. For identification of other echoes of Yeats in "Und Drang" (the sequence which "Au Jardin" ends), see Terence Diggory, *Yeats and American Poetry* (Princeton: Princeton University Press, 1983), p. 42.

"*I had a thought*"   VP 206.

p. 19   *"There is little"* Pound, *This Generation* (typescript in the
          Pound Archive, Beinecke Library, Yale University), pp. 36–
          37.

          "misprints" Yeats to Lady Gregory, 8 January 1913. For an ac-
          count of Pound's minor revisions of the poems Yeats pub-
          lished in the December 1912 issue of *Poetry*, see Richard
          Ellmann, *Eminent Domain: Yeats Among Wilde, Joyce,
          Pound, Eliot, and Auden* (New York: Oxford University
          Press, 1967), pp. 64–65, or Ellen Williams, *Harriet Monroe
          and the Poetry Renaissance* (Urbana: University of Illinois
          Press, 1977), pp. 62–63. Thomas Parkinson has shown that
          Yeats had begun the process of "modernization" long before
          Pound began to tinker with his verse. See "Yeats and Pound:
          The Illusion of Influence," *passim*.

          "He is full" Yeats to Lady Gregory, 3 January 1913, in A. Nor-
          man Jeffares, *W. B. Yeats: Man and Poet* (London: Rout-
          ledge & Kegan Paul, 1949), p. 167.

          "had a young man" UPII 414.

p. 20   *"run with the"* Pound, *This Generation*, p. 37.

          "What is astonishing" George Mills Harper, *W. B. Yeats and
          W. T. Horton: The Record of an Occult Friendship* (New
          York: Macmillan, 1980), p. 129.

          "I find Mr. Yeats" Pound, "Status Rerum," *Poetry* 1 (January
          1913): 123. For Pound's revision of the essay see Williams,
          Harriet Monroe, p. 36.

          "distinguished" PSL 111.

          "The Eagle is" PSL 113.

p. 21   *"half a million"* Pound to his mother, 19 February 1910 (152).
          Part of this letter is quoted in Noel Stock, *The Life of Ezra
          Pound* (San Francisco: North Point Press, 1982), pp. 81–82.

          "Yeats is already" PL 21 (21).

          "the good sense" Pound to Harriet Monroe, August 1913, in
          Williams, *Harriet Monroe*, p. 47.

          "is not the greatest" Pound, "The Approach to Paris" [letter],
          New Age 13 (25 September 1913): 647.

          "stay in Stone Cottage" PL 25 (28).

          "we who are artists" Pound to Yone Noguchi, 2 September
          1911; in *Yone Noguchi: Collected English Letters*, ed. Ikuko
          Atsumi (Tokyo: Yone Noguchi Society, 1975), p. 211.

          "promote investigation" PSL 62.

p. 22   *"In vain, in vain"* VP 311.

          "to say we are" Pound, "On the 'Decline of Faith'" [letter],
          New Age 10 (21 December 1911): 191.

          "a re-incarnation so" PSL 61.

"visionary interpretation" SR 90.

"the consciousness of" SR 92.

"It is what Imagination" Pound to Harriet Monroe, April 1913.

"I know, I mean" SR 92.

p. 23 *"compares interestingly"* Pound to his father, 1909 (119).

"how the world" Robert Hugh Benson, *The Light Invisible* (New York: Benzinger Brothers, 1906), pp. 61, 65.

"that the memories" E&I 41, 43.

"the cleverest boom" PL 106 (118).

"someone greater than" Pound to Harriet Monroe, October 1912, in Harriet Monroe, *A Poet's Life* (New York: Macmillan, 1938), p. 262. The importance of both Mead and Tagore for Pound and Yeats has been considered by Herbert N. Schneidau in "Pound and Yeats: The Question of Symbolism," *ELH* 32 (1965): 220–37. For more information on the two poets' relationships with Tagore, see two articles by Harold M. Hurwitz: "Yeats and Tagore," *Comparative Literature* 16 (1964): 55–64, and "Ezra Pound and Rabindranath Tagore," *American Literature* 36 (1964): 53–63.

"To take part" Hurwitz, "Yeats and Tagore," p. 57.

p. 24 *"try to get some"* PL 10 (6).

"And we feel" Pound, "Tagore's Poems," *Poetry* 1 (December 1912): 93.

"Boccaccio must have" Pound, "Rabindranath Tagore," *Fortnightly Review* 93 (1 March 1913): 573, 574.

"I have carried" E&I 390.

"It is made" Marianne Moore, "To William Butler Yeats on Tagore," *Egoist* 2 (1 May 1915): 77.

p. 25 *"is unequal and there"* YL 572–73. Yeats's remark about imperialism is disingenuous. See his letter to Lady Gregory, 1 January 1913, in which he explains that Tagore wrote a poem addressed to God but allowed it to be interpreted as a poem addressed to the king. Yeats told Lady Gregory not to tell Gosse the story "as I want Tagore either elected or given a public reception" ("Some New Letters from W. B. Yeats to Lady Gregory," ed. Donald T. Torchiana and Glenn O'Malley, *Review of English Studies* 4, 3 [1963]: 15).

"world-fellowship is" Pound, "Tagore's Poems," p. 94.

"who have been" Pound, "Rabindranath Tagore," p. 573.

"the only real" Pound to Harriet Monroe, October 1912, in Monroe, *A Poet's Life*, p. 262; my emphasis.

"this occasion" PSL 232.

"wasn't allowed to" Richard Aldington, *Life for Life's Sake* (New York: Viking, 1941), p. 109.

p. 26   " 'Grey Rock' is very"   PSL 224.
           "the whirl of"   PJ 44.
           "I have longed"   Pound, "The Order of the Brothers Minor"
               [letter], *New Freewoman* 1 (15 October 1913): 176.
p. 27   "It must be offered"   Pound to Harriet Monroe, 10 June 1913.
p. 28   "ought to be enough"   Pound to Harriet Monroe, 15 October
               1912.
           "My first thought"   Yeats to Lady Gregory, 11 November 1913,
               in Hone, *W. B. Yeats*, p. 292.
           "some unknown needy"   YL 585.
           "I am very glad"   Pound to Harriet Monroe, 8 November 1913,
               in Williams, *Harriet Monroe*, p. 93.
p. 29   "I want to arrange"   Yeats to Lady Gregory, 7 July 1913.
           "Mrs Fowler has lent"   Yeats to Lady Gregory, 16 July 1913, in
               Torchiana and O'Malley, eds., "Some New Letters," pp. 33–
               34.
           "on the edge of Ashdown"   Yeats to Lady Gregory, 17 August
               1913; in Torchiana and O'Malley, eds., "Some New Letters,"
               p. 39.
           "a signed photograph"   PSL 245.
p. 30   "insisted on talking"   PSL 180.
           "great controversy"   "Ghosts and Dreams, Lecture by Mr. W. B.
               Yeats," *Irish Times*, 1 November 1913, p. 7. See Yeats's
               "Preliminary Examination of the Script of E. R.," ed. George
               Mills Harper and John S. Kelly, in *Yeats and the Occult*, ed.
               George Mills Harper (Niagara Falls: Maclean-Hunter Press,
               1975), pp. 130–71. The editors of the manuscript point out
               that Pound helped Yeats to identify several Provençal lines
               that emerged in the automatic writing.
p. 31   "go in fear"   LE 5.
           "held also a certain"   F. S. Flint, "Imagisme," *Poetry* 1 (March
               1913): 199.
           "we had a doctrine"   F. S. Flint, "The Appreciation of Poetry",
               in J. B. Harmer, *Victory in Limbo: Imagism 1908–1917*
               (London: Secker & Warburg, 1975), p. 168.
           "It is in art"   PSL 227–78.
p. 32   "The image—a cross"   VP 807.
           "Is Mr. Yeats an"   LE 378.
           "Now as at all"   VP 318.
p. 33   "getting our little"   PL 27 (31).

Initiation

p. 37   *"experiment"*   Yeats to Lady Gregory, 16 July 1913, in Torchiana and O'Malley, eds., "Some New Letters," p. 33.

"not be in"   PL 25 (28).

"Ezra is a"   Yeats to Lady Gregory, 20 November 1913, in Hone, *W. B. Yeats*, p. 290, where it is conflated with a letter written on 3 January 1913.

"Yeats is much"   PL 27 (31).

"elderish female"   PSL 293.

p. 38   *"aristocracy of entail"*   Pound, "The New Sculpture," *Egoist* 1 (16 February 1914): 68.

"at Stone Cottage"   83/534.

"the prerogative of"   Yeats to Mabel Beardsley, November 1913.

p. 39   *"Because of his"*   Ezra Pound, "Ford Madox Hueffer," *New Freewoman* 1 (15 December 1913): 251.

"Past all the"   Ford Madox Ford, *Collected Poems* (New York: Oxford University Press, 1936), p. 199.

"such an expression"   LE 5.

"the best poem"   LE 373, 374.

p. 40   *"old Ford's conversation"*   82/525.

"goes wrong because"   Ezra Pound, "On Criticism in General," *Criterion* 1 (January 1923): 146, 145.

"the word delicate"   PSL 293.

"She stands by"   Aldington's parodies are reprinted in the appendix to Hugh Witemeyer, *The Poetry of Ezra Pound: Forms and Renewal* (Berkeley: University of California Press, 1969), pp. 198–99.

p. 41   *"much improved one"*   PSL 293.

"a new thing"   Yeats to Lady Gregory, 3 January 1913, in Jeffares, *Yeats: Man and Poet*, p. 167.

"the elaborate"   VP 278.

"I shouldn't think"   PSL 296.

"The rustling of"   P 108.

"The sound of"   H. A. Giles, *A History of Chinese Literature* (New York: D. Appleton, 1901), p. 100. For more information on Pound's reworkings of Giles's translations, see Wai-lim Yip, *Ezra Pound's Cathay* (Princeton: Princeton University Press, 1969), pp. 60–64.

p. 42   *"practically useless"*   YL 585.

"The Irish Players"   UPII 408–409.

p. 43   *"The Playboy has been"*   UPII 409–10.

"Mr. Yeats has been"   PJ 17–18.

p. 44 "*I wrote this book*" PJ 22.
"*W.B.Y. says*" PJ 18.
"*found some consolation*" PSL 297.
"*when I remember*" E&I 236.
"*we may start*" GK 80.

p. 45 "*was not merely*" Frank Brinkley, *Japan: Its History Arts and Literature* (Boston: J. B. Millet Co., 1901), 3: 1–2, 4.
"*all old Fenollosa's*" PL 27 (31).
"*charming*" PSL 287.
"*a few cultivated*" E&I 229.

p. 46 "*princes, nobles, and high*" Brinkley, *Japan*, pp. 29, 50.
"*with the help*" E&I 221.
"*have been skilfully*" Brinkley, *Japan*, p. 35.
"*earlier attempts to do*" PL 31 (36).
"*It is this very*" Quoted from the Fenollosa material in the Pound Archive, Beinecke Library, Yale University in Yoko Chiba, "Ezra Pound's Versions of Fenollosa's Noh Manuscripts and Yeats's Unpublished 'Suggestions & Corrections,'" *Yeats Annual* 4 (1986): 130.
"*Times out of mind*" T 286.

p. 47 "*These plays are full*" T 222, 236.
"*his nose kept*" PSL 287.
"*In Nishikigi, the ghosts*" T 226.
"*And she said*" V&B 79, 359.

p. 48 "*Last winter Mr. Ezra Pound*" Ex 64–65. This essay ("Swedenborg, Mediums, and the Desolate Places"), along with "Witches and Wizards and Irish Folklore," was originally published in Lady Gregory's *Visions and Beliefs*.
"*bore [him] to death*" PL 25 (28).
"*repeat . . . the prophecy*" Harper, *Yeats and Horton*, pp. 121, 119.
"*mood*" of "*Mr. Yeats*" CEP 8.

p. 49 "*Yeats is doing*" PSL 305.
"*Were these beings*" V&B 340. Yeats's "The Priest and the Fairy" differs from Sinistrari's tale (as Yeats notes in Lady Gregory's *Visions and Beliefs*) in that the Priest declares that the souls of fairies are not redeemable: the fairy asks, "'Man of wisdom, dost thou know / Where the souls of fairies go?" but "The father dropt his rosary— / 'They are lost, they are lost, each one,' cried he" (VP 729–30).
"*glean anything you*" PSL 275.

p. 50 "*intellectual vision*" PSL 276.
"*fix her attention*" Mem 27, 28.
"*a desert and black Titan*" Au 125.

"*The Kakemono grows*"   83/533–34.

p. 51   "*drunk with intellectual*"   E&I 119.

"*What's riches to*"   VP 310–11.

"*a drippy kind of*"   PSL 269.

"*a great peacock ten*"   E. R. and J. Pennell, *The Life of James McNeill Whistler* (London: William Heinemann, 1911), pp. 306, 301. See Hugh Kenner, *A Colder Eye: The Modern Irish Writers* (New York: Knopf, 1983), pp. 54–55.

p. 52   "*perception by symbolic*"   SP 359.

"*found a black panther*"   PSL 276.

"*The black panther*"   P 109.

p. 53   "*The title is*"   Pound to his father, 12 October 1916 (439).

"*A brown, fat babe*"   P 147.

"*a small, fat, brown*"   PSL 118.

"*They call you*"   This version of "His Vision of a Certain Lady Post Mortem" (which was eventually titled "Post Mortem Conspectu" in the 1926 edition of *Personae*) was sent to Harriet Monroe in 1913 bearing the title "Madonna e desiato in sommo cielo." Its opening line appears in K. K. Ruthven, *A Guide to Ezra Pound's Personae* (Berkeley: University of California Press, 1969), p. 198.

p. 54   "*a technical and*"   PJ 38.

"*the clash of fallen*"   VP 161.

"*I hear an army*"   James Joyce, *Chamber Music*, ed. William York Tindall (New York: Columbia University Press, 1954), p. 179.

"*phantom vision*"   PJ 138.

"*an attitude*"   John Gould Fletcher to Harriet Monroe, 29 August 1913, in Harmer, *Victory in Limbo*, p. 95.

"*were not bound*"   T 222.

The Bourgeois State of Mind

p. 56   "*hearing nearly all*"   83/534.

"*You gave, but will*"   VP 287–88.

p. 57   "*emended by W.B.Y.*"   Pound's copy of *Responsibilities* is owned by Donald Gallup; the marginalia appears here with his permission. The version of "The Witch" which Pound remembered is printed in Jeffares, *Yeats: Man and Poet*, p. 175.

"*What need you*"   VP 289.

"*the little bright boxes*"   P 117.

"*honorable debt*"   Pound, "On Criticism in General," p. 144.

p. 58   *"One could respect"*   VP 819.
           "You gave, but will"   VP 287–88.
p. 59   *"Against all this"*   VP 819.
           "the good of the greatest"   LE 41, 42, 44.
p. 60   *"As W.B.Y. says"*   Pound to his father, 27 August 1912 (252).
           "As soon as the applause"   George Moore, "Yeats, Lady Gregory,
               and Synge," *English Review* 16 (January 1914): 167.
           "George Moore in"   Mem 269, 270.
p. 61   *"does nowt but write"*   PSL 302.
           "surmise companions"   This version of "Notoriety" appeared in
               the *New Statesman* 2 (February 1914): 563.
p. 62   *"in the inconceivable"*   Yeats to Lady Gregory, 4 January 1914.
           Yeats dissuaded him: Yeats to Mabel Beardsley, 4 January 1914.
           "The English Review"   PJ 24.
p. 63   *"One of the boudoir"*   Bastien von Helmholtz [Pound], "The
               Bourgeois," *Egoist* 1 (2 February 1914): 53.
           "middle class"   UPII 241.
           "The word 'bourgeois'"   Mem 270.
p. 64   *"He has mistaken"*   Pound, "The Bourgeois," p. 53.
           "democracy of commentators"   Bastien von Helmholtz [Pound],
               "John Synge and the Habits of Cricitism," *Egoist* 1 (2 Feb-
               ruary 1914): 53–54.
           "the only true religion"   Bastien von Helmholtz [Pound], "On
               the Imbecility of the Rich," *Egoist* 1 (15 October 1914):
               389.
p. 65   *"The duty of literate"*   Bastien von Helmholtz [Pound], "Suf-
               fragettes," *Egoist* 1 (1 July 1914): 254–55.
           "Mr. Yeats? Ah"   PSL 282.
p. 66   *"when I first"*   A transcript of Yeats's speech appears in *Royal
               Society of Literature, The Academic Committee Addresses
               of Reception* (London: Oxford University Press, 1914), pp.
               37–42.
           "must be a terrible"   PSL 280.
           "talks of the academic"   PSL 283.
p. 67   *"the grandest of old"*   Pound, "Status Rerum," p. 127.
           "the first Englishman"   William T. Going, "A Peacock Dinner:
               The Homage of Pound and Yeats to Wilfrid Scawen Blunt,"
               Journal of Modern Literature 1 (March 1971): 306.
           "if you think"   Yeats to Lady Gregory, 24 November 1913, in
               Augusta Gregory, *Seventy Years: Being the Autobiography
               of Lady Gregory* (Gerrards Cross: Colin Smythe, 1974),
               p. 479.
           "if it is as dammmmM"   PSL 297.

"*a more divine*" Yeats to Lady Gregory, February 1914, in Gregory, *Seventy Years*, p. 480.

"*went very well*" Pound to his mother, 20 February 1914, in A. Walton Litz, " 'Remember that I have remembered': Traces of the past in *The Pisan Cantos*," *Yale Review* 75 (1986): 367.

p. 68 "*We have cried*" VP 293.

"*dreamed this thought*" Au 353.

"*Because you have gone*" CEP 281.

p. 69 *When Pound was:* Yeats to Lady Gregory, 15 January 1914.

"*the last man*" Pound, "Homage to Wilfrid Blunt" *Poetry* 3 (March 1914): 221.

"*an attitude*" Yeats to Lady Gregory, 16 January 1914.

"*a fairly complete*" Pound, "Homage to Wilfrid Blunt," p. 222.

"*Tell Lady Gregory*" Hone, W. B. *Yeats*, p. 291. Yeats's article on the dinner, originally published in the 20 January 1914 issue of the London *Times*, is reprinted in UPII 410–11.

"BELLIGERENTS WILL" PL 46 (58).

"*of a man who is*" Richard Aldington, "Presentation to Mr. W. S. Blunt," *Egoist* 1 (2 February 1914): 57.

p. 70 "*trembles for my*" Pound to Harriet Monroe, 10 April 1913, in Williams, *Harriet Monroe*, p. 54.

"*Let us deride*" P 145.

"*into all sorts*" AV-A 62–63.

p. 71 "*Time to put off*" VP 299–300.

p. 72 "*said to Yeats*" 80/504.

"*old enough*" GK 227.

"*My gracious, superior*" Ferrex [Pound], "Ferrex on Petulance," *Egoist* 1 (1 January 1914): 9.

p. 73 "*It may be*" Porrex [Pound], "Porrex on Ferrex," *Egoist* 1 (1 January 1914): 10.

"*Mr. Pound is one*" Richard Aldington, "Blast," *Egoist* 1 (15 July 1914): 273.

"*break up of the*" T. E. Hulme, "Modern Art and its Philosophy," *Speculations*, ed. Herbert Read (London: Routledge and Kegan Paul, 1965), p. 78.

p. 74 "*The artist has*" Pound, "The New Sculpture," p. 68.

"*Sir Hugh Lane tried*" Pound, "Affirmations II: Vorticism," *New Age* 16 (14 January 1915): 277.

"*to date no one*" LE 378.

p. 75 *when Yeats completed:* Yeats to Lady Gregory, 25 December 1912.

"*print this as soon*" Pound to Harriet Monroe, Autumn 1913.

"*a bit of propaganda*"   Pound to Harriet Monroe, Autumn 1913.
"*And when they drove*"   VP 288.
"*gracious*" and "*dignified*"   PL 28 (31).
"*scholars of the*"   LE 220.
"*specialist in renaissances*"   CEP 313.

p. 76   "*we will rebuild*"   SP 107.
"*a thing made*"   LE 220.
"*That there can*"   8/28–29.

p. 77   "*the mysteries*"   GK 145.

Symbolism in Its Profounder Sense

p. 78   "*the generic term*"   Pound to Harriet Monroe, 17 August 1914.
"Vorticism" was originally published in the *Fortnightly Review* 96 (1 September 1914): 461–71.
"*one does not*"   GB 84–85.

p. 79   "*What do you mean*"   PSL 302. Parkinson, in "Yeats and Pound: The Illusion of Influence," has shown convincingly that "Yeats himself—before meeting Pound—had outgrown the early Yeats." Parkinson errs, however, when he states that Pound "could not stomach Yeats's occult experiments" (pp. 258–60). Schneidau, in "Pound and Yeats: The Question of Symbolism," states correctly that Pound "developed a peculiar variety of metaphysical mysticism which . . . was to some extent shaped by Yeats" but like Parkinson he is mistaken when he claims that "Pound was tying together spiritualism, suggestiveness and Symbolism in order to reject them more emphatically" (pp. 221, 232).
"*not necessarily*"   GB 84.

p. 80   "*almost anyone can*"   GB 86, 84.
"*The image is the word*"   GB 88.
"*had last night*"   PSL 150.
"*Dark eyed*"   P 91. "Contemporania" was published in *Poetry* 2 (April 1913): 1–12, and included "Tenzone," "The Condolence," "The Garret," "The Garden," "Ortus," "Dance Figure," "Salutation," "Salutation the Second," "Pax Saturni," "Commission," "A Pact," and "In a Station of the Metro."

p. 81   "*beautiful face and*"   GB 86–87.
"*The apparition*"   GB 89.
"*call down among us*"   E&I 157.
"*perfectly symbolical*"   E&I 155.
"*one image poem*"   GB 89.

"*evoke an emotion*"   E&I 156.

"*an intellectual and*"   LE 4.

p. 82   "*has been known*"   GB 82. Pound mentions both *Le Comte de Gabalis* (1670) and *The History of Magic* (1854) in his response to Dorothy Shakespear's questions about symbolism. In Canto 83 Pound recalled that at Stone Cottage Yeats preferred "Ennemoser on Witches" to Wordsworth. Robert Kirk's *Secret Commonwealth; or, a treatise displaying the chiefe Curiosities as they are in use among diverse of the People of Scotland to this day* (1691) was another esoteric work Pound and Yeats read during the winter of 1913–14. On November 21, 1913 Pound wrote to Dorothy Shakespear that he had "started Kirk's 'Secret Commonwealth' which is diverting" (PSL 276). Kirk justifies the existence of "SEERS, or Men of a 2d or more exhalted Sight than others" (*The Secret Commonwealth*, ed. Andrew Lang [London: David Nutt, 1893], p. 28), and Pound no doubt found support for his visionary conception of symbolism in these doctrines.

"*which both in*"   The Poems of Alexander Pope, ed. Geoffrey Tillotson (New Haven: Yale University Press, 1962), 2: 142–43.

"*been reading The Comte*"   PSL 293. On March 21, 1914, Dorothy Shakespear wrote to Pound saying that Olivia Shakespear "has done another Gabalis entretien which I shall bring back with me for you" (PSL 334). The five "conversations" of Olivia Shakespear's translation of *Le Comte de Gabalis* (retitled "Memoirs of a Charming Person") appeared in five issues of the *Egoist*:

"Conversation the First," *Egoist* 1 (16 March 1914): 112–13.

"Second Conversation," *Egoist* 1 (15 April 1914): 153–54.

"Third Conversation," *Egoist* 1 (1 May 1914): 171–73.

"Fourth Conversation," *Egoist* 1 (15 May 1914): 189–90.

"V.," *Egoist* 1 (1 June 1914): 207–208.

Olivia Shakespear translated only the original five dialogues by the Abbé de Montfaucon de Villars and included none of the appended notes and commentary that are present in most French and English editions of the book. In the "Third Conversation," p. 173, when the Count mentions the "Jewish Teraphim," Olivia Shakespear adds a footnote: "Translator's Note: Judges xvii.; Ezekiel xxi., 21; Hosea iii, 4."

p. 83   "*I think you have*"   YL 234.

"*most absorbing old*"   Olivia Shakespear, "Beauty's Hour," *Savoy* 5 (September 1896): 15.

p. 84 *"Diana Vernon tried"*   Mem 87–88. For a fuller discussion of
Yeats's relationship with Shakespear, see John Harwood,
"Olivia Shakespear and W. B. Yeats," *Yeats Annual* 4
(1986): 75–98.

"of a single"   Pound made this comment about Yeats's poems
in his commentary to the anthology he edited with Marcella
Spann: *Confucius to Cummings: An Anthology of Poetry*
(New York: New Directions, 1964), p. 327.

"Pale brows, still"   VP 152.

"For more than"   YL 916.

"The vision is correct"   YL 256.

p. 85 *"in a room all"*   PSL 16.

"You told me"   PSL 153–54.

p. 86 *"two qualities"*   Olivia Shakespear, "The Poetry of D. H. Lawrence," *Egoist* 2 (1 May 1915): 81.

p. 87 *"the Cabalistic extravaganza"*   Henry Bryan Binns, "The Dangers
of Occultism" [letter], *Egoist* 1 (15 May 1914): 200.

"I trust no one"   Pound, "The Dangers of Occultism" [letter],
Egoist 1 (1 June 1914): 220.

"I have some religion"   PSL 307.

p. 88 *"artist has been"*   Pound, "The New Sculpture," pp. 67–68.

p. 89 *"When you are one"*   Shakespear, "Memoirs of a Charming
Person, Second Conversation," pp. 153–54.

"If Adam had not"   Shakespear, "Memoirs of a Charming Person, Fourth Conversation," p. 189.

p. 90 *"There was no use"*   Shakespear, "Memoirs of a Charming Person, Third Conversation," p. 171.

"we find sex"   SR 93.

"I think a superficial"   PSL 302.

"To give concrete"   CEP 295–96.

"when a thing is hidden"   I quote this translation of Tertullian
from another English translation of *Le Comte de Gabalis*
published in 1914: *Comte de Gabalis by the Abbe N. de
Villars Rendered out of French into English with a Commentary, published by The Brothers* (London: W. H.
Broome, 1914), p. [iii].

" 'Then,' cried I"   Shakespear, "Memoirs of a Charming Person,
Fourth Conversation," p. 189.

p. 91 *"As for the obscurity"*   Shakespear, "Memoirs of a Charming
Person, Third Conversation," p. 173.

"Greek myth arose"   SR 92.

"Therein especially"   Joseph Ennemoser, *The History of Magic*,
trans. William Howitt (London: Henry G. Bohn, 1854),
2: 8.

"*is dead of*" Shakespear, "Memoirs of a Charming Person, Conversation the First," p. 112.

p. 92 "*I do not think*" Pound, "Editorial," *Little Review* 4 (May 1917): 5.

"*The art of allusion*" T 214.

"*invented a form*" E&I 221.

"*an unpopular theatre*" Ex 254; my emphasis.

"*the public will*" Pound, "The New Sculpture," p. 68.

p. 93 "*What the analytic*" SP 362.

"*every two thousand*" AV-B 29.

"*See, they return*" P 74.

p. 94 "*We die with the dying*" T. S. Eliot, *Complete Poems and Plays* 1909–1950 (New York: Harcourt, Brace, 1971), p. 144.

"*The hells move*" 113/787.

"*I learned from*" E&I 10.

p. 95 "*The people have*" Pound, "John Synge and the Habits of Criticism," p. 54.

"*Le Paradis n'est*" 83/528–29.

p. 96 "*and Tullio Romano*" 76/460. The most influential and canonical reading of Pound's comments about Yeats and symbolism in the *Pisan Cantos* is by Donald Davie, *Ezra Pound: Poet as Sculptor* (New York: Oxford University Press, 1964), pp. 178–81. See also Ellmann, *Eminent Domain*, p. 86.

"*That the body*" 113/788–89.

"*It becomes evil*" Edwin John Ellis and William Butler Yeats, eds., *The Works of William Blake: Poetic, Symbolic, and Critical* (London: Bernard Quaritch, 1893), 1: 243.

p. 97 "*but that kind*" 113/789. Pound quotes from Yeats's *On the Boiler* (Ex 412).

"*We young writers*" UPII 412–14.

p. 99 "*a subtle change*" J. B. Yeats, *Letters to his Son W. B. Yeats and Others*, ed. Joseph Hone (New York: E. P. Dutton, 1946), p. 174.

"*breakdown*" YL 526.

"*[Pound] is to marry*" J. B. Yeats, *Letters*, p. 175.

"*I perceive that*" PSL 304.

"*heard from W.B.Y.*" PSL 320.

"*see how you've*" PSL 323.

"*You will have*" PSL 332.

"*Yesterday I got*" Yeats to Lady Gregory, 8 March 1914, in Torchiana and O'Malley, eds., "Some New Letters," p. 41.

p. 100 "*much praised but*" P 100.

"*you can not*" PSL 235.

"*much more in*" PSL 307.

"Thanks, [for] your" Pound, "Letters to William Butler
Yeats," ed. C. F. Terrell, *Antaeus* 21 (1976): 34. For Dorothy Shakespear's recollections of Blunt, see Michael Reck,
Ezra Pound: A Close-up (New York: McGraw Hill, 1976),
p. 27.

p. 101   *"I live, so far"* LE 378.
"Romantic Ireland's Dead" LE 379–80.
"Tell me, do" See LE 380 and Mem 221.
"constant element" LE 379.

War Poets by the Waste Moor

p. 105   *"With minds still"* P 148.
"a magazine" PSL 316.
p. 106   *"Ricketts has made"* PL 46–47 (58).
"own kind" CEP 86.
p. 107   *"Pound exaggerated"* See Ronald Bush, "Pound and Li Po:
What Becomes a Man," in *Ezra Pound Among the Poets*,
ed. George Bornstein (Chicago: University of Chicago
Press, 1985), pp. 35–62. Pound completed *Cathay* before
returning to Sussex but proofed the volume while he was
living in Stone Cottage: he wrote his father on 30 November 1914 that he had begun the Chinese poems and wrote
again on 20 December 1914 that he had finished them; he
wrote his mother from Stone Cottage on 12 February 1915
that he was reading proof.
"And with them" P 134.
"a scheme to enable" PL 47 (58).
"at an intellectual" Pound, "Preliminary Announcement of the
College of the Arts," *Egoist* 1 (2 November 1914): 413.
"the war is eating" Pound to Harriet Monroe, 29 August 1914.
"people do nothing" Yeats to Lady Gregory, 30 August 1914,
in Gregory, *Seventy Years*, p. 513.
p. 108   *"how the war"* Yeats to Lennox Robinson, 5 August 1914.
"owing to the" Yeats to Lady Gregory, 30 August 1914, in
Gregory, *Seventy Years*, p. 481.
"It seems impossible" Yeats to John Quinn, 31 October 1914.
"losing interest" Pound to his father, 30 November 1914 (358).
"I walk Verona" Pound, "Three Cantos I," *Poetry* 10 (June
1917): 115.
p. 109   *"priceless imp has"* Yeats to John Quinn, 21 March 1915.
"I hope they" Yeats to Lady Gregory, 27 October 1914.
"as if her face" Yeats to Mabel Beardsley, 15 January 1915.

Pound wrote his mother on 12 February 1915 that Dorothy
Pound had completed a new cover for *Ripostes*.

p. 110 "*I have a distaste*" Yeats, Introduction to *The Oxford Book
of Modern Verse* (Oxford: Clarendon Press, 1936), pp.
xxxiv–xxxv.

p. 112 "*Those five years*" Virginia Woolf, *Mrs. Dalloway* (New York:
Harcourt, Brace, 1953 [1925]), p. 108.

"*The war, people*" Virginia Woolf, *To the Lighthouse* (New
York: Harcourt, Brace, 1955 [1927]), p. 202.

"*his great eyes*" Simon Nowell-Smith, ed., *The Legend of the
Master* (London: Constable, 1947), pp. 166–67.

p. 113 "*Death's nobility again*" Wallace Stevens, *Opus Posthumous*
(New York: Knopf, 1977), pp. 4–5.

"*the war-poem scandal*" PL 63 (75).

"VERY glad" Pound to Harriet Monroe, 15 September 1914.

p. 114 "*Great is King George*" P 237.

p. 115 "*appeared just at*" Pound to Harriet Monroe, 29 August 1914.

"*a complaint against*" PL 64 (76).

"*not submitted*" Written by Pound on the manuscript of
"War Verse" sent to Harriet Monroe.

"*O two-penny*" Pound, "War Verse," manuscript poem in the
Poetry magazine papers, Department of Special Collections,
University of Chicago Library.

p. 116 "*Good poetry is*" Pound, "Webster Ford," *Egoist* 1 (1 January
1915): 11. For a fuller discussion of *Cathay* as a war book,
see Hugh Kenner, *The Pound Era* (Berkeley: University of
California Press, 1971), pp. 192–222.

"*Mind and spirit*" P 139.

"*poems depict*" GB 58.

"*I think you*" Yeats to Pound, 8 May 1915.

p. 117 "*I don't suppose*" Pound to his father, January 1915 (366).

"*I wonder if*" Yeats to Lady Gregory, 18 February 1915, in
Gregory, *Seventy Years*, p. 521.

"*been promoted*" Pound to his father, 16 January 1915 (367).

"*nursing the wounded*" *Letters to W. B. Yeats*, ed. Richard
J. Finneran, et al. (New York: Columbia University Press,
1977), 2: 308.

p. 118 "*The country is*" Pound to Harriet Monroe, 31 January 1915.

"*Regiment came over*" Pound to his mother, 7 February and
12 February 1915 (371, 372).

"*I think it better*" This version of the poem appeared in *The
Book of the Homeless*, ed. Edith Wharton (New York:
Charles Scribner's Sons, 1916), p. 45.

"*is the only*" YL 600.

p. 119   *"this anyhow"*   Pound to Harriet Monroe, 1 August 1917.
　　　　"we may as well"   Pound to Harriet Monroe, 20 February 1915.
　　　　"I think it has"   PL 51 (62).
　　　　"The smeared, leather"   Pound, "1915: February," manuscript
　　　　　　poem in the *Poetry* magazine papers, Department of Special
　　　　　　Collections, University of Chicago Library.

p. 120   *"a symptom of"*   PL 47 (58).
　　　　"I do not like"   Pound to Harriet Monroe, May 1915.
　　　　"I don't know"   Pound to his father, January 1915 (366).

p. 121   *"To-day is magnificent"*   GB 70.
　　　　"real artists who"   Pound, "A Flock from Oxford," *Poetry* 10
　　　　　　(April 1917): 42.
　　　　"The host with"   Eliot, *Complete Poems and Plays*, p. 36.

p. 122   *"in the great"*   Yeats, Introduction to *The Oxford Book of
　　　　　　Modern Verse*, p. xxii.
　　　　"public controversies"   VP 818.

p. 123   *"Only a man"*   *The Complete Poetical Works of Thomas
　　　　　　Hardy*, ed. Samuel Hynes (Oxford: Clarendon Press, 1984),
　　　　　　2: 295–96.
　　　　"convinced that"   Pound to Harriet Monroe, 5 June 1915.
　　　　"The war 1915"   Pound to Harriet Monroe, Autumn 1915.
　　　　"You can also"   Pound to Harriet Monroe, 24 December 1915.
　　　　"the one about"   Pound to Harriet Monroe, 1916.
　　　　"An image of"   P 107.

p. 125   *"Over the flat"*   CEP 286.
　　　　"the ground between"   T. E. Hulme, *Further Speculations*, ed.
　　　　　　Samuel Hynes (Minneapolis: University of Minnesota
　　　　　　Press, 1955), pp. 157, 169.

p. 126   *"Emotion is born"*   P 139.
　　　　"Life to make"   7/27.
　　　　"He was killed"   Pound to Harriet Monroe, 28 June 1915.

p. 127   *"Is it a love poem?"*   P 153–54.
　　　　"I am trying"   YL 646.
　　　　"He stayed for"   VP 341–42.

p. 128   *"Major Robert Gregory"*   VP 323.
　　　　"companions of my youth"   VP 323–24.
　　　　"In balance with"   VP 328.
　　　　"treated Ireland"   YL 654.

p. 129   *"You say that we"*   VP 395.
　　　　"Half-drunk or"   VP 791.
　　　　"drunken soldiery"   VP 429.

p. 130   *"Died some, pro patria"*   P 190.
　　　　"crimes of the war"   SP 420.

p. 131   *"The soul starts"*   Quoted in Christine Froula, *To Write Para-*

dise: *Style and Error in Ezra Pound's Cantos* (New Haven: Yale University Press, 1984), pp. 74–75.

"*The falcon cannot*" These drafts of "The Second Coming" appear in Jon Stallworthy, *Between the Lines: Yeats's Poetry in the Making* (Oxford: Clarendon Press, 1971), p. 17.

"*And Henri Gaudier*" 16/71.

"*serious curiosity*" EPWL 250.

p. 132   "*began investigation*" *Selected Poems of Ezra Pound* (New York: New Directions, 1957), p. viii.

"*remember that I have*" 80/506.

"*the tradition of*" Pound, "How I Began," *T. P.'s Weekly* 21 (6 June 1913): 707.

"*keep the neighbourhood*" YL 600.

p. 133   "*What wholesome sun*" VP 442.

"*at Phase 22*" AV-A 210.

"*an unnatural story*" AV-B 19.

p. 134   "*story of Griselda*" AV-A xv–xvi. For a different discussion of *A Vision* as a war book, see Elizabeth Cullingford, *Yeats, Ireland, and Fascism* (London: Macmillan, 1981), pp. 115–40.

"*order is a*" YL 692.

"*In mockery of*" VP 480.

"*half dead at*" 79/487.

Poems Cold and Passionate as the Dawn

p. 135   "*I wish I was*" Pound sent these lines to Harriet Monroe on February 19, 1915, and they are now part of the *Poetry* magazine papers in the University of Chicago Library. Under the name "Abel Sanders," Pound published a similar parody of Lindsay in 1918: "Mr. Lindsay," *Little Review* 4 (January 1918): 54–55.

p. 136   "*Mr. Lindsay is*" Pound to Harriet Monroe, 19 February 1915.

"*stripped bare*" UPII 412.

"*deliberately tries*" Pound to Harriet Monroe, 5 January 1915.

p. 137   "*In the Imagist*" PL 48 (59). This letter is dated 31 January 1915 in the *Poetry* papers at the University of Chicago; the two paragraphs which I have deleted from the text as it appears in Pound's *Selected Letters* were inserted from another letter dated 5 January 1915.

"*I should not*" Pound to Harriet Monroe, 1 February 1915, in Williams, *Harriet Monroe*, p. 134.

" '*Mr. Prufrock*' *does*" PL 50 (61).

p. 139   *"Eliot has sent"* EPWL 8–9.
    "Yeats says there" EPWL 9.
    "not be in town" Noel Stock, ed. *Ezra Pound: Perspectives* (Chicago: Henry Regnery, 1965), pp. 110–11.

p. 140   *"for the sake"* LE 80.
    "appeared as it were" Pound, *Profile*, p. 47.
    "All shuffle there" VP 337.
    "They'll cough in" This version of "The Scholars" appeared in *Catholic Anthology 1914–1915*, ed. Ezra Pound (London: Elkin Mathews, 1915), p. 1.

p. 141   *"If a man owned"* SP 22.
    "I would much rather" LE 9.

p. 142   nothing but *"facts"* Yeats to Jack Yeats, 3 May 1913.
    "Scholarship is but" PL 48 (59), 47 (58).
    "The best poetry" Pound, *Instigations* (New York: Boni and Liveright, 1920), p. 376. For the dating of Pound's work on the Fenollosa essay, see Kenner, *Pound Era*, pp. 291, 579.
    "is as old and" Pound, "Imagisme and England," *T. P.'s Weekly* 25 (20 February 1915): 185. Pound wrote his father on 20 December 1914 (before leaving for Sussex) that he had completed this essay; however, its contents suggest that he continued to revise the essay at Stone Cottage.

p. 143   *"by reading Wordsworth"* Yeats to Lady Gregory, 23 January 1915, in Gregory, *Seventy Years*, p. 491.
    "to raise his" Yeats to Quinn, 19 December 1915.
    "There was a certain" Charles Doughty, *Travels in Arabia Deserta* (London: Jonathan Cape Ltd., 1924), 2: 193. Pound mentions reading *Travels in Arabia Deserta* in a letter to his mother, 1 February 1915. Although he recalled reading Doughty's *The Dawn in Britain* in the *Pisan Cantos*, neither he nor Yeats mentioned the work in any of their letters from Stone Cottage.

p. 144   *"I have walked"* P 121–23. For a reading of "Provincia Deserta" in the context of Pound's quarrel with philological method, see James Longenbach, *Modernist Poetics of History: Pound, Eliot, and the Sense of the Past* (Princeton: Princeton University Press, 1987), pp. 80–86.

p. 145   *"Upon a moonless night"* VP 467.
    "All those gyres" VP 830. For a more complete study of Yeats's interest in Arabian literature, see S. B. Bushrui, "Yeats's Arabic Interests," in *In Excited Reverie*, ed. A. Norman Jeffares and K.G.W. Cross (New York: St. Martin's Press, 1965), pp. 280–314.

p. 146   *"the number of people"*   Pound, "Studies in Contemporary
            Mentality XI," *New Age* 22 (8 November 1917): 29.
            "Yeats has sent"   PL 50 (61). When these three poems ap-
            peared in *Poetry* in February 1916, their titles were "The
            Thorn Tree," "The Phoenix," and "There is a Queen in
            China," respectively.
p. 147   *"The lineaments"*   VP 315.
            "W.B.Y. at his"   Pound to Harriet Monroe, 26 October 1912.
            Part of this letter is quoted by Ellmann in *Eminent Do-
            main*, p. 65.
p. 148   *"What can books"*   VP 309.
            "One is so tired"   PJ 28–29.
            "think about old"   VP 173.
            " 'Time's bitter flood'!"   CEP 182.
p. 149   *"She is foremost"*   VP 350–51.
            "I cannot remember"   Pound, "Affirmations VII: The Non-
            Existence of Ireland," *New Age* 16 (25 February 1915):
            453.
p. 150   *"There's Margaret"*   VP 354. For Ellmann's suggestion see
            Eminent Domain, p. 73.
            "There is grey"   VP 355.
p. 151   *"My dear is angry"*   Mem 145.
            "What have I earned"   VP 351–52.
p. 152   *"Two friends: a breath"*   P 158.
p. 153   *"such men seldom"*   Amy Lowell, *A Critical Fable* (Boston:
            Houghton Mifflin, 1922), pp. 92, 95.
p. 154   *"The living men"*   VP 347–48.
            "I have even seen"   Pound, "Affirmations II: Vorticism," p. 277.
            "ceased, quite simply"   Pound, "Affirmations VII: The Non-
            Existence of Ireland," p. 452.
            "Maybe a twelvemonth"   VP 348.
p. 155   *"I once boasted"*   E&I 523.
            "one of the best"   Pound to Harriet Monroe, 20 February 1916.
            "the best English"   Pound, "Books Current," *Future* 2 (De-
            cember 1918): 311.

Tragic Generations

p. 156   *"alone in modern times"*   VP 603.
            "old William was"   80/507.
p. 157   *"Subject for poem"*   Mem 225.
            "How should the world"   VP 264.
            "This house has"   In A. Norman Jeffares, *A Commentary on*

the Collected Poems of W. B. Yeats (Stanford: Stanford
University Press, 1968), p. 109.

"Eagle has done two" PSL 183.

p. 158 "Although she has turned" In Jeffares, A Commentary, p. 194.

"Yeats gives me" SR 50.

"The Eagle has been" PSL 186.

"Mabel's red head" 80/507.

"on one occasion" Moore, "Yeats, Lady Gregory, and Synge,"
pp. 167–68.

p. 159 "get himself proclaimed" PSL 302.

"some sort of" Yeats to Susan Mary [Lily] Yeats, 29 December 1914, in Hone, W. B. Yeats, p. 308.

"you that did not" VP 270.

Yeats originally planned: Yeats to Elizabeth Corbet [Lollie]
Yeats, January 1914.

p. 160 "How am I fallen" VP 269.

"For a long time" Allen Upward, "Sayings of K'ung the Master," New Freewoman 1 (1 November 1913): 190.

"I desire to go" PL 128 (142).

"the gray steps" 3/11.

"Confucius later taught" Pound, "Three Cantos I," p. 119.

"the dynastic temple" 13/58–59.

p. 161 he had never written: Yeats to Mabel Beardsley, 28 August
1914.

"Yesterday I finished" YL 589.

"Ezra Pound and his wife" YL 590.

still patching: Yeats to Mabel Beardsley, 15 January 1915.

"modern autobiography" AV-A 199.

p. 162 "Certainly it will" The Life of Lord Herbert of Cherbury (New
York: Cassell and Co., Ltd., n.d.), p. 17. Pound told his
mother on 31 December 1914 that he and Yeats were reading the autobiography of Herbert of Cherbury.

"Hitherto Lord Herbert" The Life of Lord Herbert of Cherbury, pp. 9–10.

p. 163 "She was full" Au 11.

"some sort of" Hone, W. B. Yeats, p. 308.

"I am handing" YL 606–7.

"very much" liked J. B. Yeats, Letters, p. 133.

"a very clear" PL 52 (63).

p. 164 "his, William's, old" 80/507.

"I make no excuse" Pound, "The Yeats Letters," Poetry 11
(January 1918): 223.

"Mr. Yeats understands" T. S. Eliot, "The Letters of J. B.
Yeats," Egoist 4 (July 1917): 90, 84.

"I am going"   YL 603.

"Private. A first"   Mem 19. For Curtis Bradford's attempt to
    date this manuscript more precisely, see Yeats at Work
    (Carbondale: Southern Illinois University Press, 1965),
    p. 348. See also Joseph Ronsley, Yeats's Autobiography:
    Life as Symbolic Pattern (Cambridge: Harvard University
    Press, 1968).

p. 165   "too late for the first"   Pound to John Quinn, 26 August 1915.

"living artists"   Pound, "How I began," p. 707.

"Young Mr. Ezra Pound"   Victor Plarr, Ernest Dowson (Lon-
    don: Elkin Mathews, 1914), p. 28.

p. 166   "Wilde had arrived"   Au 219.

"first chapters are"   Pound, "[A review of] Ernest Dowson by
    Victor Plarr," Poetry 6 (April 1915): 43.

"Sell my ring"   Mem 93.

p. 167   "You had to face"   VP 273.

p. 168   "outweighs this by a"   LE 379.

"more than all"   Mem 96–97.

p. 169   "For two hours"   P 193.

"the delirium of"   Passages from the Letters of John Butler
    Yeats, ed. Ezra Pound (Churchtown, Ireland: Cuala Press,
    1916), p. 28.

"Gladstone was still"   P 192.

"Accept opinion"   P 194.

p. 170   "For three years"   P 187.

"Mr. Yeats' recent"   T. S. Eliot, "Contemporary English Prose,"
    Vanity Fair 20 (July 1923): 51.

"Wells, Bennett"   T. S. Eliot, "A Preface to Modern Litera-
    ture," Vanity Fair 21 (November 1923): 118, 44.

p. 171   "extraordinary distinction"   Yeats to Pound, 20 August 1920.

"always discussed life"   Au 214.

"that he is"   Matthew Arnold, On the Classical Tradition, ed.
    R. H. Super (Ann Arbor: University of Michigan Press,
    1960), pp. 102, 188.

p. 172   "spends his life"   AV-A 63.

"more deliberate nobility"   Yeats, Introduction to The Oxford
    Book of Modern Verse, p. xxv.

"Lordly men are"   74/432–33.

"La beauté"   80/511.

p. 173   "I said to [Beardsley]"   Au 223.

"Men like Sir Edward"   Mem 284.

"'beauty is difficult' sd/ Mr Beardsley"   74/444. For Perloff's
    reading of this passage see The Poetics of Indeterminacy
    (Princeton: Princeton University Press, 1981), pp. 189–95.

p. 174   *"beauty is difficult"*   74/444–45.
p. 175   *"a man passed him"*   74/445.
        "I know so many"   GK 226.
p. 176   *"certain images be formed"*   74/446.

Dialogues with the Dead

p. 179   *"The arrival of"*   Pound to his father, June 1915 (390).

        Violet Hunt: See Violet Hunt, *I Have This to Say* (London: Boni and Liveright, 1926), p. 114: "The portrait of Ezra Pound in stone by this young Frenchman . . . is actually supposed to have guaranteed my immunity from German bombs during the raids."

        "An exciting event"   Yeats to Lady Gregory, 13 October 1915, in Gregory, *Seventy Years*, p. 524.

p. 180   *"the mob cheered"*   YL 588. This letter is misdated 12 September 1914; the first zepellin raid took place on 31 May 1915, making 12 September 1915 the probable date of the letter.

        "I believe one"   Pound to his father, 25 September 1915 (398).

        "Let it then"   PD 145–46.

        "My proposition"   Pound to John Quinn, August 1915.

        "last raid of"   Richard Ellmann, ed., *Letters of James Joyce*, (London: Faber and Faber, 1966), 2: 353.

        "obscurity and poverty"   PJ 39.

p. 182   *"I have just heard"*   YL 596–97.

        "to make perfectly"   PJ 36–37.

        "Joyce says"   Ellmann, ed., *Letters of James Joyce*, 2: 354.

        "typed passages"   YL 597.

        "My dear Gosse"   YL 600–601.

        When Yeats wrote: Yeats to Pound, 28 August 1915.

        "has had an amusing"   PJ 42.

p. 183   *"I am glad"*   PJ 42.

        "I am very glad indeed"   PJ 40.

        "I am down here"   PJ 62.

        "in the first"   Pound to Harriet Monroe, 15 December 1915, Williams, *Harriet Monroe*, p. 164.

        "too old"   Yeats recorded this conversation with Joyce in a retracted preface for *Ideas of Good and Evil*, printed in Richard Ellmann, *The Identity of Yeats* (New York: Oxford University Press, 1964), pp. 86–88.

        "Yeats knows life"   Pound to Harriet Monroe, 15 December 1915, in Williams, *Harriet Monroe*, p. 165.

p. 184   *"at home in town"*   Yeats to Lady Gregory, 5 March 1915, in Gregory, *Seventy Years*, p. 491.

"[*Pound*] *has a beautiful*"   Yeats to John Quinn, 19 December
1915.

"*I find I can*"   Yeats to John Quinn, 12 September 1915.

"*Last Monday Madame*"   Mem 271.

p. 185   "*Mlle de Pratz says*"   Pound to his father, 18 December 1915
(406).

"*Flammarion or someone*"   PJ 70–71.

"*the war is bound*"   Sigmund Freud, *Character and Culture*,
ed. Philip Rieff (New York: Collier Books, 1963), p. 124.

"*while the great battle*"   Ex 51.

"*Nowadays I'm often*"   *The Diary of Virginia Woolf*, ed. Anne
Oliver Bell (New York: Harcourt, Brace, 1978), 2: 47.

"*There are so many dead*"   D. H. Lawrence, *The Complete
Poems*, ed. Vivian de Sola Pinto and F. Warren Roberts
(New York: Penguin, 1980), p. 739.

p. 186   "*I have endeavored*"   Oliver J. Lodge, *Raymond or Life after
Death* (New York: George H. Doran, 1916), p. 85.

"*Oh, take a heaven*"   Quoted in Froula, pp. 74–75.

p. 187   "*ghosts [that] move about*"   Pound, "Three Cantos I," p. 114.

"*a whole culture*"   PL 89 (103). Pound remarked in a letter to
his mother dated 31 December 1914 that he and Yeats were
reading Landor.

p. 188   " '*Are' as Uncle*"   95/645.

"*The Muses are*"   74/445.

"*The Muses were*"   T 340.

"*A poet, when he*"   Myth 342.

"*I know what wages*"   VP 336.

"*I shall dine late*"   Walter Savage Landor, *Imaginary Conversations*, ed. Charles G. Crump (London: J. M. Dent, 1891),
4: 427.

p. 189   "*Yet to walk*"   113/786.

"*literature dwindles*"   E&I 185.

"*When we delight*"   E&I 352.

"*centuries of race*"   SP 34.

"*no man has ever*"   SP 387, 386.

p. 190   "*You will find me*"   Yeats, "The Manuscript of 'Leo Africanus,' "
ed. Steve L. Adams and George Mills Harper, *Yeats Annual*
1 (1982): 19.

"*He was no secondary*"   Yeats, "Leo Africanus," p. 13.

"*doctrine of 'the mask*' "   Au 102.

p. 191   "*his opposite, instead*"   Richard Ellmann, *Yeats: The Man and
the Masks* (New York: W. W. Norton, 1979), p. 199.

"*You were my opposite*"   Yeats, "Leo Africanus," p. 21.

"*I call to the mysterious*"   VP 371.

"*not convinced that*"   Yeats, "Leo Africanus," p. 38.

p. 192   "We [*the spirits of the dead*]"   Yeats, "Leo Africanus," p. 38.

"*the Daimon comes not*"   Myth 335.

"*immortality of the soul*"   T 340.

"*Henry More who has*"   Yeats, "Leo Africanus," p. 33.

p, 193   "*a Great Memory passing*"   Myth 345.

"*I am your opposite*"   Yeats, "Leo Africanus," p. 38.

"*antipodes of our*"   Pound to Harriet Monroe, 24 December 1915, in Ellmann, *Eminent Domain*, p. 68.

"*Sometimes when you*"   Yeats, "Leo Africanus," p. 29.

"*I sometimes fence*"   Myth 337.

By the end of February: On 28 February 1916 Pound told John Quinn that he was sending the twelve dialogues to the *Egoist*.

p. 194   "*he who would paint*"   PD 142.

"*Be on your guard*"   PD 120.

"*but accept the inheritance*"   Pound, "Pastiche: The Regional VIII," *New Age* 25 (28 August 1919): 300.

p. 195   "*they have not rung*"   PD 88–89.

"*Student: And yet*"   PD 86.

"*Even my dialogues*"   PJ 118.

p. 196   "*sulk and leave*"   Pound, "Three Cantos I," p. 118.

The Player Queen: Yeats to Lady Gregory, 12 February 1915; Yeats to John Quinn, 4 February 1916. Although it has often been suggested that Pound persuaded Yeats to rewrite *The Player Queen* as a comedy, Curtis Bradford has shown that the play had a tragic ending only in the earliest scenarios. Yeats did not begin to speak of the play as a "wild comedy" (YL 588; Yeats to his father, 12 September 1915 [misdated 1914]) until September 1915 when he was at Coole and away from Pound; when he returned to London he read Pound this new version of the play in December 1915 and did not remark that Pound offered suggestions (Yeats to Lady Gregory, 23 December 1915). Consequently, Pound's advice was probably restricted to just what Yeats told Lady Gregory on 12 February 1915: a reduction of the play to two acts. These 1915–16 versions of the play are printed as drafts 18 through 21 in *The Writing of the Player Queen*, ed. Curtis Bradford (DeKalb, Illinois: Northern Illinois University Press, 1977), pp. 269–346.

Theatre Business

p. 197　"*the work of*"　Frank Kermode, *Forms of Attention* (Chicago: University of Chicago Press, 1985), p. 17.

"*Being a writer*"　UPII 401. For Pound's praise of the lecture see Yeats's letter to Lady Gregory, 8 March 1914, in Torchiana and O'Malley, eds., "Some New Letters," p. 41.

p. 198　"*the fascination of*"　VP 260.

"*I went to Paris*"　This and the following recollections by Itow are taken from Ian Carruthers, "A Translation of Fifteen Pages of Ito Michio's Autobiography 'Utsukushiku Naru Kyoshitsu,'" *Canadian Journal of Irish Studies* 2 (1976): 32–43. See also Helen Caldwell, *Michio Itow: The Dancer and his Dances* (Berkeley: University of California Press, 1977).

p. 201　"*So Miscio sat*"　77/469.

"*made possible by*"　E&I 224.

"*Michio Itow is*"　PJ 58.

"*the finer movements*"　Pound, "Sword-Dance and Spear-Dance: Texts of the Poems used with Michio Itow's Dances," *Future* 1 (December 1916): 54.

"*Beneath the pale*"　This poem, along with four others ("Song for a Foiled Vendetta," "The Sole Surviver," "Honogi," and "Yamadera"), was printed in Pound's "Sword-Dance and Spear-Dance."

p. 202　"*The translation*"　Pound, "Sword-Dance and Spear-Dance," p. 54.

"*Each dance was*"　Pound, "Sword-Dance and Spear-Dance," p. 54.

"*To me the*"　PL 3–4 (2).

p. 203　"*It is a sad*"　Pound, "The Classical Stage of Japan," *Drama* 18 (May 1915): 215.

"*Synge and the*"　Marie Stopes, *Plays of Old Japan: The Nō* (London: Heinemann, 1913), p. 1. Pound referred to this volume in the notes to '*Noh*' *or Accomplishment*.

"*I've a sad*"　T 227.

"*the least interesting*"　T. S. Eliot, "The Noh and the Image," *Egoist* 4 (August 1917): 103.

p. 204　"*Yeats is booming*"　Pound to John Quinn, 28 February 1916.

"*I do not*"　Almost all of Yeats's "Suggestions & Corrections" for *Certain Noble Plays of Japan* (which are held in the Pound Archive, Beinecke Library, Yale University) are reprinted in Yoko Chiba, "Ezra Pound's Versions of Fenollosa's Noh Manuscripts and Yeats's Unpublished 'Suggestions & Corrections,' " *Yeats Annual* 4 (1986): 121–44.

p. 205 "*the scattered fragments*" PL 214 (227).

"*Yeats is making*" PL 72 (84).

"*He has done*" Pound to his father, February 1916 (409).

p. 206 "*an unpopular theatre*" Ex 254.

"*has a scheme*" Pound to John Quinn, 28 February 1916.

"*Is not all*" Cited in Bradford, *Yeats at Work*, p. 215.

p. 207 "*it won't do*" PJ 45, 46.

"*Must our most*" PJ 56.

"*I have written*" E&I 221.

p. 208 "*I think you*" PJ 123.

"*I think it a*" PJ 93.

"*A novel, to be*" PJ 141–42.

p. 209 "*somewhere or other*" Pound to John Quinn, 25 April 1916.

"*on account of*" PJ 92.

"*She was so*" Pound, "John Synge and the Habits of Criticism," p. 53.

p. 210 "*so that you*" 77/469.

"*James: Do you mind*" Pound's *The Consolations of Matrimony* (along with three other plays, *The Protagonist, De Musset's "A Supper at the House of Madamoiselle Rachel,"* and *Tristan*) was recently published in PMN 13–22.

p. 211 "*As you are*" PSL 326.

"*Of course divorce*" PSL 327.

p. 212 "*was solemn and*" Brinkley, pp. 31, 50.

Yoro: The text of *Yoro*, Yeats's model for *At the Hawk's Well*, is reprinted in Richard Taylor, *The Drama of W. B. Yeats: Irish Myth and the Japanese Nō* (New Haven: Yale University Press, 1976), pp. 121–27.

p. 213 "*The night is*" Yeats's prose draft of *At the Hawk's Well* (titled *The Well of Immortality*) is reprinted in Bradford, *Yeats at Work*, pp. 176–82; this passage occurs on p. 177.

"*Night falls*" VPl 400–401.

"*vers libre is*" PSL 287.

p. 214 "*in describing this*" Yeats, Introduction to *The Oxford Book of Modern Verse*, p. xxi.

"*radically naturalistic*" I. A. Richards, *Principles of Literary Criticism* (New York: Harcourt, Brace, 1925), p. 292.

"*All the wild*" VP 343–44.

p. 215 "*I remember well*" Eliot, "Ezra Pound," p. 326.

"*with the Cuchulain*" T. S. Eliot, *On Poetry and Poets* (New York: Farrar, Straus, 1957), p. 305.

"*Chorus describes*" Bradford, *Yeats at Work*, p. 180. Bradford

is mistaken when he suggests (p. 182) that Yeats's uncertainty about the dance shows that he did not yet know that
Itow would be available.

"The horror of" The draft of *At the Hawk's Well* that includes these ultimately deleted lyrics is printed in Bradford,
Yeats at Work, pp. 195–205; this passage occurs on p. 202.

p. 216 *"There falls a"* VPl 407.

"Keep me from" Bradford, *Yeats at Work,* p. 203.

p. 217 *"The anxiety of"* YL 601.

"may have to" Yeats to Lady Gregory, 23 January 1915.

"One cannot discuss" YL 611.

"waves his arms" YL 609.

"some undefined" Pound to John Quinn, 13 March 1916.

"A man who" Ex 256.

p. 218 *"modern actor"* T. S. Eliot, " 'The Duchess of Malfi' at the
Lyric: and Poetic Drama," *Art & Letters* 3 (1920): 38–39.

"certain things" *The Journals of Arnold Bennett 1921–1928,*
ed. Newman Flower (London: Cassell and Co., 1933),
p. 52.

"should be stylized" T. S. Eliot to Hallie Flanagan, 18 March
1933, in Hallie Flanagan, *Dynamo* (New York: Duell, Sloan
and Pearce, 1943), p. 83.

"cared for poetry" VPl 416.

"selected royalty" Pound to John Quinn, 4 April 1916.

"a success" Pound to John Quinn, 5 April 1916.

p. 219 *"we found a"* VPl 416.

"No press, no" YL 610.

"upon a single" E&I 234.

p. 220 *"I am often"* GB 94.

"unity of the image" Eliot, "The Noh and the Image," p. 103.
For an examination of Pound's, Yeats's, and Eliot's interest
in the Noh and an exploration of how the idea of "ryhthm
of metaphor" made the modern long poem possible, see
Ronald Bush, "The 'Rhythm of Metaphor': Yeats, Pound,
Eliot, and the Unity of Image in Postsymbolist Poetry," in
Allegory, Myth, and Symbol, ed. Morton Bloomfield (Cam-
bridge: Harvard University Press, 1981), pp. 371–88.

p. 221 *"roughly the theme"* Cited in Myles Slatin, "A History of
Pound's Cantos I–XVI, 1915–1925," *American Literature*
35 (1963): 186. The definitive account of Pound's transformation of *Three Cantos* (1917) into *A Draft of XVI
Cantos* (1925) is Ronald Bush, *The Genesis of Ezra Pound's
Cantos* (Princeton: Princeton University Press, 1976). I
have offered a reading of *Three Cantos* as an expression of

Pound's changing historicism in *Modernist Poetics of History: Pound, Eliot, and the Sense of the Past* (Princeton: Princeton University Press, 1987), pp. 96–130.

Ghosts Patched with Histories

p. 222 "*We walked briskly* Anne Moberly and Eleanor Jourdain, *An Adventure* (1911; rpt. New York: Coward McCann, 1935), p. 41.

p. 223 "*retrocognition*" See, for instance, W.H.W. Sabine, "Is There a Case for Retrocognition?", *Journal of the American Society for Psychical Research* 44 (1950): 43–64.

"*'Tis as in midmost*" CEP 71.

p. 224 "*an elaborate vision*" V&B 348.

"*I was once talking*" V&B 351.

p. 225 "*I was comparing one*" Ex 31.

"*a discovery one had*" Ex 35.

"*spiritism, whether of*" Myth 354.

p. 226 "*thinks of those apparitions*" AV-B 227.

"*you tell me*" PMN 23, 24.

p. 227 "*put himself in sympathy*" T 236–37.

"*great types of human*" T 279–80.

"*A hat and*" T 335.

"*The Muses were*" T 340.

p. 228 "*All that I believed*" PD 86.

"*I used to be told*" Cicero, *De Senectute, De Amicitia, De Divinatione*, trans. W. A. Falconer (Cambridge: Harvard University Press, Loeb Classical Library, 1959), pp. 89–91.

"*And this is the recollection*" SR 140–41.

p. 229 "*Richard of St. Victor*" Pound, "The Approach to Paris VI," *New Age* 13 (9 October 1913): 695.

"*had two sets of*" LE 433; my emphasis.

"*I have seen the God*" LE 431.

p. 230 "*These things are*" SR 92.

"*When any man is*" LE 432.

"*at work on a*" Pound to his father, 25 September 1915, in Slatin, "A History of Cantos I–XVI," p. 185.

"*allowed him to*" Yeats to John Quinn, 19 December 1915.

"*If you like*" Pound to his father, 18 December 1915. This passage has been cited in numerous places, most fully in George Bornstein, "Pound's Parleyings with Robert Browning," *Ezra Pound Among the Poets*, ed. George Bornstein (Chicago: University of Chicago Press, 1985), pp. 119–20.

p. 231   "*I must have*"   Pound to his father, 18 December 1915, in
                Slatin, "A History of Cantos I–XVI," p. 185.
         "*And the place*"   Pound, "Three Cantos I," pp. 116, 118.
p. 232   "*Spiritism . . . will*"   Myth 354.
         "*Chinese poetry is*"   Pound, "Chinese Poetry II," *To-day* 3
                (May 1918): 93.
p. 233   "*Why does my heart*"   VPl 762–3.
         "*So the murk*"   Pound, "Three Cantos II," *Poetry* 10 (July
                1917): 182.
p. 234   "*neither alone, nor*"   PMN 37, 38.
         "*Now I will fall*"   These drafts of the so-called "Ur-cantos" are
                part of the Pound Archive, Beinecke Library, Yale Univer-
                sity.
p. 235   "*For the gossip*"   5/20. For a discussion of Pound's use of
                Roscoe, see Wendy Flory, *Ezra Pound and the Cantos: A
                Record of Struggle* (New Haven: Yale University Press,
                1980), pp. 118–20, 290–91.
         "*Turn to Vyasa's*"   Draft of the Ur-cantos, Pound Archive.
p. 236   "*all over Ireland*"   VP 808, 810.
         "*hanging in a cave*"   *The Mahābhārata, book 1, The Book of
                the Beginning,* trans. and ed. J. A. B. van Buitenen (Chi-
                cago: University of Chicago Press, 1973), p. 104. The 1915
                drafts of the Ur-cantos also show that Pound was planning
                to use Sinistrari's *Demonology* (which he gave to Yeats dur-
                ing the first Stone Cottage winter) as another example of
                otherworldly experience.
p. 237   " '*All is within us*' "   Draft of the Ur-cantos, Pound Archive.
p. 238   "*Their thoughts are*"   SR 92.
         "*I dare say*"   PSL 206.
         "*Another's a half-cracked*"   Pound, "Three Cantos III," *Poetry*
                10 (August 1917): 248.
         "*A clavichord or*"   GB 127.
p. 239   "*that is acknowledged*"   John Heydon, *The Holy Guide* (Lon-
                don, 1662), 3: 88–9. For information on Heydon I am in-
                debted to Thomas Willard's unpublished essay, "John Hey-
                don's Visions: 'Pretty' or 'Polluted'?"
         "*form to come*"   GB 92.
         "*are related by*"   Ex 36.
         "*Admitting the possibility*"   LE 444.
p. 240   "*This liquid is certainly*"   74/449.
         "*the painting is done*"   Pound, "Affirmations II: Vorticism,"
                p. 278.
p. 241   "*I made it out of*"   GK 152.
         "*But weigh this song*"   VP 166.

"a portable substitute"   PL 257 (277).

"The vast mnemonic"   Richard Sieburth, "The Design of *The Cantos:* An Introduction," *Iowa Review* 15 (1985): 21.

"Thus Heydon, in a"   Pound, "Three Cantos III," p. 248. For Pound's use of Heydon in the Rock-Drill Cantos, see Walter Baumann, "Secretary of Nature, J. Heydon," in *New Approaches to Ezra Pound*, ed. Eva Hesse (London: Faber and Faber, 1969), pp. 303–18.

p. 242   *"Walking upon the plain"*   Heydon, 6: 30–31.

       "Take the old way"   Pound, "Three Cantos III," p. 248.

p. 243   *"John Heydon, a servant"*   V&B 346.

       "Does in fact"   Yeats, "Leo Africanus," p. 27.

       "The soul has a plastic"   Myth 349.

p. 244   *"to prove that the"*   V&B 346–47.

       "When the white doe"   V&B 347.

       "imagine ourselves as"   Myth 334, 341.

p. 245   *"I don't want to be"*   Pound, "Letters to William Butler Yeats," p. 34.

       "Certainly in most writings"   Ex 69–70.

p. 246   *"the measure of blood"*   V&B 306.

       "All these shadows"   Ex 56.

       "One remembers also"   Yeats, "Preliminary Examination of the Script of E.R.," p. 161.

       "by building into its"   Myth 349–50.

       "Came then Anticlea"   Pound, "Three Cantos III," pp. 253–54.

p. 247   *"And now it's all"*   Pound, "Three Cantos I," p. 120.

p. 248   *"The book seems half"*   Lawrence Lipking, *The Life of the Poet: Beginnings and Endings of Poetic Careers* (Chicago: University of Chicago Press, 1981), p. 49. My examination of *Three Cantos* and *Per Amica Silentia Lunae* as "crisis odes" occupying different points of crisis in the poets' careers is indebted to Harold Bloom's theory of poetic "crossing." See especially the "Coda: Poetic Crossing" in *Wallace Stevens: The Poems of Our Climate* (Ithaca: Cornell University Press, 1977), pp. 375–406.

       "At certain moments"   Myth 364–65.

       "there came new"   81/520.

p. 249   *"I don't think Yeats"*   PL 137 (153).

       "on psychism"   PL 140 (154).

       "will be quite sensible"   PL 141 (154).

p. 250   *"made for no man's"*   LE 64–65.

Epilogue

p. 251   "*Mr. Yeats [is]*"   Pound, "Status Rerum," p. 123.

"*Looking at the*"   Pound, "Status Rerum–the Second," *Poetry* 8 (April 1916): 40.

"*[Yeats] is the only*"   Pound, "Mr. Yeats' New Book," *Poetry* 9 (December 1916): 150–51.

p. 252   "*not only men*"   PJ 283.

"*Nine adulteries*"   P 100.

"*the true quality*"   Pound wrote Yeats's remark in a note to Harriet Monroe on the manuscript of "The Temperaments" in the *Poetry* magazine papers, University of Chicago Library.

"*no asylum for*"   PL 73 (84).

p. 253   "*deletions in this*"   PJ 280–81.

"*quoted Donne*"   Pound to Harriet Monroe, 29 May 1916.

"*clean cut satire*"   PJ 282.

"*Realism is created*"   E&I 227.

"*occasional bits of*"   Pound, "Mr. Yeats' New Book," p. 151.

p. 254   "*published some of*"   Pound, "Cooperation (A Note on the Volume Completed)," *Little Review* 5 (July 1918): 54.

"*The Wind Among the Reeds is*"   Harold Bloom, *Yeats* (New York: Oxford University Press, 1970), p. 162.

"*I have looked*"   VP 322–23.

p. 255   "*for my own*"   E&I 236.

"*trying to write*"   YL 613.

"*We know their*"   VP 394.

"*I had no*"   YL 613.

p. 256   "*of a no less*"   Pound, "Mr. Yeats' New Book," p. 151.

"*going out to*"   Pound to John Quinn, 1 May 1916.

"*There seems to*"   Pound to John Quinn, 1 June 1916.

"*Romantic Ireland's dead*"   VP 820.

"*sows eating their*"   14/62.

p. 257   "*I recognize that*"   Pound to John Quinn, 19 July 1916. See also Ellmann, *Eminent Domain*, p. 72.

p. 258   "*Beneath the broad*"   A. E. Waite, *The Real History of the Rosicrucians* (London: Redway, 1887), p. 1.

"*arts are . . . about*"   E&I 193.

"*all of Wm.*"   Pound, "Letters to Viola Baxter Jordan," ed. Donald Gallup, *Paideuma* 1 (1972): 109.

"*Thus ends the*"   *Le Comte de Gabalis by the Abbe N. de Villars Rendered out of French into English with a Commentary, published by The Brothers*, p. 201.

p. 259   *"Thus he ended our"*   Shakespear, "Memoirs of a Charming
           Person, V.," p. 207.
p. 260   *"did we ever"*   83/534.
           "I think people"   Yeats to John Quinn, 4 February 1916.
           "Pound's experience"   *The letters of John Quinn to William
           Butler Yeats*, ed. Alan Himber with George Mills Harper
           (Ann Arbor: UMI Research Press, 1983), p. 168.
           "I am so unused"   Pound to Lucy Masterman, 4 February 1916;
           in *Illustrated Catalogue, English Literature, Comprising
           Printed Books, Autograph Letters and Manuscripts*, for sale
           on July 21 and 22, 1983 (London: Sotheby Parke Bernet &
           Co.), p. 170.
p. 261   *"When I arrived"*   Yeats to G. H. Mair, February 1916, Berg
           Collection, New York Public Library. Pound typed this let-
           ter and made several brief insertions by hand which I have not
           included in this transcription.
           "The Home Office"   Pound to his father, February 1916 (409).
p. 262   *"My dear Yeats"*   Robert Bridges to Yeats, 8 February 1916,
           Pound Archive, Beinecke Library, Yale University; the let-
           ter appears here by permission of Thomas Bridges.
           "cop appeared this"   Pound to C. F. G. Masterman, February
           1916; in *Illustrated Catalogue*, p. 170.
p. 263   *"A fat moon"*   83/535.
           "I don't believe"   Pound to John Quinn, 27 July 1916.
p. 264   *"I have not"*   *The Letters of John Keats 1814–1821*, ed. Hyder
           Edward Rollins (Cambridge: Harvard University Press,
           1958), 1: 266.
           "art and poetry"   Algernon Charles Swinburne, *William Blake:
           A Critical Study*, ed. Hugh J. Luke (1868; rpt. Lincoln,
           Nebraska: Nebraska University Press, 1970), p. 36.
           "The fascist revolution"   J/M 127.
p. 265   *"the most individual"*   T. S. Eliot, *The Sacred Wood* (New
           York: Methuen, 1972), p. 48.
           "The problem"   T. S. Eliot, *After Strange Gods* (New York:
           Harcourt, Brace, 1934), pp. 15, 18.
           "vers libre does"   T. S. Eliot, *To Criticize the Critic* (London:
           Faber and Faber, 1985), pp. 183, 189.
           "artificial simplification"   Eliot, *Sacred Wood*, pp. viii, ix, x.
           "Nietzsche has done"   SP 421.
           "real intelligence"   J/M 18.
           "the extent to"   Jeffrey Perl, *The Tradition of Return: The Im-
           plicit History of Modern Literature* (Princeton: Princeton
           University Press, 1984), p. 266.
p. 266   *"Ireland that reacts"*   YL 693.

"*All through the*" YL 872. For an examination of Yeats's interest in Mussolini see Cullingford, *Yeats, Ireland, and Fascism*, pp. 144–60. For the subtlest examination of Pound's self-entrapping commitment to Mussolini, see Flory, *Pound and the Cantos*, pp. 179–80.

p. 267 "*there is no longer*" PL 158 (170).

"*my glory was*" VP 604.

p. 268 "*their prominent part*" VP 565–67.

p. 269 "*But to have done*" 81/521–22.

Index